No Strings Attached

The Unconditional Love of the Savior

Rick & Sylvia
Best blessings!
& hugs)! *Karen*
June 2021

Karen Hutchins

ISBN 978-1-64670-379-1 (Paperback)
ISBN 978-1-64670-380-7 (Digital)

All Scriptures are NKJV unless otherwise noted.
All commentators quoted are taken from E-sword unless
otherwise noted.
No Strings Attached: The Unconditional Love of the Savior

Covenant Books, Inc.
11661 Hwy 707
Murrells Inlet, SC 29576
www.covenantbooks.com

Writing this book has truly been a labor of love, but only possible because of the love that was poured into me by so many mentors over the years: Norman and Sandra Howell, Jerry and Kathy Baker, Ruth Richardson, the late Stephen Wallace, Donya Wallace Perez, Ron Richardson, Nash and Rosa Vallone, Don and Pat De Jong, John and Carol Wright. I'm eternally grateful that they followed God in guiding me through some rough times. I dedicate this book to them and to my family. Thank you for all the sacrifices you've made on my behalf!

Contents

Introduction

Being raised in a loving home, I always felt secure, even though that home was not a Christian home. My mom was a Christian when I was growing up, but it wasn't until Daddy was sixty-two years old that he finally accepted Jesus as his Lord and Savior. Two years after that, my dear wonderful mom moved to her heavenly home. Daddy was always a "bigger than life" kind of guy, and becoming a Christian didn't change that. It did, however, change his focus. His focus, as far as I was concerned, was to get me back in church! And I am so glad he vocalized his opinion!

I had been saved in Church Camp when I was nine years old, but adult life and its challenges had not been particularly kind to me. I made a few wrong choices which led me to drift away from my salvation and my Lord. Daddy knew that and told me it was time I got myself "back in church," because he wanted the same band in heaven that he'd had on earth.

(After I got out of the Marine Corps, I lived in my hometown, which had been nicknamed the Gem City. After my son was born, Daddy compiled a family band—Bill Uppinghouse and The Gems—he played piano, my cousin played bass, my brother was on drums, and my older sister and I sang. We were together for nine years, until I moved to Texas, and we were considered one of the top bands in the tristate area of Missouri, Illinois, and Iowa.)

So when Daddy started "strongly encouraging" me to come back to the Lord, I decided he was right. We only got to serve the Lord together a few times, because I lived in Texas at the time and he lived in Illinois. But every day, we shared by phone what God was doing in his life and in mine, until he went home to meet Jesus face-to-face over twenty years ago.

It was after his passing that I lived through the heartache that resulted in my first book, *Protective Custody: Miracles Can Happen When God Has You Right Where He Wants You.* That was the first time I experienced firsthand the absolute and unconditional love of my Savior, Jesus Christ. In the years since, God has continually revealed His grace and mercy to me, guiding me, sometimes gently and sometimes prodding me, into becoming the woman of God that I am today. Occasionally, I can still hear my daddy's voice encouraging me and sometimes reminding me that I haven't yet arrived. God isn't finished with me, by any means. It continues to be my joy, every morning, to sit in His presence, as He speaks softly to my heart. I have grown to know Him as so much more than the Savior I met at age nine and the Lord I finally submitted to in my thirties...so much more. I can't imagine going even one step without the wonderful, merciful, loving God who sees me through every step I take.

Over the years, as I felt the Holy Spirit nudging me to share more of the story since my Protective Custody days. I have started, hesitantly, by writing accounts of teachings, messages, stories, anything the Lord leads me to write, always with a foggy view of the path ahead, but never with true conviction and focus, until now.

Several months ago at a Women's Camp, I sat with thirty other women, listening to the sweet testimony of God's marvelous work in a young woman's life. It was during her testimony that I heard her say, "No strings attached." At that moment, I lost touch with anything else she said. To my heart, beyond a shadow of a doubt, my Lord also spoke, "The unconditional love of the Savior." I knew the time had come to arrange the notes of my continuing story and I knew the God-given title.

I have personally experienced His unconditional love and witnessed it time and again in the lives of others.

It strikes me as sad that Daddy never got to meet my one and only—the one man that God Himself prepared for me. But I know they will meet one day in heaven. In the meantime, I serve God beside my husband, Wayne (Hutch) Hutchins. Sometimes God uses us together, sometimes He uses us separately, and sometimes we feel like a tag team. We are both totally sold out to God, following Him wherever he leads and participating in whatever His plans for us entail, knowing that God never gives us more than we can handle, and that He always prepares and enables us to do what He asks us to do!

I have been a writer since I was a child. So, as we go through our lives here on earth, I write a lot of what goes on in our lives. But I write even more about what God wants us to learn. It is my prayer that readers will hear God's heart through my writings. He is all I will ever have to offer anyone. I share my experience now, in these pages, for your good and His glory. I hope you are blessed.

Chapter 1
Somewhere along the Way

I pour my heart and soul into everything I do. I wasn't always like this, but somewhere along the way I absorbed thoughts and beliefs that have contributed to this characteristic. Things like, "Anything worth doing, is worth doing well," or, "If you aren't going to do it right, don't do it at all." I wasn't always a "neat nut." But somewhere along the way, I developed that characteristic too. There was a time in my life when I could look at a picture hanging on the wall in my home and remind myself to straighten it later. I didn't feel the need to stop what I was doing to get up and straighten it. I don't remember ever walking up to an askew hanging in a public building and straightening it. Somewhere along the way, I developed a bit of OCD (obsessive-compulsive disorder). I have noticed that if I indulge it, it only becomes worse! Sometimes, I am a neat freak, but not always. I am definitely one, when the mess I am cleaning up is not my own. I don't know when these changes began, if they were gradual transitions or overnight changes. I do know that there is solid evidence of me not being me anymore—at least not the me I used to be.

I was born in the Midwest, but I spent most of my adult life in Texas, so I consider myself a transplanted Texan. I was saved at Church Camp when I was nine years old. My first definitive "Christian" memory after that is a picture I've seen of my older sister and my younger brother and me, taken after VBS. I remember it very well because *they* both wore glittered paper crowns, and I wasn't wearing one. Why? You may ask. Because my sweet baby brother had ripped it off, thrown it in the dirt, and stomped on it. You know, typical little brother antics. To this day I can't believe he did it! But I think Christian or non-Christian families alike, you can appreciate why I still remember it! Living through life moments, we generally don't consider how situations in life affect our character, but they do. Somewhere along the way, I grew up and became the me I am now. Looking back, I see that many changes came from my relationship with my first husband.

After high school graduation I experienced an unsuccessful attempt at college. Before they had a chance to flunk me out, I quit and joined the United States Marine Corps. That's where I met my first husband. I married at the tender age of eighteen and had my son at age twenty. When I completed my tour in the Marine Corps, we bought a little house in my hometown of Quincy, Illinois, and later moved to Texas. I was a working mother and trying my best to be a good Christian wife. My husband was a Christian but declined to attend church with us. After a while I became too apathetic to go myself. I thank God I had sense to at least continue taking my son to church before I went back home to finish the housework, laundry, and cooking for the week!

I went into my first marriage as a young, invincible, usually happy-go-lucky young woman who frequently wore "rose-colored glasses" (as Daddy called them). But I also harbored a serious sub-surface knowledge that I was

1) expected to be a "good person";
2) raised to be honest, kind, and considerate;
3) responsible for my own actions; and
4) accountable to God and family for my decisions.

I am not sure I did very well in any of those departments. If I were to rate myself best in a category, I guess I would rate myself top in #2. I paid a heavy price for some pretty poor decisions (#3). The first one was when I asked my first husband for a divorce. In all honesty, I just wanted to get his attention. I was hoping he'd say, "Wait, we can work this out!" Unfortunately, he didn't even suggest it; thus I was stuck with my decision. He let me know in the middle of the divorce process that I was an evil person and a horrible mother, so I guess I wasn't kind or considerate to him. In his opinion, I was definitely not a good person.

When we give the enemy of our souls a little room, he subtly and gradually takes more and more. Before I knew it, I was a lot further from God that I ever intended to be. Suffice it to say that, in hindsight, I see where the enemy of our souls convinced me to believe several lies, or exaggerated truths, and I chose to walk away from the marriage, after having "drifted away" from the Christian upbringing to which I have since returned.

I was the only one of my siblings who had been married more than fifteen years. It was difficult to swallow my pride and tell my family that I had let them down. I let God down even more so. It became rather difficult to even face Him, so I "kinda" didn't. Somewhere along the way, I just stopped thinking about God much. The emotional stress, regret, and disillusionment became way too much for my rose-colored glasses to handle. And somewhere along the way, I began to ease the pain by drinking more than I ever had…in fact, a *lot* more than I ever had. It was the most difficult time of my life, and I was going through it without leaning on God. I hate to think of how many times, after a few too many drinks, I lost track of the time. Or how often I left my twelve-year-old son to take care of himself, do his homework, fix his own supper, and "page me if he needed me."

Somewhere along the way, I decided it would be a good idea to marry my drinking buddy. After all, he was the one who was taking care of me and making sure I got home okay. What a mistake that proved to be. Up until our wedding day, he and my son got along pretty well, or so I thought. The minute we said "I do," their relationship changed drastically. Suddenly, my new husband and I were at odds all the time because I wouldn't make my son do chores that I didn't see as his responsibility. He accused me of treating his kids differently than I treated my own. I found that I was defending myself and my son at every turn. It became obvious that our marriage was a huge mistake. His frequent violent temper tantrums caused serious concern for the welfare of myself as well as that of my son. I was heading for another divorce. Although this time, my family also thought it best. Once again I failed:

> #1—I didn't consider myself a good person, after letting my son raise himself for five years.
> #2—I wasn't even being honest with myself anymore.
> #3—Not only I paid for my actions but my son did too.
> #4—I still hadn't figured out a way to tell God.

My son, Jason, and I had struggled through another marriage. He was (and still is) an amazingly talented musician and he withdrew into his music. When that marriage ended in divorce after five years of drama, verbal abuse and anger, Jason's girlfriend, Jennifer (now his wife), and her family were tremendously important in his life and stability and I am eternally grateful to them for helping to raise my son!

Shortly afterward, I ran into a man I had known for ten years. He was very much like my daddy—handsome, meticulous, deep thinker, a man of integrity…and a nonbeliever. We had been a great team when we worked together. Our families had been friends when I was married to my first husband. We started spending time together and somewhere along the way, we realized that we were very compatible. We were the "flip side" of each other, yin and yang, so to speak. Finally, a happy peaceful life and the future looked promising, or so I thought at the time. Two years later, he called Daddy and asked for my hand in marriage. He and my son not only got along, they actually enjoyed spending time together and they respected each other. His kids enjoyed being with us too. It really was a nice situation all round. With him, I found it easy to live up to my four ground rules for living.

Six weeks after our wedding, my mom died. This was the woman whom I so adored, that it was a long time after she passed that I could even talk about her, even to my husband, because her memory was too precious to mar with human words. She was the believer in the family from the beginning. She insisted that we kids go to church, while we were growing up, when she felt obliged to stay home with my nonbelieving father.

She was the strong woman who allowed me to be a Daddy's girl. She was the tender woman who could show me how to be tender as well as how to be strong. She was the woman who insisted I sing in a talent show in eighth grade, when I was too shy to do it. I can remember being so angry at her for "making me" sing a solo with my guitar. I was so grateful in later years that she had been wise enough (and stern enough) to do it. It wasn't until she told me later that she had been as shy as I was and wished someone had pushed her to "shine" as she had pushed me, that I truly appreciated her wisdom. She had been the solid, nonjudgmental, loving Christian influence through all of my life.

Although I have said, "I wasn't thinking much about God," truth be known, I was. After being saved at age nine, I had tried to convince Daddy to come to Jesus every moment since then. After accepting Christ, he began asking me to help him understand the Bible. His questions were wearing on my conscience and forced me to get back into God's Word, so I could answer them. I was thrilled, but since I was no longer walking with the Lord, it kind of stung. (I still hadn't told God about my divorces…and yes, I realized he already knew…) When my mom died, two years after Daddy gave his life to Jesus, I decided I didn't want to spend forever without seeing her again, so I pulled my prodigal son move and came back to the Lord.

After nine years of carousing, I stopped drinking—that was the easy part. But I had been singing in smoky bars—I had started smoking when I was in the Marine Corps, and I was up to three packs a day by that time. I wanted to sing for Jesus again, but my voice was shot. I don't recommend it, but I made a deal with God. I told Him if He would give me back my voice, I would sing for no one but Him. On March 19, 1995, He delivered me from smoking. The damage I had done to my lungs was in the form of emphysema, but the doctors have said it is dormant, and other than lacking a bit of lung capacity, it is being treated successfully with inhalers.

Contemplating how this return to Jesus would work, I began looking at churches in the area. One Saturday, as I was praying, I asked the Lord to lead me to the church He wanted me to go to. I opened the local phone book and, in fact, tore out the yellow page ad and laid it on the nightstand beside my Bible. I said, "Lord, unless you tell me otherwise, this is the church I am going to tomorrow morning." Later that afternoon, my husband came home from work and we were walking out to the mailbox. As we talked, he stepped over a bright pink flyer that had found its way into the yard.

I thought it unusual that he stepped over it, because he was quite a "neat nut" and his norm would have been to pick it up (and probably throw it away without looking at it). When I picked it up, it was a flyer announcing "Kick-off" Sunday scheduled for the next day for a new church opening in a vacant building a few blocks away. Obviously, God wanted me to go there instead of the church from the yellow pages!

I prayed that night in a different way. I knew God was in this plan to return to Him. I knew that if I didn't find "a job" in this church, in which I felt like I was contributing something, I would go for a few weeks, maybe even a month or two, and then dwindle away again. So I prayed that God would make me feel needed.

When I walked in the door the next morning, to this church plant, I was met by a gentle-looking young woman holding a baby boy, about five months old. She introduced herself as the pastor's wife. Being the baby-person that I am, I immediately held out my hands and he came to me happily. That's pretty much where he stayed for the next year or so.

Understand that I am a person who needs to feel needed. If I feel like the church can run perfectly well without me, I will let it do just that! (God is still working on me in that regard!) That pastor's wife became a very dear friend, and later told me that one of their concerns about starting the church had been someone to watch the baby while Pastor did the preaching and teaching and she led the worship! So when this cuddle bug became so much a part of me, from the very first day, she knew I was the answer to their prayer. (In reality, he was an answer to mine, because I would never disappoint him by not attending!)

It wasn't long before I was helping with the church in a number of different ways, and my son and Jennifer started going to church with me. My husband knew I had started going to church again, and would frequently join us after Sunday evening service, as we all went out to one of the local restaurants for supper, and this generally coincided with the time he got off work. I was busily doing something for the church almost every moment that my husband was at work, helping with events, doing the bulletins, etc. This went on for several years, and our lives were as close to "normal" as I can remember up to that point. Jason and Jennifer were living with us when my first granddaughter was born. As my husband said often, life was good. However, after some traumatic events, primarily stemming from my husband's volatile work situation, we decided to move to a city about three hours away.

The pastor's wife was saddened by the news that I would soon be moving, and she told me that she just didn't think it was God's plan for us to move. As we were preparing to move, she and Jennifer were shopping for supplies for Vacation Bible School, when they pulled into a parking place at the mall facing a van that had a bumper sticker on it that said "God bless Laredo, Texas." That convinced her. As soon as she could get to a phone she called me and said she had been convinced that God was in this move. When we got to Laredo, my first priority was to find a church. As it happened, the Lord led me to the church that had actually produced those bumper stickers! Another sign to me that God was "all into" my return to Jesus!

My husband had been working two jobs, so we didn't see each other much on weekends. When I came back to the Lord, he didn't have much time to notice. He did, however, take note that I started drinking pop when we went out dancing. He didn't think much of it because I frequently got migraines from drinking alcohol. He also noticed when I quit smoking. I was singing in a band at the time, so he just thought the reason was that I was trying to save my voice. When we moved he didn't work weekends anymore. That's when he really started noticing. I never pushed him into going to church with me. I believe that if we are living the life Christ calls us to, people will see it every day, not just on Sundays!

Even though I was married to a nonbeliever, he was very supportive about my serving God. He even went so far as suggesting that I tithe on half of his income. (He said that half of what he made was mine anyway). He joined the church family for potlucks and after-church lunches. He didn't participate in the Christian activities I was involved in, but he watched. He was watching as I slipped into the bedroom to pray on the phone with someone who was trying to keep her family together, or with someone who had just lost a loved one to cancer. He watched when I came back into the living room with red eyes, and he knew I had been crying. He didn't understand why I cry when I pray. He hated it when I cried, and he didn't understand that the tears weren't tears of sadness. I didn't realize how close he was watching, how deeply he was effected, or how much he misunderstood.

One night, after working late, he came home, and I could smell the courage in the form of the alcohol he had been drinking. He confessed that he had been having an affair for the past six months and wanted a divorce. I literally felt the angels surrounding me as I tried to steady my heart and I heard myself say, "We can work this out." To this he replied that he couldn't handle "the God thing" and repeated that he wanted a divorce. No warning. I never saw it coming. Just six weeks prior to that night, he had sent me roses on our fifth anniversary with a card that read, "To the inspiration of my life." I felt shattered, broken, and found myself unable to breathe.

By this point in time, I had seriously trashed the four ground rules I was trying to live by. Somewhere along the way, I had re-developed a relationship with Jesus, which instilled in me that my help was to be found in Him, not in four rules. It was to Jesus I found myself retreating to. Somewhere along the way, I learned that there are no rules that can be followed 100 percent of the time. God and His love, grace, and mercy are the answers. When I learned to extend a little grace to myself, I felt His love and mercy. I learned many of the ways of God, from my pastors, one of whom I worked for. They opened their hearts to me, and my life began to change. The next three years were spent in what was fondly referred to as the Prophet's Chambers—a haven studio apartment above their garage. It was a loving, healing, and learning environment, where I rediscovered who I was and who God was. I continued moving forward on the road to becoming what God wanted me to be.

Those were times I felt so broken that I could do nothing more than fall at Jesus's feet and cry. Other times I'd crawl into Daddy God's lap and weep and receive His healing. The journal entries I made during that period led me to write a book called *Protective Custody: Miracles Can Happen When God Has You Right Where He Wants You.* God used the writing of that book to heal me. He has healed many others as they read it. One valuable thing I began to recognize there is that the quiet times with my Great Shepherd—those times when I can be still and know that He is God—those are the times I regain my strength. That's when He again puts the wind back in my sails. It was in those desperate moments when I began to understand what it means to be totally dependent on Him, His provision, His love, and His sovereignty, and how reliable His character is! He picked me up and brushed me off, and led me to attend Christian Leadership University. This time around, I was a much better student! I earned my bachelor's in ministry, my master's degree in theology and my doctorate's degree in Christian counseling.

After university, I spent the next two years working as a personal assistant to my pastor in Texas, and that's where I was when, one day, she invited me to go with her to a revival in a church three hours away. While I was at that service, a woman whom I had never met approached me and said she had a word from the Lord for me. Now, I have been on the giving and the receiving ends of "Thus saith the Lord," and I know that when someone says that, it is vital that we test that word against the written Word of God. When she began speaking, I was listening very closely. She said something along the lines of, "The Lord is preparing a man for you…" Instantly, I stopped listening. To this well-meaning, sweet little old lady, I said, albeit respectfully, "He can keep him. I don't want him." I thanked her. I even hugged her as I walked away.

When I got back to the Prophet's Chambers that night, I laid in bed, contemplating my encounter with that dear servant of God. I remember praying that the words that sprang from my wounded heart did not wound her heart! At this point, the thought of remarrying hadn't even occurred to me. I was still horribly wounded, and, truth be told, I was a bit angry with God. I had faithfully prayed for my former husband. I had clung to the words in 1 Corinthians 7:14 that the unbelieving spouse was sanctified by the believing spouse, by me… but the very next verse says if the unbelieving spouse leaves, let him depart. Besides, somewhere deep in my broken heart, I still expected God to save him and send him back to me!

My former husband's remarriage, seventeen days after our divorce was final, doused any hope I had of us reuniting. My goal was now clearer: I was going forward as a single woman. I felt verse 15 helped me accept it as a clean separation (a brother or a sister is not under bondage in such cases). I was thinking about the woman's word that "God was preparing someone for me." So…maybe it *wasn't* God's plan for me to be single for the rest of my life. With that thought in mind, I decided I would stay out of it and let God Himself choose my next husband. But you know I couldn't stay out of it completely, because he would have to be a man that I would find at least slightly attractive, right?

Out of my broken heart, I did have a few suggestions. I asked the Lord for someone who loved God at least as much as I did…and someone that I could sing duets with would be great.

I probably should have stopped there, but I didn't. I asked God for someone who had blond hair and blue eyes, and I actually like long hair on men, so that would be acceptable, and laugh lines—you know, crinkles around his eyes, and he had to be taller than I am.

Not only did God, in his kindness, not strike me dead for being so flippant, rather He brought me exactly what I had asked for! Right down to the long blond hair—it was in a neat braid down past the middle of his back. He is barely an inch taller than I am. His blue eyes twinkle when he laughs and he does laugh a lot. He loves God and we sing duets as often as we can! In fact the first year we were married we were nick-named the Worship Warriors because we led worship for all the Christian Motorcyclist's Association Gold Wing motorcycle rallies in Washington state and we did that for the next three years. There, we entered the ministry full time. Somewhere along the way, I learned a thing or two about submission and truly being a godly wife, but that's an ongoing lesson.

Somewhere along the way, I wrote a couple of books and I realized that my story could help other women, who had suffered in some way. I began speaking at women's events. If anything good can come of a bad experience, my God can make it happen. So I share my story. And my voice? God gave me a wider range than I had ever had, and He put me under the tutelage of a gifted and anointed Christian choir director who stretched me into using the voice that God restored! Today, age has taken some toll on that voice, but I still lead worship at First Baptist Church in Lisbon, North Dakota, although from the alto, and I still do duets with my husband, occasionally.

Somewhere along the way, I have learned to accept that I am good at some things and lousy at others. In the end, it balances out. I trust God to use me where He wants. He never asks me to do something that He isn't going to enable me to do.

Together, my God-given husband and I have pastored churches and ministered in both Washington state and North Dakota. We're seeking God's face, for everything He has for us to do together as a team as well as individually. Out of this seeking, God is sharing with me what He wants me to share with others...that is my heart's desire. I am learning that I truly love people. I genuinely enjoy helping them work their way through the problems that come along with us living in a fallen world. It is with joyful anticipation that I am looking forward to continuing to live, love, serve, and learn somewhere along the way.

Chapter 2
Listening for the Shepherd's Voice

When we spend time with the Lord daily, we generally call it our devotional time, prayer time, or our personal time with the Lord. Whatever we call it, the quality of that time has a direct link with our peace, joy, and our victorious walk with God. There was a time several years ago when the events of my life, which you just read about, led me to view my prayer life as the lifeline it truly is. Maybe some of you have discovered that truth about your own prayer life. I hope so. But, if you haven't, it is my prayer that before you have finished reading this book, you will realize that there is nothing as important as daily quality time with the One who is always waiting to spend time with you.

I once led the ladies in my church in a study called *A Woman's Walk with God* by Sheila Cragg.[1] It is a great way to train or re-train yourself, if need be, in establishing and keeping a daily devotional time. I was reviewing that study a few weeks ago, when I felt the Lord leading me to ask a very important question. Why do we want and need to spend quiet time with the Lord? There are six reasons:

1.   Love: This one works in three different directions: God's love for you, your love for Him, and our quiet time teaches us how to love others—even those who aren't easy to love.

2. Confession: When we're alone with God, He so gently brings to mind anything we need to repent of. If we don't act on that gentle nudging—if we don't repent, God won't be so likely to talk to us. After all, if we haven't acted on what He has already told us, why would He give us something else to do!

3. Direction: Jeremiah 29:11 tells us that God has plans for us—plans for good and not calamity, to give us a future and a hope. Why do you think God would share *that* with us, if He wasn't intending to tell us what His plans are? Our quiet time is a perfect one-on-one time for that type of intimacy.

4. Service: Galatians 5:13 tells us to serve one another in love. 1 Peter 4:10 tells us to do that, by using whatever abilities God has given us. Again, our personal time with the Lord is a great opportunity for Him to move us into the area of service He wants for us.

5. Prayer: God needs our full attention when we pray. (See Chapter 9)

6. Rest: This is discussed in detail, later in this chapter.

The secondary question to *why* is *why me?* Why would God want to talk to me?

I am the Good Shepherd, and I know those that are Mine, and I am known by those who are Mine. Even as the Father knows Me, I also know the Father. And I lay down My life for the sheep. And I have other sheep who

are not of this fold. I must also lead those,
and they shall hear My voice, and there shall
be one flock, one Shepherd. (John 10:14–16,
NJKV)

I prefer the NKJV, but no matter which version you prefer,
the word *shepherd* is used quite frequently. In each reference, it
is used to illustrate that sheep cannot take care of themselves
in one way or another. Jesus used this illustration many times
throughout scripture. That tells me that it is important to Him.

"As a shepherd seeks out his flock in the day that he is
among his scattered sheep, so I will seek out My sheep and will
deliver them out of all places where they have been scattered in
the cloudy and dark day" (Ezek. 34:12, NKJV).

One reason they might get scattered is that sheep have
poor eyesight. During a dreary or cloudy day, their vision is
very poor. It is vital that they are able to follow the shepherd by
voice alone.

And I will bring them out from the peoples,
and gather them from the lands, and will bring
them to their own land and feed them on the
mountain of Israel by the rivers, and in all the
places of the land where people live. I will feed
them in a good pasture, and their fold shall be
on the high mountains of Israel. There they
shall lie in a good fold, and in a fat pasture
they shall feed on the mountains of Israel. I
will feed My flock, and I will cause them to lie
down, says the Lord Jehovah. I will seek the
lost, and bring again those driven away, and
will bind up the broken, and will strengthen
the sick… (Ezek. 34:13–16a, NKJV)

This passage delineates the different aspects of a shepherd's responsibilities. A shepherd herds and rounds up the flock; he prompts his sheep to follow him through speaking to them; he will make sure his flock has the necessary food and rest.

"Truly, truly, I say to you, He who does not enter into the sheepfold by the door, but going up by another way, that one is a thief and a robber" (John 10:1, NKJV).

You may be familiar with a book by Phillip Keller called *A Shepherd Looks at the 23rd Psalm*.[2] He also wrote *A Shepherd Looks at the Good Shepherd and His Sheep*.[3] It's from those books that I want to share with you, because he writes such a wonderful description of a sheepfold.

> What is a sheepfold? It is an enclosure open to the wind. It is an enclosure open to the scrutiny of the owner. It is an enclosure not covered in, roofed over, or shielded from the eyes of the shepherd. It is not a barn, shed, or closed-in structure. Its walls, open to the sun, the sky, stars, rain and wind, may be made of rough-laid stones, sun-dried bricks, timber, mud and wattle, or even tightly placed thorn brush, called a coral in some places, a kraal in others and a boma in parts of Africa. The main purpose of the sheepfold is to provide protection for the sheep—especially at night and in stormy weather. Its high thick walls are a barrier that prevents thieves or, to use a modern parlance, rustlers from invading the flock to plunder the defenseless sheep. The enclosing walls are also a safeguard for the sheep against all sorts of predators.

Jesus gives us a wonderful example of a sheepfold, when He often takes His disciples to a quiet place to rest and pray. Next time you go to your prayer closet, look at it as a sheepfold, where you and the Great Shepherd are spending time together and you have His undivided attention!

A shepherd gathers the scattered or lost sheep. The difference between scattered and lost: *scattered* sheep are those who have wandered so that they're not right near the shepherd, but they are within his sight from one side of the valley to another. A *lost* sheep cannot see the shepherd and is out of range of the sound of his voice. That sheep may be beyond the valley, stuck in a thicket or behind a bush. The shepherd gathers both, which means he has to go after some and hunt for them. A shepherd feeds his sheep healthy food. In our analogy here, we can rest assured that Jesus feeds us physical food (He provides our every need) but also spiritual food!

Frequently, lost lambs are wounded or fall and suffer broken bones. It is the shepherd's responsibility to bind up the wound with a makeshift splint made from whatever sticks he can find and cloth (maybe torn from his own robe). He would then nurse the sheep back to health. When we speak of the role of our Great Shepherd, we can't get very far into this, without going to the 23rd Psalm, which is also known as the Shepherd's Psalm.

"The Lord is my Shepherd, I shall not want. He makes me lie down in green pasture. He leads me beside quiet waters. He restores my soul. He guides me in the paths of righteousness for His Name's sake" (Ps. 23:1–3, NKJV).

Chapter 3

Is God Still Speaking?

Many Christians have been taught that God doesn't speak to us today—that He only speaks through His written Word. I believe in 100 percent of the Bible from Genesis in the beginning to maps in the back of the Book! That's why I believe that He *does* still speak to His people. Let me ask you a few questions. These are not trick questions, just a simple yes or no: Did God speak to Adam and Eve? Abraham and Sarah? Mary? John? Paul? Old Testament or New, man or woman, God communicated with His people. After all, He created us for the supreme purpose of having an agape love relationship with Him. Hebrews 13:8 tells us that God is the same God now that He has always been. His mode of communication may have changed a bit since biblical times, but God can make himself heard any way He wants to.

Henry Blackaby and his son, Richard, wrote a book called *Hearing God's Voice*,[4] in which they discuss four general views on God's communication with His people, today and in biblical times:

> 1. *Bible only: Some people believe that the Written Word of God is the only method God communicates with people.* (Saul would have represented that one well. He was a stickler for biblical detail.)

2. *Experience over the Bible: Some more liberal believers believe that God speaks directly and clearly to His people, and that what He says NOW doesn't necessarily line up with the Written Word.* (Several years ago there was a man named David Koresh, who developed quite a following for himself, based on this theory. Another well-known example is Jim Jones. ["They drank the Kool-Aid" came from his cultist activities which eventually resulted in mass murder of his followers.] Understand that God never contradicts His written word when he communicates with us!)

3. *Doctrine above experience:* (This would have suited the Pharisees well. The Pharisees added more rules and regulations to Scripture and expected the Jews of the day to follow them all, sometimes even above Scripture.)

4. *Experiencing God Personally:* (Represents the true God experience, one that was also portrayed by Saul on the road to Damascus, when he was changed miraculously to our beloved Apostle Paul (Acts 9:3–8)! Understand that you cannot experience God without being miraculously changed!)

Several years ago in Texas, I was facing a hard decision and I went to a godly couple I was very close to. I told them about my dilemma and asked them to pray that I would hear God's voice and make the right choice. They said something that I will never forget: "God is big enough to make Himself heard!" Sounds so simple, yet so true! In our humanness, we don't always trust our spiritual hearing!

Let's look at the logistics of a daily devotional time. How many of you have kids? How important is it to you to spend quality time with them? What does that quality time look like for you? Playing games, pretend tea parties, picnics? Sports? Mealtime conversations? We all have a different perspective of quality time, right?

I have two granddaughters in Texas. Hayley and I once sat in the middle of the parking lot and spent the whole afternoon making chalk drawings, and she was thrilled. I think I enjoyed it as much as she did! She lived with me for the first five months of her life, so I established a relationship with her before I left Texas. Her sister, Hannah, was only two months old when I moved from Texas to Washington. I don't know her as well as I do Hayley. I don't know if she would enjoy the quiet restful and silly atmosphere of creating an entire city out of chalk, or if she'd rather be dancing through that same parking lot or showing me her latest basketball moves!

The point is, God knows us. He doesn't always expect us to sit with Him and talk, if you'd rather be walking through the woods! He wants your time and company. Sometimes He may nudge you to look outside and in your heart (in your spiritual ears) you hear Him saying, "Let's go for a walk. Come and see what I have created for you to enjoy." God isn't going to force you to sit and do chalk drawings in the parking lot! But if that's what you want to do *and you invite Him,* He will meet you there. I guarantee it. *HE guarantees it!*

So, you get up and grab your jacket and go outside. You don't have to call your girlfriends and go on a group prayer walk, although those can be great fun and very powerful. Think of this as a date night with God. You and God alone, walking along a path that *He* created, with you in mind, just so you and He could enjoy it together. That was His plan, you know. Think of the wonders God showed Adam and Eve in those first days, or weeks or however long it was, before they chose to sin and mess it up for all of us! Just moseying around, enjoying the beautiful garden that God created—the absolute vibrant colors, exhilarating smells, no sneezing or running eyes. Envision them watching the birds fly around, and maybe even landing on Eve's outstretched hand, animals being comfortable around them and vice versa, without fear of being attacked. That's what God had planned for us!

Maybe it's those times with God, sitting in our prayer closet with Him that direct us to be different. Maybe it's on a bench down by the lake, or a walk along a path. Whatever it looks like in your life, your time with God—that quality time can guide you to do things differently, to live a different life, to see things differently, because you'll be seeing things in God's perspective. What is important to Him becomes important to you. What used to be important to you, may become trivial, because you'll be looking at things the way God sees them—with an eternal perspective.

Our time alone with God enables God to have an influence in our lives. I can look at my adult son and see so much of me in him. He has his own thoughts and ideas, but because he and I spent a lot of quality time together, I had an influence in his life. God's influence in our lives changes us. Specific activities in our lives become of the Spirit, and not of the flesh, because God is there. In his book *Praying in the Spirit*, Neil Anderson puts it this way:

> When our daily prayers are no longer all about me—me—me; when they stop being self-indulgent Christmas lists; when they are flexible enough to pose the question "does God have something He wants to talk to me

about?" then our prayers become two-way dialogues with Our Sovereign Lord.

That's what these chapters is all about: learning what it takes on *our* part, to be still and hear the voice of our Great Shepherd and to hear what He wants to say to *you!*

Chapter 4
How to Listen

When I was twelve or so, my grandmother gave me a five-year diary. I wrote in it every single day, even if it was only to write "nothing new." Nothing new was pretty normal for a preteen in a small town with nothing happening! There were some days when I literally wrote volumes! Even though I was saved as a child, there wasn't much of a godly or spiritual nature in my diary entries. As a young adult, I called my diaries "journals." Writing has always helped me maintain my focus and clarify my thoughts. It helps me put everything in perspective. (My memory isn't what it once was, and I don't think it was ever very good.) So if God wants to talk to me (and it is my firm belief that He wants to talk to *all* of us), I don't want to forget a thing He has to say! So I write it down.

When I still lived in Texas, there was a period of four or five days straight that I woke up at about three o'clock in the morning, with the name "Irene" on my mind. I was clueless. I didn't know anyone named Irene. But the Holy Spirit prompted me to pray for her, so I did. Having no idea who she was, let alone how to pray, I just prayed that God would bless her with His presence, that He would make Himself huge in her life and give her peace. (I found out later that the word Irene means peace!) After several nights of this, I called my dad and asked if we had any relatives named Irene, possibly relatives that I didn't know.

He didn't know of any either, but when I explained to him what was happening, he laughed and said that God knew he could get my attention in the middle of the night, because that was the only time I wasn't doing all the talking! Like I said, God is big enough to make Himself heard!

"Be still, and know that I am God: I will be exalted among the nations, I will be exalted in the earth" (Ps. 46:10, NKJV).

"Be still and know that I am God." I've always used that very phrase to calm my anxieties. Sometimes I even paraphrase it to suit my crisis: "Be still, take a break, settle down, cease striving, let it go, calm down, inhale, exhale and know that I am God, I have always been God and I will always be God so chill out and let me be God!"

It may be more appropriate to let it say, "Stop! Calm down and listen. It's my turn to talk," says God! Okay, so we finally sit down and shut up and we're ready to listen for our Shepherd's voice. And what do we hear? "Oh, I was supposed to call my sister this morning...wonder how she's feeling today... Or I need to pick up cat litter this afternoon...maybe I'll stop and get a latte on my way home, I wonder if Donna would have time to meet me there...it's my turn to buy..."

Such distracting thoughts may be from Satan—after all, he certainly doesn't want you to go through with this crazy plan of yours to hear from God! But those thoughts may just be our own flesh!

The following is an excerpt from the book *Having a Mary Heart in a Martha World*:

> As never before, my will and I stood face to face. I asked my will the straight question, "Will, are you ready for an hour of prayer?" Will answered, "Here I am, and I'm quite ready, if you are." So Will and I linked arms

35

and turned to go for our time of prayer. At
once all the emotions began pulling the other
way and protesting. "We're not coming," I
saw Will stagger a bit, so I asked. "Can you
stick it out, Will?" and Will replied, "Yes, if
you can." So Will went, and we got down to
prayer... It was a struggle all the way through.
At one point... one of those traitorous emotions had snared my imagination and had run
off to the golf course; and it was all I could
do to drag the wicked rascal back... At the
end of the hour, if you had asked me, "Have
you had a 'good time'?" I would have to reply,
"No, it has been a wearying wrestle with contrary emotions and a truant imagination from
beginning to end." What is more, that battle
with the emotions continued for between
two and three weeks, and if you had asked
me at the end of that period, "Have you had
a good time in your daily praying?" I would
still have had to confess, "No, at times it has
seemed as though the heavens were brass,
and God too distant to hear, and the Lord
Jesus strangely aloof, and prayer accomplish-
ing nothing." Yet something was happening.
For one thing, Will and I really taught the
emotions that we were completely independent of them. Also, one morning, about two
weeks after the contest began, just about the
time Will and I were going for another hour
of prayer, I overheard one of the emotions
whisper to another, "Come on, guys, it's no
use wasting any more time resisting. They'll

go just the same." ...Then, another couple of weeks later, what do you think happened? During one of our prayer times, when Will and I were no more thinking of the emotions than of the man in the moon, one of the most vigorous of the emotions unexpectedly sprang up and shouted, "Hallelujah!" at which all the other emotions exclaimed, "Amen!" And for the first time all the whole of my being—intellect, will and emotions—was united in one coordinated prayer operation. All at once, God was real, heaven was open, the Lord Jesus was luminously present, the Holy Spirit was indeed moving through my longings, and prayer was surprisingly vital. Moreover, in that instant there came a sudden realization that heaven had been watching and listening all the way through those days of struggle against chilling moods and mutinous emotions; also that I had been undergoing necessary tutoring by my heavenly Teacher.

Now, throughout the piece you just read, the author refers to the weeks—and by the end of the third week—so that tells you that this is not going to be an overnight process, right? This is not going to be a change that takes place today. But my hope is to establish a firm starting point here today, for you to cultivate into something that transforms your life!

Those distracting thoughts that keep us from quieting our hearts may be our enemy trying to prevent us from spending time with God. However, it is vital to remember that the primary source of those thoughts *might just be God*! It might be

Him telling me to call my sister! After all, she has had some health concerns lately! Remember my friend's advice: God is big enough to make Himself heard! That's a promise to remember!

> And the child Samuel served Jehovah before Eli. And the Word of Jehovah was rare in those days. *There was* no open vision. {God rarely spoke to people openly or in visions at that time.} And it happened at that time, when Eli *was* lying down in his place, and his eyes began to become dim so that he could not see. And the lamp of God had not gone out. And Samuel was lying down in the temple of Jehovah, where the ark of God *was*. And Jehovah called Samuel. And he answered, Here *am* I. And he ran to Eli, and said, Here *am* I. For you called me. And he said, I did not call. Go and lie down again. And he went to lie down. (1 Sam. 3:1–5, NKJV)

These verses indicate that God spoke in an audible voice to Samuel, do you agree? A voice, in fact, that was so loud that Samuel thought it was Eli calling from another room.

> And Jehovah called again, Samuel! And Samuel arose and went to Eli and said, Here am I, for you called me. And he answered, I did not call, my son. Go back, lie down. And Samuel did not yet know Jehovah, and the Word of Jehovah had not yet been revealed to him. And Jehovah called Samuel again, the third time. And he arose and went to Eli and said, Here am I, for you called me. And Eli

saw that Jehovah had called the child. And Eli said to Samuel, Go, lie down; and it shall be, if One calls you, you shall say, Speak, Jehovah, for Your servant hears. And Samuel went to lie down in his place. (1 Sam. 3:6–9, NKJV)

If we don't recognize God's voice, He doesn't just give up His quest to talk with us! He called Samuel again and again, and then laid it on Eli's heart in verse 8–9, to explain to Samuel what was really happening here! Finally, in verse 10, Samuel gets it!

"And Jehovah came and stood, and called as at other times, Samuel, Samuel! Then Samuel answered, Speak, for Your servant is listening" (1 Sam. 3:10, NKJV).

That's what we want our response to be, right? But if you're like me, my own thoughts get in the way! So I've learned a couple of tricks that help me quiet my spirit, and I think they'll help you too.

1. Ask God to open the eyes and ears of your heart.

    Therefore I speak to them in parables, because seeing they see not, and hearing they hear not; nor do they understand. And in them is fulfilled the prophecy of Isaiah which said, "By hearing you shall hear and shall not understand; and seeing you shall see and shall not perceive; for this people's heart has become gross, and their ears are dull of hearing, and they have closed their eyes, lest at any time they should see with their eyes and hear with their ears and should understand with their heart, and should be converted, and I should heal them." But blessed are your eyes, for they see; and your ears, for they hear. (Matt. 13:13–16, NKJV)

2. When you are getting ready to listen for God's voice, have a tablet handy. If something you forgot to do comes into your mind, write it down. If your doctor's appointment later that afternoon comes to mind, write it down. If you need to take the dog to the vet, write it down. Do you get the idea?

3. If a *person* comes into your mind, pray for that person right then and there. Don't wait. After all, it's probably a safe assumption that if one of God's children needs prayer in Florida, and another is listening for God's voice in Washington, that God would connect the two, right? Even if you don't know the person…don't forget Irene!

4. Then, put the list aside and pray. Now is when you get out your journal. During your quiet time, you can come back to the list. Lift it to God. Tell Him this is what *you* have planned for your day, and ask Him what *He* has in mind! Then listen and make any necessary changes!

Maybe you already journal. Maybe you don't. Maybe you used to but haven't for a while. Maybe you don't think the Bible tells us to journal. Let's look and see for ourselves what Scripture says about it.

So speaks Jehovah, the God of Israel, saying, Write all the Words that I have spoken to you in a book. (Jer. 30:2, NKJV)

…saying, I am the Alpha and Omega, the First and the Last. Also, What you see, write *in a book* and send it to the seven churches. (Rev. 1:11, NKJV; italics mine)

I will stand on my watch and set myself on the tower, and will watch to see what He will say to me, and what I shall answer when I am reproved. And Jehovah answered me and said, Write *the vision*, and make it plain on the tablets, that he who reads it may run. (Hab. 2:1–2, NKJV; italics mine)

I want to assure you that if you are one of those people who really don't want to journal, you are not being commanded to do so. What we have here is an example that we can follow. One of the General Principles of Biblical Interpretation is that a teaching that is merely *implied* in Scripture may be considered biblical when a comparison of related passages support it. The three passages we just read support the teaching of journaling. In another version, the verses in Habakkuk read this way: I will stand at my *guard post* and I will *watch and see* what He will speak to me. Then the Lord said, record the vision.

A *guard post* is any place that you can be still and hear from the Lord.

Watch and see: Obviously we're going to be listening, but it tells us to watch; to see—to look for God's vision or perspective as we pray. You may remember a Focus on the Family radio theater production called *Adventures in Odyssey*. Another similar program was *Insights for Living's Paws and Tails*. These are good examples of what your imagination is capable of doing. When you are listening, you turn on your "mind's eye," not just your ears. You have a mental picture of what the characters or the places look like. The story comes to life!

What He will speak to me: that involves recognizing the voice of the Shepherd, which comes with practice, as you will see!

Record the vision: That's the journaling we're talking about. There were no tape recorders back then. The scribes (similar to secretarial staff) wrote everything down on their scrolls with pen and ink. Write what God shows you. Don't be concerned at this point with what you're writing. Just write what comes into your heart.

We use our hearts or spirits, to learn truth, rather than our minds. God reveals things to us that our natural eyes and ears could never sense. He does this through His Spirit speaking directly to our spirits. God says that there are some things that He "reveals through the Spirit," which we must then take and test against the Bible, using our minds. Through the indwelling of the Holy Spirit in us, God has given us direct communion with Himself. We hear His voice within our hearts.

"Call to Me, and I will answer you, and show you great and inscrutable things which you do not know" (Jer. 33:3, NKJV).

How exciting that in the word given hundreds of years before Christ was born, God invited us to ask Him questions, so He could tell us about things we didn't know!

"My son, listen to my words; bow down your ear to my sayings" (Prov. 4:20, NKJV).

Open the *ears* of my heart, incline your ear...lean in to hear what He is saying. When we sit in a busy restaurant, it can be hard to carry on a conversation. So we have a tendency to lean in, toward the person we are trying to hear. God is not hard of hearing, but He is so interested in what you are saying to Him that I picture Him leaning in, out of interest and excitement that you are talking with Him!

Open the *eyes* of my heart, Lord... If we focus our eyes on ourselves as we listen for God's voice, the intuitive flow from our spirits is most likely going to be the voice or the desire of our own hearts. Yet if we "fix our eyes on Jesus, the Author and Perfecter of our faith," the intuitive flow will most likely be from Jesus, and not ourselves.

Chapter 5
Verifying That Voice

The more you know God's Word, the more you'll learn to recognize God's heart. When you know someone very well, you can sense the essence of who they are coming through their conversation. When you know God's Word, you'll know God's character, His essence. God will never tell you anything out of character.

By the way, that Irene I was talking about earlier that God led me to pray for was to become my landlady a few months later. She also became my very dear friend, whom I was privileged to lead to a relationship with Christ. She supported me in prayer for years, until she passed away. When we still our hearts to listen for the Shepherd's voice, it is important to understand that although there are times when you may actually hear God's voice audibly, we are actually listening with our spirits to hear God's Spirit. So we're listening for thoughts, more than an audible voice.

In his book, *Communion with God*, Dr. Mark Virkler[6] lists six characteristics to look for in order to recognize the thoughts that come into our hearts as God trying to tell us something. He calls them "interjecting" thoughts:

1. They are like our own thoughts, except that you sense them as coming from the heart, not the brain; they will be spontaneous, not analytical.
2. They can come easily as God speaking in the first person.
3. They are often light and gentle, and can be easily cut off by any exertion of your own thoughts.
4. They will have an unusual content to them, in that they will be wiser, more loving and more motive-oriented than your own thoughts.
5. They will cause a special reaction within your being, such as peace, excitement, conviction, faith, life, awe.
6. When embraced, they carry with them a fullness of strength to perform them, as well as a joy in doing so.

When we come to the Lord in prayer, we must decrease into nothing. We are to be living sacrifices. We must lay down our wills and be totally sold out to God's will concerning the issue about which we are praying. If our attitude isn't at that place yet, we need to pray for God to change our thinking, before we begin praying about the issue at hand.

Let me explain: If I pray about something while I still have a definite desire or direction about that matter in my own heart, my desires interfere with my ability to hear God's true direction on the issue. It may cause me to believe that God is confirming the direction I felt, whether He is or not. In other words, if I pray about an item and the item is more prominent in the eyes of my heart than my vision of the Lord, the answer will most likely be from my heart rather than from the Lord's. On the other hand, if my vision of God is more prominent in my consciousness than my vision of the issue I am praying about, then the answer I receive will most likely be from the Lord, and not contaminated by my own desires on the subject. The principle is that the intuitive flow comes out of the vision I hold before my eyes. That's why it is imperative to fix our eyes on Jesus. Then the vision will be pure.

I want to share another excerpt from Joanna Weaver's *Having a Mary Heart in a Martha World*:

> Suddenly my eyes were open to what true devotion was. It is not a duty; it is a delight! It is not an exercise in piety; it is a privilege. And it is not so much a visit, as it is a homecoming. Without question, one of the most remarkable Christian doctrines is that Jesus Christ himself through the presence of the Holy Spirit will actually enter a heart, settle down and be at home there.

Then she quotes Robert Munger's article "My Heart Christ's Home"[7]:

> We invited Jesus into our hearts, but imagine asking Him to move in there! To live there! Jesus came into the darkness of my heart and turned on the light. He built a fire in the cold hearth and banished the chill. He started the music where there had been stillness and He filled the emptiness with His own loving, wonderful fellowship.
>
> As Munger described each room, Joanna Weaver continues: they reflected my heart as well. But it was his description of the drawing room that would forever change the way

I viewed my time with the Lord: We walked into the drawing room. This room was rather intimate and comfortable. I liked it. It had a fireplace, overstuffed chairs, a bookcase, a sofa and a quiet atmosphere. He also seemed pleased with it. He said, "This is indeed a delightful room. Let us come here often. It is secluded and quiet and we can have fellowship together." Well naturally as a young Christian I was thrilled! I could not think of anything I would rather do than have a few minutes apart with Christ in intimate comradeship. He promised, "I will be here every morning early. Meet with me here and we will start the day together." So morning after morning I would come downstairs to the drawing room and He would take a book of the Bible, open it and we would read together. He would tell me of its riches and unfold to me its truths... They were wonderful hours together! In fact, we called the drawing room our "withdrawing room." It was a period when we had our quiet time together. But little by little, under the pressure of many responsibilities, this time began to be shortened... I began to miss a day now and then... I would miss it two days in a row and often more... I remember one morning when I was in a hurry... As I passed the drawing room, the door was ajar. Looking in, I saw a fire in the fireplace and the Lord sitting there... "Blessed Master forgive me. Have you been here all these mornings?" "Yes," he replied. "I told you I would be here every morning to meet with you." Then I was even more ashamed. He had been faithful to me in spite of my unfaithfulness. I asked His forgiveness and He readily forgave me... He said, "The trouble with you is this: You have been thinking of the quiet time, of the Bible study and prayer time, as a factor in your own spiritual progress. But you have forgotten that this hour means something to Me also!" What an amazing thought! That Christ wants to spend quality time with me! That He looks forward to our time together and misses me when I don't show up!

The Bible tells us not to give in to our vain imaginations. But this is a positive use of your imagination. This is something you can do in your quiet time with the Lord. Imagine yourself inviting God into each room of your heart and turning over to Him everything you do in your kitchen, when you spill sugar all over the floor, everything you do in your bedroom. If it's important to you, it's important to God! Oh, it isn't easy to schedule regular "drawing room" time with our Lord. Believe me, I struggle with it too, and I don't have children at home!

My outlook changed by author Mark Buchanan from Vancouver Canada. In his book *The Rest of God*,[8] he has some insight into that very problem. His research showed that the root of the Hebrew word for "sanctify" means to betroth, to pledge as in marriage. Mr. Buchanan's definition changed my thinking. We define "sanctify" as set apart. If I am going to set apart time for daily quiet time with the Lord, I "sanctify" that time. I set it apart. In the original language, then, I pledge that time, as if in marriage! That means commitment! If you pledge something to God, you must take that commitment as seriously as marriage! You are pledging to God that you will set and keep this Drawing Room appointment, whether it is convenient or not! It is time betrothed to God! We will be convicted if we miss that time, but we will not be condemned. If we miss it because of an emergency, He'll willingly come along with us to take care of that emergency, if we remember to invite Him along.

Our Drawing Room time doesn't have to be a huge block of time. When God takes charge of our time, he can stretch a fifteen-minute meeting into a fulfilling encouraging date that keeps us flying all day long! He stretches the time so you are still able to accomplish what He wants you to get done!

Let's eavesdrop on the journaling of a king, in Psalm 61.

> Hear my cry, O God; Attend to my prayer. From the end of the earth I will cry to You, When my heart is overwhelmed; Lead me to the rock that is higher than I. For You have been a shelter for me, A strong tower from the enemy. I will abide in Your tabernacle forever; I will trust in the shelter of Your wings. Selah (Psalm 61:1–4, NKJV)

These first four verses of this psalm portray King David in a desperate pleading state—he is crying out to the Lord. His heart is overwhelmed, but He knows the name of the Lord is His strong tower, and He trusts in the shelter of God's wings. That's why he's turning to God in the first place! He knows where his strength lies! Then at the end of verse 4, there is the word *Selah*. It's in the psalm quite frequently, and we often go right past it, without even reading it. It's a short word but it's a huge word. It means *stop, pause and consider, take a second look. Think about what you just read.* In this case, it means, "Think, David, about what you just *wrote*! Is God truly your strength?" I believe, in this case, David did take a second look at what he had just written—this desperate cry from his heart—God was right there listening, waiting for this little lamb to stop talking...to be still so God could get a word in edgewise! We don't know how long David paused before continuing to write the psalm. We don't know what He might have heard the Great Shepherd say to this lowly shepherd, but the very next line gives us a good idea! His whole outlook has changed:

> For You, O God, have heard my vows; You have given me the heritage of those who fear Your name. You will prolong the king's life, His years as many generations. He shall abide before God forever. Oh, prepare mercy and truth, which may preserve him! So I will sing praise to Your name forever, That I may daily perform my vows. (Ps. 61:5–8, NKJV)

David's circumstances didn't change. But he was seeing them with God's perspective, so his outlook is what changed. David wasn't always a king. He started out as a shepherd. He knew sheep. It was the most natural thing in the world for him to relate to his Heavenly Father as his Great Shepherd. David knew how much he himself would care for one of his sheep. The psalm we just read tells us that David knew how much God loved him. So he knew that God would care for him even more than he would have cared for one of his own sheep. David knew the daily needs of his sheep. He had learned to recognize his sheep's contented sounds, as opposed to the bleating of a sheep that was in trouble, so he could respond immediately.

When I was living in Texas, I knew a modern-day shepherd who shared a lot of his knowledge of sheep...actually how dumb they really are. But they knew their shepherd's voice. He told us that if he spoke softly to them when he talked to them, they came toward his voice. He invited some of the church leaders to what he called a shepherd's luncheon. Wes had set a lovely table in a pecan orchard, and after we ate, he asked us to sit quietly for a few minutes. As he started speaking, raising his voice only slightly, the sheep came out of a pasture and started across the pecan orchard toward us. They came closer so they could hear him, and feel safe and secure, knowing he was close to them. They looked at us and made a wide circle around us, ignoring the strangers, trying to coax them over to where we were sitting. But they would have none of it. They moved toward their shepherd. He could turn his sheep away from trouble with a voice near a whisper! He didn't have to yell. He didn't even have to raise his voice.

> To him the gatekeeper opens. The sheep hear his voice, and he calls his own sheep by name and leads them out. When he has brought out all his own, he goes before them, and the sheep follow him, for they know his voice. A stranger they will not follow, but they will flee from him, for they do not know the voice of strangers. (John 10:3–5, NKJV)

Jesus went on to say "the sheep know My voice." Jesus is talking about *His* sheep. The sheep that recognize His voice are the ones that belong to Him. If we don't belong to Jesus, we're never going to recognize His voice! Once we give our lives to Him, we desire to get closer to Him, to lean in toward Him, so we can hear His voice, just as Wes's sheep drew nearer, to hear Him better. No matter how long we have been one of the Great Shepherd's sheep, the Holy Spirit indwells us. When we are born again, our spirits are made alive to God's Holy Spirit.

His Spirit lives in our hearts. The only way we can successfully run the race God has placed before us is to learn how to receive guidance from the Holy Spirit, as you listen to your spirit.

"What does it say? [This is the message Paul preached everywhere he went] 'The word is near you, in your mouth and in your heart'" (Rom. 10:8, NKJV).

Obviously, this scripture isn't talking about that pinkish miracle inside your chest that goes ba-thump, ba-thump! It refers to our spiritual hearts, our inner man or our spirit. God communicates with us through the spirit man inside us. That's what we want to learn to listen to. You can be led by the Holy Spirit in every situation of your life if you learn to listen to your heart—your spirit. One of the pastors I studied under had a saying, "If it pleases you to please God, do as you please." To be successful in life, we as Christians must decide ahead of time to listen to our hearts *only* if our hearts' desire is to please God! Then to always do what the Holy Spirit is leading us to do! That's why it is so important to train ourselves to be able to hear the Holy Spirit!

Chapter 6
Spiritual Fitness

You can drive through even a tiny town almost anywhere in America and see physical fitness centers and gyms. Millions of dollars are spent every year by Americans trying to get their physical bodies into shape! Millions more are being spent at colleges and universities to train us intellectually, to get the educations that are so valuable! Our spirits must be trained as well. We have to train the eyes and ears of our hearts to listen and hear the Holy Spirit talking to our spirit! We must train our bodies physically, intellectually, and spiritually!

Besides the written Word of God, I want to address three general ways that the Holy Spirit communicates with us.

1. **The Inward witness**. Romans 8:16—The Spirit Himself bears witness with our spirit. Sometimes that's called the "check" in our spirit. The conviction that we shouldn't be doing what we're doing. This is what enables us to live every day of our lives. Maybe the Holy Spirit nudges us to turn and take a different route on our way home one day. We may never know what we were saved from by changing routes, or what blessing or divine appointment God's Holy Spirit led us to.

   Prophets from the Old Testament would say, "The Word of the Lord came to me saying..." The Word didn't come to them in an audible voice, or else the whole village would have heard it too and there would have been no need for prophets! They were Old Testament prophets because they "had" the Spirit of God. Today, a Christian doesn't need to go to the prophets or the priests to hear from God. We have the Spirit of God in us. We just have to train ourselves to listen.

2. **The Inward Voice**. The inward man, our spirit man has a voice. It tells us what is right and wrong. It is commonly called our conscience, our still small voice

3. **The voice of the Holy Spirit**. There is a difference between the still small voice of our own spirits and the inward voice of the Holy Spirit. When the Holy Spirit communicates with your spirit, it is an authoritative voice. It can be so real it almost sounds like an audible voice. You may even look behind you to see who is talking to you. Remember Samuel's first conversation with the Lord? He thought it was his mentor, Eli, calling him from another room. (1 Samuel 3)

The phrase "he who has an ear let him hear" is used several times in Scripture. Jesus uses it when He teaches in parables. He uses it when He writes to the end-time churches through John. Jesus is not talking about physical ears here. I believe He is saying "turn on your spiritual ears"—the ears of our hearts—and really get this!

In Revelation 2:7 John is writing as Jesus is dictating the first of the letters to the seven churches: He who has an ear, let him hear what the Spirit says to the churches (NKJV).

In Revelation 3:20, Christ is addressing the last letter to the Laodicean Church. My Bible calls that church the lukewarm one. In *Escape the Coming Night* by Dr. David Jeremiah[9], it's called the "disgusting church." In this letter, Jesus adds a phrase. He says, "If anyone hears My voice..."

It's like a call to order. Class is starting. Pay attention! Wake up. Okay, now at least some of you have turned on your spiritual ears... Then in verse 22, he goes on, "he who has an ear, let him hear."

Jesus uses that same phrase in each of the seven letters. Who were those letters addressed to? The churches, right? What were those churches comprised of? Saints. Christians. If population demographics are similar then as what they are now, more than half of those Christians are women! There really is a reason God gave us two ears and one mouth! I don't want to be so busy talking or so distracted doing other things, even ministry that I don't hear Jesus! I don't think you do either! I don't want to be so preoccupied that Jesus doubts I still have the spiritual ears He gave me! I want to hear Jesus the first time He speaks. I want to be so in tune to Jesus that I hear His every sigh. John's spirit was trained to see the visions, to hear the revelation he was given! This is the same John who rested his head against Jesus's breast at the Last Supper. I want to hear every heartbeat! Don't you?!

I know evolution isn't a popular topic among Christians, but it is very relevant. The definition of evolution is this: any process of formation or growth, a process of gradual, progressive change and development. That's what happens when journaling occurs on a regular basis. It evolves, but not on its own. You have to make it happen, by spending drawing room time with the Lord, and practicing hearing from God.

> The wisest of women builds her house, but folly with her own hands tears it down. Whoever walks in uprightness fears the LORD, but he who is devious in his ways despises him. By the mouth of a fool comes a

rod for his back, but the lips of the wise will preserve them. Where there are no oxen, the manger is clean, but abundant crops come by the strength of the ox. A faithful witness does not lie, but a false witness breathes out lies. A scoffer seeks wisdom in vain, but knowledge is easy for a man of understanding. Leave the presence of a fool, for there you do not meet words of knowledge. (Prov. 14:1–7, NKJV)

These were the writings of a king. They were wise words, but there's no flow, is there? They just seem to be random thoughts. Undoubtedly wise, but disconnected statements from the wisest and richest king ever—King Solomon. A far cry from the poetic form of his father, King David, in the Psalms we read a few pages back. Here's the point: Your journal will be totally different from mine, from anyone else's! It may be as different as these two forms of writing are, and one entry is different from the next. Journaling is not an exercise in grammar or in English composition. This is your love letter to God and His response to your letter! This is where evolution can begin in your journaling and in your spiritual life.

In one of my old journal entries, written shortly after my divorce, I was whimpering to God about something, probably about my being alone and feeling vulnerable. He led me specifically to 2 Kings 11. This is the story about Baby Joash being kidnapped by his aunt and protected by her and the priest. His wicked grandmother went on a crazed rampage and practically wiped out the entire royal line. She would have succeeded too if it hadn't been for God stepping in and leading baby Joash into the protective arms of his aunt and the priest for seven years, until she could be dealt with and he could take his rightful place on the throne.

God took that one short Old Testament chapter and so brought it to life in one drawing room visit that I could apply those seemingly unrelated truths to what I was going through in my own life. That's where my book (*Protective Custody*) came from. This isn't a book about a baby being kidnapped out of harm's way. It isn't a book about a woman whose love for God cost her her marriage! This is a book about God's never failing, never wavering faithfulness and commitment to His children! To you! A story about His strength and protection for us to lean on every single day of our lives! He wants to talk to you about it!

When I look ahead a few years into the midpoint of my healing after that devastating blow, I see tremendous growth in my journaling. Your journaling cannot develop without your relationship with God deepening and increasingly becoming what God created you for—that personal intimacy with your Great Shepherd! That's evolution at its finest! The growth I see in my journaling directly coincides with my spiritual growth. I see visible improvement in my spiritual well-being and I know you will see the change in yours!

In Joanna Weaver's book she states, "Some people feel uneasy in the presence of God. They dismiss the act of worship as too emotional, preferring the intellectual pursuit of Bible study. Or they simply have trouble being still, because that's their personality. But regardless of our temperament, regardless of our emotional preference, we are all called to intimacy with God. That's why He created us!"

> But Martha was distracted with much serving. And she went up to him and said, "Lord, do you not care that my sister has left me to serve alone? Tell her then to help me." But the Lord answered her, "Martha, Martha, you are anxious and troubled about many things, but one

thing is necessary. Mary has chosen the good portion, which will not be taken away from her." (Luke 10:40, NKJV)

The "one thing" Martha needed—the one thing Mary found at Jesus's feet—is the one thing *we* all need, as well. God actually wants us close and is willing to do whatever it takes to make sure it happens.

I have a friend who was working with her husband when a heavy piece of equipment fell on her foot. She was laid up for several weeks! She believes it was God telling her she needed to spend more time in the drawing room with Him. She spent much of her recuperation seeking God's face, studying His Word, and "just" spending time with Him! I myself recently fell and ended up with a badly sprained ankle and a bruised hip. That jump restarted my quiet time with Him! I'm not saying God will make you spend time with Him, but when you begin this new deepening in your prayer life, you can rest assured God is on your side! He wants it to happen as much as you do, if not more!

There are some important safeguards I always share, when I'm teaching about listening for God's voice.

1. The more you know the Bible, the more you know the character of God. The more you know God's character, the more you will recognize that you are indeed listening to *His* voice.

2. God may chastise, correct, or teach you through your journaling, but He does it in love and is never condemning. He will convict and convince. Only our enemy condemns.

3. What God tells you in your quiet time will never contradict anything He has already said in His

written word. As I mentioned earlier, you have to know what's in there! 1 Thessalonians 5:21 tells us to examine everything carefully and to hold onto that which is good. We are to test what we hear, against the Word of God, not our own theology. The lawful use of scripture, according to Romans 15:4, is to cause one to persevere and be encouraged to hope. We are not to beat someone over the head with it, nor are we to beat ourselves up in testing our journaling.

4. God will never tell you to sin. Again, that would be contrary to His written word.

5. He will never speak against His children. So if you go venting to Him about something one of your Christian friends said or did, He's not going to take sides with you against them. More than likely He's going to tell you to go to them and love them through whatever difficulty they are going through! That goes back to God's character.

6. Develop a humble attitude and a teachable spirit. Never say "God told me and that's that." Remember you are human and fallible! All revelation must be tested.

7. As you begin journaling, you will find the Holy Spirit grants you healing, love, and affirmation when He speaks edification, exhortation, and comfort to your heart (1 Cor. 14:3). Look for them. Expect them. Accept them. Enjoy them. Remember, He delights in you. Share all your emotions with God. If it matters to you, it matters to Him.

8. As you progress in your journaling, you may be tempted to ask God for specific dates, names, and places. Don't bother. (When I've done this, I've found that His answer is usually, "Soon," which can mean any time over the next one thousand years, or, "Trust me.") I do trust Him! The better you know God's heart and character, the more you know He is worthy of our trust!

9. If you feel the Lord has revealed something to you that you need to act on immediately, always seek godly counsel. We are all called to be obedient, but also to be wise.

10. Remember that God is not going to tell you to do something that He has not given you authority to do. Husbands, fathers, and elders of the church are your authorities.

11. If your journaling becomes discouraging or destructive to you, instead of leading you to greater wholeness, stop journaling and talk to a godly man or woman you are comfortable with, who will be honest with you. Ephesians 5:21 tells us to submit ourselves to one another. If you submit your journaling to another saint, you won't go off on a wrong path. Women, don't forget that the person God leads you to, to discuss your journaling may just be your husband.

The five steps to testing each journal entry are the following:

1. What is its origin? The more you know the Bible, the more you know the character of God. The more you know God's character, the more you

will recognize His voice. Remember God is convicting and convincing but never condemning.

2. What is its content? It will never contradict anything God has already said in His written Word! God will never tell you to sin and He will never speak against His children.

3. What is its fruit? It will be instructive, encouraging, helpful, and will always lead you back to Scripture.

4. Compare it with Scripture. That means you have to know Scripture! Study it!

5. Submit it to your spiritual sound board. If you don't have one, look around you. Look at maybe someone you are sharing a room with. Talk about it, pray about it. God will give you good advice.

If any part of what I have shared thus far has made it sound like I have it all together and have this "Hearing from God" thing down pat, believe me nothing could be further from the truth. Every date I plan with God sets off all kinds of attacks—not just from the enemy of our souls, but from my own will and emotions as well. Everything I've been able to share, I learned from the school of hard knocks, until I finally figured out that God's way is easier. Even after learning that, I still miss it occasionally!

Just because we become Christians, those hard knocks don't necessarily come to an end. We just have the Holy Spirit's help going through them! I can't leave you thinking that once I made the decision to let God choose my mate, it all worked out like the story book ending. When my husband, Hutch, and I got married on Valentine's Day 2003, we both had been alone for several years, so we had pretty much learned the ins and outs of being in control of our own lives. I was kind of a neat freak, and he was definitely not…you know, that kind of thing that you don't know about someone until you live with them. It was pretty obvious right from the start that our marriage was not the happy ever after that we had both expected.

I can only speak from my own perspective here, but you have to understand, I had been married to a Christian man who didn't understand how to be the spiritual lead in our family, a man who claimed to be a Christian and lived a totally different life and an adamant nonbeliever! Did you hear the words "godly man" in that mess? No, because I'd never been married to one! When Hutch and I got married, I had no idea how to be a godly wife, and I didn't have any desire whatsoever how to be a submissive one, even to a godly husband who was willing to take the spiritual lead in our lives. I was ordained at the time, preaching and teaching and leading the choir! I think you can understand why I felt I didn't need a spiritual leader! Those early months were a constant struggle, that I knew I wasn't winning. I was miserable, he was miserable, we were both in shock. The hardest part was I really loved this man and I knew he wasn't winning either! Nobody wins in a struggle like that!

I made decisions for the wrong reasons. I did what I had to do to protect my Christian witness. Wrong motive, but I was being submissive to my husband in public, so at least that was a good thing. And I never really outright rebelled in private either, but boy my heart! My heart was another matter entirely! I resented being under his authority—and I taught spiritual authority! I knew God sees the heart! And in all honesty I even resented God putting me there. But in the midst of it all I didn't realize what was happening.

Now you don't know this so you'll just have to take my word for it when I say that my husband is the most honest godly man of integrity I have ever known. But I was really struggling with God putting him in charge, over me, can you tell? I was angry on the outside and rebellious in my heart. I can remember about eight months into our marriage, sitting on the couch having a "discussion" with my husband. Hutch has a "pseudo-calm" voice that he uses when he knows that what he's about to say is not going to sit well with me. That's the voice he used that evening. I can remember him saying, in this "sickening-sweet" voice, "Honey, God talks to you, why don't you pray about it and see what He has to say." I immediately spouted back. (Oh my poor husband.) "Apparently God has nothing to say to me because I *have* been praying and *God isn't talking to me right now*."

It was an unexpected truth that was so upsetting to me that tears instantly poured, the conversation ended, and I went to bed crying. What I didn't know was that my husband stayed up most the night praying…for me. Poor guy didn't have a clue what he'd gotten into with this "woman God gave him." And I couldn't shed any light on it because I didn't get it myself. Psalm 32 let the light of God's Word shed some light on the situation:

> Blessed is the one whose transgression is forgiven, whose sin is covered. Blessed is the man against whom the LORD counts no iniquity, and in whose spirit there is no deceit. For when I kept silent, my bones wasted away through my groaning all day long. For day and night your hand was heavy upon me; my strength was dried up as by the heat of summer. Selah. (Ps. 32:1–4, ESV)

Remember what "selah" means? Pause and consider. I knew that I was dealing with some heavy stuff. I felt horrible all the time, physically! I had recently been diagnosed with fibromyalgia syndrome—unexplained widespread pain—but when I read this verse and really paused and considered what it meant, I realized my heaviness was the very hand of God and He wasn't happy with me. I knew I needed to get on my face and repent! And I did. I didn't want to! I wanted to get rid of my battle, but I didn't want to give up control! I didn't want to repent. Because I knew that meant I had to turn away from my power struggle with my husband! I wanted to maintain control, even though I absolutely positively knew that control was not rightfully *or scripturally* mine!

"I acknowledged my sin to you, and I did not cover my iniquity; I said, 'I will confess my transgressions to the LORD,' and you forgave the iniquity of my sin. Selah" (Ps. 32:5, ESV).

When you pause and consider *that* phrase, after you have humbled yourself, and turned away from your sin and turned back to God's arms, you find such love and forgiveness there! That's when you feel how big and loving and warm God really is! That's when you experience His grace and mercy!

Chapter 7
A Mother-In-Law's Story

You're probably familiar with the story of Naomi and her daughter-in-law, Ruth. There was a time in my life, when it was very easy for me to put myself in Naomi's shoes. While my son was on the road with his job, my daughter-in-law lived with me. I was honored to lead her to the Lord. I treasure this biblical story and I am still learning the many lessons found there. The applicable lesson here is something that we don't study too much about. We're told Naomi is a widow, but let's back up a minute and look at her marriage.

Ruth's husband's name was Elimelech. He and Naomi and their two sons were living in Israel when the famine started seriously affecting them. So, Elimelech decided to pack up his family and move to Moab, where there was plenty of food. Now Moab was a pagan territory, far different from Israel's religion-based culture, even though it was only thirty miles away. That move took Naomi's sons out of their homeland, where they could marry Israelite women, and set them up to marry pagan women. Both Naomi and Elimelech knew that marrying these women was strictly forbidden by God. As head of the family, Elimelech could have, and in my opinion, should have confessed. He should have confessed his first decision to move the family out of Israel and away from their faith. He should have confessed his second wrong decision to allow his oldest son marry a pagan woman. And he should have confessed his third wrong decision when he repeated his mistake and allowed his youngest son to marry one as well. But he didn't. As a result, not only did Elimelech die but both of his sons did as well.

Now look at all this from Naomi's viewpoint. She is a widow, with two pagan daughters-in-law. They don't believe what she believes. She is a strange land, with no ties to her Jewish heritage. She's brokenhearted and bitter. She's probably angry with her deceased husband for bringing her here and for dying and making her a widow, let alone for making her and her sons abandon the God of their fathers, and now she feels like God has deserted her as well. I'm thinking she's pretty depressed, don't you think? It would be perfectly understandable if she had (1) refused to move in the first place; (2) packed her and her sons up and moved back to Israel; or (3) she could have nagged Elimelech and made his life miserable right up until the day he died, trying to convince him to move back to Israel. But she didn't do that. She chose—and it's always a choice—to trust God to take care of the situation. God did, just not in the same way we might have. Maybe not in the way that Naomi would have chosen. But God, in His sovereignty, advised Naomi to step into her daughter-in-law's situation. God had Naomi position Ruth so He could place her in the bloodline of our Lord Jesus Christ.

There is another pause in verse 7. Then God answers: "I will instruct you and teach you in the way you should go; I will counsel you with My eye upon you" (Ps. 32:8, ESV).

God honored Naomi's decision to be obedient to Him by being submissive to her husband, even though she thought he was wrong. Even when she believed he was not listening to God. Ruth was brought to a point where she would marry Boaz, the kinsman redeemer, because of the godly guidance and the obedience of Naomi. Do you think that plan was Naomi's?

Of course not, it was God's. Is it possible that Naomi had to be still in order to hear God, to hear that plan?

Within a month from that tearful outburst with my husband, our women's group at church began teaching their fall Bible study. The had decided to study a book by Martha Peace called *Becoming a Titus Two Woman—all* about submission! You can imagine how absolutely thrilled I was to attend that! I hadn't missed a Bible study yet, so how would it look if I didn't go to this one! Another right decision with a wrong motive! I prayed and earnestly asked the Lord to open my heart to what he wanted me to see, because I really didn't want to go. I did go…and my heart was softened…a little. God had my undivided attention, and He started talking to me again. I started listening again, humbly.

Then several months later, I was asked to teach that same study, and I learned even more about being a godly wife. In the midst of teaching that study, my Women's Ministry director and I decided to go through Martha Peace's next book *The Excellent Wife*. More godly instruction.

"I will instruct you and teach you in the way you should go; I will counsel you with My eye upon you." God instructed Naomi about submission and she listened and learned and acted on God's Word! She was rewarded! God instructed me to the hilt about submission, and I have grown in leaps and bounds and I am learning that there is true joy in submitting to my husband! I am learning that even if he isn't perfect. God is! I had to relax, be still, calm down, breathe…and you know what? God is still being God! When we repent of our rebellion, or whatever sin we are in, He listens to us again and He talks to us again! When we have any sin that hasn't been dealt with—lies, gossip, addictions, rebellion, whatever this book calls sin—if we're doing it, God turns a deaf ear to us and He doesn't talk to us.

"Be not like a horse or a mule, without understanding, whose mouth must be curbed with bit and bridle, or it will not stay near you. Many are the sorrows of the wicked, but mercy embraces the one who trusts in the LORD" (Ps. 32:9–10, ESV).

Don't be discouraged if you are in a difficult position. You have a hope to cling to. No matter what your situation is, God is not only big enough to *handle* it all, He's big enough to *fix* it all! No matter what you're dealing with, God is big enough! All we have to do is (1) trust Him, (2) get out of His way, and (3) let God be God!

"Be still and know that I am God." Do you believe Him yet? It means we have to stop mumbling and grumbling and whimpering and whining. It means we have to be still...it means we have to listen...so we can learn...so we can be still and know. It is in our weakness, when we come to God out of total desperation, that He can be strong in our lives! When we come to Him in tears or grief, He consoles us and comforts us. When we come to Him in turmoil and anxiety, He gives us peace. Whatever your problem, He has the solution. Whatever your need, He has the answer. But if we come to Him excited about something that is happening in our lives, He can share that excitement with you! God wants to be a part of your life, whether you are happy, sad, mixed up, or right in focus! He just wants to spend time with you!

And finally, Psalm 32:11 says, "Be glad in the LORD, and rejoice, O righteous, and shout for joy, all you upright in heart!"

He's talking to you! You are the righteous one He's talking about because you are in Christ. Shout for joy! Whatever it is you've been going through, whatever it is you've been struggling with or wrestling with, God knew about it from the beginning of time. This is the time and place He chose for your healing—maybe He chose for you to be healed here completely once and for all, as you read this chapter. Maybe this is the removal of the bandage—healing complete. But this has been a very important chapter for you! This has been important to Him too!

You may have physical wounds or emotional ones. If you've been wounded by family, friends, Christians, or non-Christians, crawl up in Daddy God's lap and give that wound to Him. Let Him be God, lay those troubles in His lap, and leave them there. If God has brought to your mind an area where repentance is needed, do that now, while you are in His lap in His loving arms. Repent and receive His forgiveness. Feel His mercy and love comfort you and encourage you.

Chapter 8

Jacob: Speckled Sheep, Boundaries

Have you ever sat and watched children play—especially when they don't know you're watching them? Quite often you hear one of them say, "Mine," and then you'll hear a reply, "No, mine!" Then an argument ensues and sometimes screaming and crying and tears and, well, you'd better step in about then.

When Jacob saw Rachel, he wanted her for his wife. He bargained with Laban, her father, who agreed to let him marry Rachel only after Jacob worked for him for seven years. In this chapter, we will learn that Laban is a selfish man and basically, he said, "Rachel is *mine*." Jacob works for Laban tending his sheep, taking care of his property, and after seven years there is a wedding. But many of you know Laban still says "mine." Unbeknownst to Jacob, Laban substitutes his older daughter, Leah, and Jacob marries her instead of Rachel. (Jacob must really have wanted Rachel for his wife, because he agrees to work another seven years so that he can marry her and it happened just that way.) Fast forward a few years, Jacob's family grows and he approaches Laban and requests they be allowed to return to his own country, but Laban asks him to stay and they renegotiate their agreement.

In Genesis 30:32, Laban agrees to let Jacob have all the sheep with streaks and spots. About *those* sheep, Laban does not say "mine." He sees them as imperfect, and he tells Jacob that

70

he can have those sheep as his wages. So the agreement is that Laban gets all the nice, pretty sheep and Jacob gets all the seemingly flawed ones—the streaked or spotted ones, because Laban sees them as imperfect. He doesn't want those, even though there isn't a thing wrong with them, similar to people who have freckles. (My freckles don't mean I am flawed, although as a kid, I thought they did.)

Jacob moves with his family and his flocks, about three days journey from Laban. God increases Jacob's flocks tremendously. God is always watching and waiting to bless His children. Suddenly there are a lot more speckled sheep…so many more that Laban's sons begin to be jealous. Laban is not happy. God's blessing on His children isn't always viewed favorably by others. It may be resentment, jealousy, even our brothers and sisters, and fellow believers can be envious of God's blessings on us.

In Genesis 31:13, God tells Jacob to get out of his land and return to his own family. Jacob talks to both of his wives, Leah and Rachel, and he tells them that God has given them instructions to leave. After he reminds them how deviously Laban has dealt with him, even before the weddings, they agree that it's best to leave. But they also know that Laban is probably not going to let them go quietly, so they pack up their belongings and plan to leave after dark. In the process of packing their belongings, Rachel takes it upon herself to pack a few things that do not belong to her. The household idols she chooses to take with her in Genesis 31:19 belong to her father. Scripture tells us that Laban spent what inheritance should have been his daughters, so maybe Rachel justified stealing them by convincing herself the idols were rightfully hers. They are pagan idols and are not valuable to Jacob, but they certainly were to Laban and you can bet he is going to notice they are missing and say, "mine."

Understand that God has blessed Jacob, his wives, children, and flocks, so much so that they are not going to be able to go anywhere without being noticed. Laban pursues them. In verse 24, God appears to Laban and tells him to speak neither good nor bad to Jacob. When he catches up to their caravan Laban questions Jacob about sneaking out in the middle of the night and asks "why have you stolen my gods from me?" (Gen. 31:30).

Jacob knows nothing about this, so he declares his innocence and instructs Laban to search his whole caravan. Whoever is found with them is to be killed. Rachel had them hidden and claimed that she could not get up so they didn't search the blanket on her camel and therefore, they didn't find them. Jacob, thinking they are in the clear, begins to get angry at the accusation and he starts spewing his anger—it's what we do naturally when we're unjustly accused. All of the old hurts that Laban had caused came to the surface from Jacob's heart and spewed out his mouth.

In verse 43, Jacob and Laban agree to disagree, and Jacob builds an altar in verse 52, honoring a covenant to designate that altar as the boundary that neither one shall pass. Boundaries are important. Physical boundaries protect your property from your neighbor's property and vice versa. Spiritual boundaries are crucial to your walk with the Lord. Jacob was able to maintain his, although Rachel's desire for her father's idols indicates he had not established the same for her. Emotional boundaries are necessary too to protect your heart. The emotional boundaries are really what this is about between Laban and Jacob. Jacob had learned that Laban was a man who would take what he wanted and who would guard what he had. Jacob had worked hard and God had blessed him and prospered him. He wanted to protect that, but Jacob also wanted to protect himself and his wives from their father's devious dealings. Laban had already proven himself not to be a trustworthy man—not someone you would want to open yourself up to, because his history shows that you will be hurt. But you have to be careful when you set up too many boundaries, as Jacob would soon learn. As soon as Jacob sets up this boundary and the two men say their good-byes, Laban returns home and Jacob turns to continue his journey and he comes to the boundary of his brother Esau.

Now, turn the tables here in your mind for a minute. Esau was the firstborn of Isaac. If you remember, Jacob tricked Isaac into giving *him* the blessing intended for the firstborn—the blessing that should have rightfully gone to Esau. Realizing he had been duped, Esau threatened to kill Jacob. Their mother Rebecca instructed Jacob to flee and that's how Jacob ended up living with Laban's people in the first place. With that history between brothers, you can understand why it was a fairly safe assumption on Jacob's part that he might not have been welcomed, if he crossed Esau's boundary unannounced. Jacob sends a generous gift to his brother Esau. Then he sits and waits. Now, Jacob is in a place where he can't return and he can't continue forward. He's between a rock and a hard place. I call it limbo. We've all been there at one time or another. It's a time of reflection, considering choices, making plans, and, hopefully, renewing our relationship with God.

Sometimes, it's really good to be alone. When we are alone we can turn off the TV, open our Bibles, read, and truly understand some of the lessons there and how to apply them to our situations. When we allow Him to, God meets us there. Whatever comes to our minds when we are alone, we can talk to God about. We can listen for His viewpoint on our situation. We can just rest in the presence of God, or we can wrestle with Him as Jacob did. In Genesis 32:24 Jacob is all alone when he has an encounter with God.

As a side note and generally speaking…no one gets to see the face of God. Even Moses on Mount Sinai wasn't permitted to see him. Maybe, it's because Jacob dealt honorably with Laban. Maybe it's because Jacob was Isaac's son, who was Abraham's son, whom God promised He would bless and multiply. It may be for all of those reasons or it may simply be because God blesses his children. Whatever the reason, God allowed His face to be seen by Jacob. God is sovereign and He can do whatever He wants to do. He can show Himself to whomever He wants to show Himself.

"So Jacob called the name of the place Peniel: 'For I have seen God face to face, and my life is preserved'" (Gen. 32:30, NKJV).

Getting back to Jacob and his story, this wrestling between God and Jacob lasted until daybreak. As the sun rose Jacob looked up and saw his brother coming toward him. I imagine at that moment Jacob's heart started pounding—partly in excitement, partly in fear. Jacob had wronged his brother many years ago and he knew it. Sometimes, when we have been wronged, we have to accept that we may never get an apology. Scripture doesn't tell us if there was any apology between these brothers. It appears that even without an apology, Esau had forgiven Jacob and welcomed Jacob with open arms.

"But Esau ran to meet him, and embraced him, and fell on his neck and kissed him, and they wept" (Gen. 33:4, NKJV).

There are so many lessons in the above passage—so many pictures of God's heart, and how He wants us to live. These are such great examples of how God will bless us, and how we need to forgive, whether we think someone deserves it or not; whether they apologize or not. Jacob and Laban set up an altar to delineate the boundary between them. They agreed to disagree. There were no apologies. There was a level of forgiveness on Jacob's part. It does not demand that Jacob forget the type of person his father-in-law had proved himself to be. Jacob didn't forgive *and forget*. He forgave, so he could go forward peacefully.

We all have struggles. Every possible issue that we encounter in our lives is in this Book (the Bible). Maybe it doesn't have your name written on it. Maybe it has Jacob's name or Rachel's name. If their story fits your situation, you can use it as an example of how to live your life. But if you don't know what's in there, you won't be able to use it. I encourage you to grab one of those "Through the Bible in a Year" plans (in the back of the book) and start following it. You will learn so much about God, so much about yourself and how you should live. I guarantee you your life will be so much better if you spend just a little time every day in God's word.

Chapter 9

Joseph—What a Story

Everyone is familiar with some aspect of the story of Joseph. Maybe you remember the coat of many colors that made him the envy of his brothers. His father was Jacob. Yes, the same Jacob you just read about. Joseph's mother, Rachel, was Jacob's favorite wife—the same Rachel that ran off with her father's idols. Jacob had ten sons with Leah, but Joseph was his first-born with the beloved Rachel and became his favorite son. Jacob wasn't very wise in his blatant display of that favoritism.

When Jacob gave Joseph his brilliant beautiful tunic (Gen 37:3) the brothers were steamed. That was just another reason for their jealousy of Joseph. As he grew, he began to have dreams and started telling his brothers what the dreams meant.

> "There we were, binding sheaves in the field. Then behold, my sheaf arose and also stood upright; and indeed your sheaves stood all around and bowed down to my sheaf." And his brothers said to him, "Shall you indeed reign over us? Or shall you indeed have dominion over us?" So they hated him even more for his dreams and for his words. (Gen. 37:7–8, NKJV)

And then Joseph's second dream:

> Then he dreamed still another dream and
> told it to his brothers, and said, "Look, I have
> dreamed another dream. And this time, the
> sun, the moon, and the eleven stars bowed
> down to me." So he told it to his father and
> his brothers; and his father rebuked him and
> said to him, "What is this dream that you
> have dreamed? Shall your mother and I and
> your brothers indeed come to bow down
> to the earth before you?" And his brothers
> envied him, but his father kept the matter in
> mind. (Gen. 37:9–11, NKJV)

From that point, the hatred that Joseph's brothers had for him only grew. Any time hatred is allowed to grow it ferments into bitterness and can spawn any number of evil actions. That's exactly what happened: Joseph's brothers started whining and complaining and they devised a plan to take care of Joseph, once and for all.

The brothers were out feeding their father's sheep, and Jacob, who has been renamed Israel by this time, sent Joseph to take their lunch out to them in the field. From the brothers' viewpoint, they could see him coming from a long way away. They decided among themselves to kill him, spread blood on his colorful coat, and tell Jacob/Israel that a wild animal had killed him. But Reuben (one of the brothers) vetoed the plan. It was decided instead to throw Joseph into an empty well, where he would be left to die.

Reuben had plans to retrieve Joseph from the pit without the knowledge of the other brothers, and return him to his father. Whether Reuben was truly hoping to save Joseph or play the hero with his father, we aren't told. So that's what they did. They took Joseph's beautiful tunic off him and threw him into the pit. They smeared the tunic with animal blood, advancing that part of the original plan. But while they were eating, some Midianite traders came by, and instead, most of the brothers decided to sell Joseph to them. When Reuben went back to get Joseph out of the pit, he was gone.

Once that happened, as far as the brothers were concerned, Joseph was out of their lives forever. *But God*—I love that phrase: but God." How many of us have stories that would have ended so differently if it hadn't been for God changing the outcome!

Now Joseph is in the hands of the Midianite traders, although Israel thinks his favored son has been killed. Joseph was taken to Egypt, where he was bought by Potiphar who was the captain of Pharaoh's army, and that's where the "but God" comes in.

> The LORD was with Joseph, and he was a successful man; and he was in the house of his master the Egyptian. And his master saw that the LORD was with him and that the LORD made all he did to prosper in his hand. So Joseph found favor in his sight, and served him. Then he made him overseer of his house, and all that he had he put under his authority. So it was, from the time that he had made him overseer of his house and all that he had, that the LORD blessed the Egyptian's house for Joseph's sake; and the blessing of the LORD was on all that he had in the house and in the field. Thus he left all that he had in Joseph's hand, and he did not know what he had except for the bread which

he ate. Now Joseph was handsome in form and appearance. And it came to pass after these things that his master's wife cast longing eyes on Joseph, and she said, "Lie with me." But he refused and said to his master's wife, "Look, my master does not know what is with me in the house, and he has committed all that he has to my hand. There is no one greater in this house than I, nor has he kept back anything from me but you, because you are his wife. How then can I do this great wickedness, and sin against God?" (Gen. 39:2–9, NKJV)

We don't know how long this went on, but Scripture tells us that finally, Potiphar's wife caught Joseph's garment and as he was fleeing from her advances one more time, he slipped out of his tunic, and left the garment with her and literally ran. With that garment in her hand, she told Potiphar the lies that landed Joseph in prison for being disloyal to his master. I imagine that the whole episode broke Potiphar's heart, but the prison warden made Joseph more or less a trustee. And it was God that made everything Joseph touched prosper, so the prison did as well. And because of that, Joseph was shown favor.

I imagine you'll remember the part of Joseph's story where the chief butler and the baker are thrown in prison with Joseph. That's when Joseph was again interpreting dreams, but in this case, the chief butler and baker were having the dreams, and Joseph was telling them what their dreams meant: one would advance in the kingdom and the other would die, and that's exactly what happened. But the chief butler was supposed to "remember him" to the Pharaoh, and he didn't, until the

Pharaoh himself had a dream and needed an interpreter...who was, of course, Joseph.

> Then it came to pass, at the end of two full years, that Pharaoh had a dream; and behold, he stood by the river. Suddenly there came up out of the river seven cows, fine looking and fat; and they fed in the meadow. Then behold, seven other cows came up after them out of the river, ugly and gaunt, and stood by the other cows on the bank of the river. And the ugly and gaunt cows ate up the seven fine looking and fat cows. So Pharaoh awoke. He slept and dreamed a second time; and suddenly seven heads of grain came up on one stalk, plump and good. Then behold, seven thin heads, blighted by the east wind, sprang up after them. And the seven thin heads devoured the seven plump and full heads. So Pharaoh awoke, and indeed, it was a dream. Now it came to pass in the morning that his spirit was troubled, and he sent and called for all the magicians of Egypt and all its wise men. And Pharaoh told them his dreams, but there was no one who could interpret them for Pharaoh. (Gen. 41:1–8, NKJV)

Suddenly the chief butler remembered Joseph and advised the Pharaoh of his ability to interpret dreams. Pharaoh called for Joseph to be brought to him from prison so he could tell him about the dreams.

Joseph told Pharaoh that both dreams foretold the famine that was coming. One dream gave specifics as to what would happen if nothing was done, and the other gave instruction as to how to survive and indeed thrive during the famine. Because Pharaoh was wise enough to believe Joseph, and because Pharaoh remembered how his house had prospered when Joseph was overseer there, he not only let him out of prison but made him governor and assigned him the storehouses.

So it was in that position that Joseph found himself facing his brothers, and being in the situation to either allow them to starve to death or help them. The older brothers are sent to him for food, but they don't recognize him, because he has taken on the appearance of the Egyptians that he has lived among for most of his adult life. After making them jump through a few hoops, that enabled Joseph to be reunited with all the brothers and Israel. Israel dies and Joseph had him embalmed and buried him and returns to Egypt.

> When Joseph's brothers saw that their father was dead, they said, "Perhaps Joseph will hate us, and may actually repay us for all the evil which we did to him." So they sent messengers to Joseph, saying, "Before your father died he commanded, saying, 'Thus you shall say to Joseph: "I beg you, please forgive the trespass of your brothers and their sin; for they did evil to you."' Now, please, forgive the trespass of the servants of the God of your father." And Joseph wept when they spoke to him. Then his brothers also went and fell down before his face, and they said, "Behold, we are your servants." Joseph said to them, "Do not be afraid, for am I in the place of God? But as for you, you meant evil against me; *but God* meant it for good, in order to

bring it about as it is this day, to save many
people alive. Now therefore, do not be afraid;
I will provide for you and your little ones."
And he comforted them and spoke kindly to
them. (Gen. 50:15–20, NKJV)

Think about a time in your life when something looked
like it had been meant for evil and God turned it for good.
Romans 8:28 states, "And we know that *all* things work together
for good to those who love God, to those who are the called
according to His purpose" (NKJV). But God always makes the
difference!

Chapter 10

Jonah

The Christian life is always a life of change as God calls us to new ministries, new people, and new places where our witness is needed. The Holy Spirit challenges us to let go of old habits, routines, preconceptions, and prejudices so that we might experience God's presence in ever-changing contexts. Whether the call is to international, national, or local mission, we are challenged to expand our vision of God's unconditional love for all people. Unfortunately, not everyone is ready to let go of preconceived notions in order to experience God's loving presence in a new way in a "new neighborhood." The prophet Jonah certainly wasn't! This reluctant prophet was called to a place where he did not want to go and how he eventually came to discover God's sustaining love in a most unlikely place—the city of Nineveh—is truly a God story!

Nineveh was the capital city of the Assyrian Empire. This empire first invaded the northern kingdom of Israel in 732 BC. It wasn't until the Assyrian's second attempt in 722 BC that they successfully conquered Samaria, which was the capital city of the northern kingdom.

"...the King of Assyria took Samaria and carried the ten tribes of Israel away to Assyria and placed them in Halah, and by the Habor, the River Gozan and in the cities of the Medes" (2 Kings 17:6, NKJV).

If you look at a map, those places mentioned in that verse surround Nineveh. Naturally, the descendants of those captive Israelites made up a part of the population of Nineveh, where Jonah is being told to go. The Israelites had suffered oppression at the hands of the Assyrians for many years. When Jonah was sent to Nineveh to preach to the people there, he must have thought, "You have got to be kidding!"

> Now the word of the LORD came to Jonah the son of Amittai, saying, "Arise, go to Nineveh, that great city, and cry out against it; for their wickedness has come up before Me." But Jonah arose to flee to Tarshish from the presence of the LORD. He went down to Joppa, and found a ship going to Tarshish; so he paid the fare, and went down into it, to go with them to Tarshish from the presence of the LORD. (Jon. 1:1–3, NKJV)

Instead of traveling the five hundred miles from his hometown of Gath-hepher to Nineveh, Jonah runs from God and travels over land to Joppa, and pays the fare to travel 2,500 miles by boat to Tarshish, Spain. Tarshish was the furthest point from God's presence. It was known to be a place where the gospel had not been spread. Jonah may have pondered that God's command would not reach him that far from Gath-hepher. These first three verses give us an example of what *not* to do when God asks us to do something! Ideally, a godly person displays instant and willing obedience to do God's bidding. Godly people are not stubborn. Why? Because stubbornness only causes trouble! Godly people *should* obey promptly.

The Assyrian Army was brutal in their conquering of Israel, torturing everyone, not just the soldiers. It is no wonder Jonah was reluctant to go to Nineveh. Warning the Ninevites of God's wrath against their wickedness would open the way for them to repent and for God to save them—and Jonah, like many of those who had lived under Assyrian oppression, would have much preferred they get their just desserts. Therefore, instead of obeying God's command, the prophet headed in exactly the opposite direction.

> But the LORD sent out a great wind on the sea, and there was a mighty tempest on the sea, so that the ship was about to be broken up. Then the mariners were afraid; and every man cried out to his god, and threw the cargo that was in the ship into the sea, to lighten the load. But Jonah had gone down into the lowest parts of the ship, had lain down, and was fast asleep. So the captain came to him, and said to him, "What do you mean, sleeper? Arise, call on your God; perhaps your God will consider us, so that we may not perish." (Jon. 1:4–6, NKJV)

Although Jonah's name means "dove" or "pigeon," his disposition describes him to be strong-willed, fretful, pouting, hasty, and clannish. He is a loyal lover of Israel, but his actions through this account show he has some struggle with God's plan to extend mercy outside of Israel.

Of course, Jonah did not get away with this act of disobedience (Bible Journeys, Judson Press, Spring 2017).[13] God sent a violent storm that threatened to break up the ship. The sailors were terrified and cried out to their gods to save them. Meanwhile, Jonah was sound asleep in the cargo hold. The ship's captain woke Jonah and ordered him to call on his God as well, so that they would not perish.

Jonah was adamant about not sharing God's love with the Ninevites, because he was generally prejudiced against anyone outside Israel, and especially against the Assyrians because of their brutal treatment of Israel when the Israelites were exiles in Assyria.

Consider the sailors. These are seasoned seamen who knew weather patterns. The storm's quickness in coming and the magnitude of it was probably very different from their average storm. This was a storm from the Creator of all storms! God knew Jonah was on that boat, and the sailors knew there was something weird going on here. Have you ever struggled with God's plans for you? When the ship's captain woke Jonah, the sailors weren't happy with him:

> And they said to one another, "Come, let us cast lots, that we may know for whose cause this trouble has come upon us." So they cast lots, and the lot fell on Jonah. Then they said to him, "Please tell us! For whose cause is this trouble upon us? What is your occupation? And where do you come from? What is your country? And of what people are you?" So he said to them, "I am a Hebrew; and I fear the LORD, the God of heaven, who made the sea and the dry land." Then the men were exceedingly afraid, and said to him, "Why have you done this?" For the men knew that he fled from the presence of the LORD, because he had told them. (Jon. 1:7–10, NKJV)

In these few short verses, both the sailors and Jonah go through some significant changes that, step by step, bring them closer to God. Initially, it is the pagan sailors, rather than the prophet Jonah, who saw the situation most clearly. They realized that the terrible storm they faced was caused by the misconduct of someone on the ship. They cast lots to see who was responsible and discovered that the culprit was Jonah!

Casting lots was a method of making a decision that could not be decided privately. Stones were placed in a bag and one was marked differently from the remaining stones. Even back in biblical days, the outcome of casting lots was the final say so and accepted by everyone concerned. It was considered fair by Jew and Gentile alike. Once they had determined that Jonah was the reason their lives were in danger, a series of questions followed. This interrogation got to the heart of the matter concerning who Jonah was and what he was supposed to be doing. With this interrogation, the sailors began to force Jonah out of his denial, making him face some hard truths about himself.

Jonah had to face the fact that his disobedience to God had resulted in catastrophe both for himself and for others. He had thought that by going to Tarshish, instead of obeying God's command to preach to the Ninevites, that he could escape doing something he did not want to do. But disobedience to the will of God is never a solution to any problem. In answering the sailor's final question, Jonah confessed his identity as a Hebrew and acknowledged God's sovereignty and power. Although it would take some time for Jonah to get right with God, he was taking a few small steps in the right direction.

The sailors also took steps in the right direction toward faith in God. When they hear Jonah's confession, they responded with fear and trembling, asking the poignant question: "What is this that you have done?" Clearly what Jonah had done was to disobey God. God had instructed him to go to Nineveh and he had refused. It was not just his disobedience that displeased God! His motive for disobedience was prejudice against the Ninevites. Prejudice is a sin against God, who created and loves *all* humanity, including our enemies.

God cannot allow known sin to remain in our lives. He will confront it because sin cannot stand in the presence of holiness He will confront it. Any prayer that we pray is in vain, until we confess and repent of our sin. Confess means to verbally recant of what we are doing. Repent means to turn from the sin and turn back to God. Remember God already sees our sin, but we have to confess it and ask forgiveness, and when we do that, God is quick to forgive. We cannot hide our sin from God.

> Then they said to him, "What shall we do to you that the sea may be calm for us?"—for the sea was growing more tempestuous. And he said to them, "Pick me up and throw me into the sea; then the sea will become calm for you. For I know that this great tempest is because of me." Nevertheless the men rowed hard to return to land, but they could not, for the sea continued to grow more tempestuous against them. Therefore they cried out to the LORD and said, "We pray, O LORD, please do not let us perish for this man's life, and do not charge us with innocent blood; for You, O LORD, have done as it pleased You." So they picked up Jonah and threw him into the sea, and the sea ceased from its raging. Then the men feared the LORD exceedingly, and offered a sacrifice to the LORD and took vows. (Jon. 1:11–16, NKJV)

Instead of throwing Jonah into the sea, as he asks them to, they first try very hard to row through the storm and get back to land. These sailors were probably Phoenicians—Canaanites, great merchants, who worshipped Baal and the goddess Ashtoreth. God allowed the Israelites to be taken captive into Assyria because they had turned their allegiance from the one true Jehovah God and started worshipping the false gods. The sailors that we are talking about here came from the area where those false gods were prevalent. Isn't it interesting that the people who worshipped these false gods now recognize the power of the one true God? They were praying to Jonah's God, before they threw him overboard. It's very possible that seeing the power that God displayed in that storm convinced them that He was not a God to be reckoned with! They prayed, offered a sacrifice to God, and threw Jonah overboard. Then scripture says they made vows. It may be that the vows they made were to add Jehovah to their list of gods!

"Now the LORD had prepared a great fish to swallow Jonah. And Jonah was in the belly of the fish three days and three nights" (Jon. 1:17, NKJV).

Maybe you've heard the stories that refer to the fish as a whale. You may have also heard some in the scientific community say it could not have been a whale, because of the whale's body structure. What does that first line say? God had prepared a great fish—may have been a whale, may have been a shark, may have been a species that God specifically created for this one purpose that we have no present knowledge of. The point is, God prepared a creature that was appropriate for Jonah to survive in, *but* not to be too comfortable in!

Strong's Concordance describes the Hebrew word used for "belly" as *mayaw*, which is translated as bowels, an extension of the stomach, or womb. Both the stomach and the intestines secrete digestive enzymes, which begin digestion. That's not where we like to think that Jonah is! But the womb? That's a life-giving place, and that's very much what was happening there! God was renewing and refreshing Jonah as he was kept in his temporary home.

"Then Jonah prayed to the LORD his God from the fish's belly. And he said: 'I cried out to the LORD because of my affliction, And He answered me. "Out of the belly of Sheol I cried, And You heard my voice."'" (Jon. 2:1–2, NKJV).

So whether he was in a stomach or womb, he had bars, right? Don't we picture Jonah peeking out from behind the ribs of that fish? He was God's captive audience for three days and three nights, and he apparently heard what God was saying to Him.

The first half of Jonah's prayer is found in Jonah 2:2–5:

> For You cast me into the deep, Into the heart of the seas, And the floods surrounded me; All Your billows and Your waves passed over me. Then I said, "I have been cast out of Your sight; Yet I will look again toward Your holy temple." The waters surrounded me, even to my soul; The deep closed around me; Weeds were wrapped around my head. (NKJV)

Sometimes we forget that Jonah was floundering in the water for at least a little while before he was taken up into the great fish. From the belly of this great fish, Jonah realizes he is in big trouble, but he also realizes that he was already in big trouble. It sounds like he was getting entangled in seaweed, out in the billows and waves of the sea, before he was swallowed up by this great creature. His comment that he "prays from the belly of Sheol (hell)" again tells us he realizes he has messed up, as that would represent the inner part of the earth—outside the presence of God.

At that point, Jonah is probably feeling pretty hopeless, a bit claustrophobic, and he realizes he is out of options. Have you ever felt you had no options? It's difficult to accept that it's time to make a U-turn in your life, isn't it? To admit that we're wrong and we need a do-over in obeying God's call on our lives.

In verse 4, Jonah realizes he was near death and yet also realizes God has snatched him out of that reality and has granted him that do-over. God is so merciful with His giving us second chances! I can't imagine Jonah ever again looking at God or God's temple in the same way. (Nor should we!)

> I went down to the moorings of the mountains; The earth with its bars closed behind me forever; Yet You have brought up my life from the pit, O LORD, my God. "When my soul fainted within me, I remembered the LORD; And my prayer went up to You, Into Your holy temple. Those who regard worthless idols forsake their own mercy. But I will sacrifice to You With the voice of thanksgiving; I will pay what I have vowed. Salvation is of the LORD." So the LORD spoke to the fish, and it vomited Jonah onto dry land. (Jon. 2:6–10, NKJV)

A wise person—a godly person understands that God responds to disobedience by making circumstances oppose us. We must understand that we must change our heart as well as our behavior. Sometimes it takes a day or two…or three for us to get it.

"For as Jonah was three days and three nights in the belly of the great fish, so will the Son of Man be three days and three nights in the heart of the earth" (Matt. 12:40).

Three days would have been considered a miraculous rescue from death and destruction. If it were anything less, the sailors and all who witnessed or heard of the account would have doubted that Jonah had actually died. Therefore it would not have been accepted as miraculous.

Verse 8 refers to those who regard worthless idols. It says they forsake their own mercy. This comment was specifically aimed toward the sailors. Jonah's prejudice extended to *anyone* outside of Israel and would have included these sailors. Obviously, the remnants of the prejudice are still there. Ironically, Jonah didn't know that the sailors had prayed to *His* God—*our* God as well. He still had not embraced God's call on his life, but he has at least re-established a connection with God.

Verse 10 tells us that God was in command of the fish as well as of Jonah and the sailors. The fish did as it was instructed and vomited Jonah up onto dry land. Tradition says that the land was probably north of Israel off the coast of Syria, north of Jonah's hometown... Not far from where he started, but heading toward and a little closer to Nineveh! I think it's interesting that God never leaves you exactly where you were before an encounter with Him. He always moves you closer to where He wants you to be.

> Now the word of the LORD came to Jonah the second time, saying, "Arise, go to Nineveh, that great city, and preach to it the message that I tell you." So Jonah arose and went to Nineveh, according to the word of the LORD. Now Nineveh was an exceedingly great city, a three-day journey. And Jonah

began to enter the city on the first day's walk. Then he cried out and said, "Yet forty days, and Nineveh shall be overthrown!" So the people of Nineveh believed God, proclaimed a fast, and put on sackcloth, from the greatest to the least of them. (Jon. 3:1–5, NKJV)

These first few verses are a perfect picture of our God as the "God of second chances!" They depict the depth of God's love, mercy, and forgiveness, even when we mess up! Notice that the second time God asked Jonah to do something, he obeyed! What a perfect example for us! When we repent and turn away from our disobedience, God puts us right back to work. Sometimes he gives us a different job to do and sometimes he tells us to go back and do what He told us to do in the first place! By giving Jonah his second chance, the people of Nineveh were also given a second chance...although they didn't even realize they had missed out on their first chance!

Notice the difference between God's first command to Jonah and this one. Both times, Jonah was told to go to Nineveh. The first time, it was to cry out against their wickedness. The second time, it was to preach the message that God would give him. The first one was laced with conviction and the second one was more merciful, offering saving grace. I believe God phrased the same command so differently because of the difference in Jonah. He is much more receptive now than before the fish! Jonah's heart toward the Ninevites may or may not have changed, but it did change toward God and he is being obedient and going where God told him to go!

It takes Jonah three days to get into the heart of Nineveh. Once again the three-day period signifies death and resurrection. We're told that it will take a "death" experience to get Nineveh turned around! Jonah now understands that this "mission" is an important one to God, so as soon as Jonah hits town, he starts preaching. It's a hard message! "Repent, or in forty days Nineveh will be destroyed." In the Bible "forty days" is often used as a time of testing. Verse 5 leads us to believe that they responded quickly! It is possible that the news of Jonah's plight reached them, and they recognized what might happen if they weren't so quick to obey! Maybe they heard of God's power from the sailors.

> Then word came to the king of Nineveh; and he arose from his throne and laid aside his robe, covered himself with sackcloth and sat in ashes. And he caused it to be proclaimed and published throughout Nineveh by the decree of the king and his nobles, saying, Let neither man nor beast, herd nor flock, taste anything; do not let them eat, or drink water. But let man and beast be covered with sackcloth, and cry mightily to God; yes, let everyone turn from his evil way and from the violence that is in his hands. Who can tell if God will turn and relent, and turn away from His fierce anger, so that we may not perish? (Jon. 3:6–9, NKJV)

The king of Assyria was wicked and bloodthirsty and ingenious in devising his ways of torture. Remember, the history of Israel's torture at the hands of these Assyrians, is why Jonah didn't want to offer God's mercy to them! Some difference we see here! This may have been a cry of fear, in hopes that God would spare them. Yet it appears sincere. Apparently, Jonah recognizes the connection between violence toward others (the

Assyrians' mistreatment for generations back of their prisoners of war as well as others) and sin against God.

The king called this fast, to get the people's attention and let them know he was sincere. His wearing the sackcloth and ashes is a sign of repentance, and acts as an example for his people to turn from their evil and wicked lifestyles. Repentance changed everything! The people heard the message of God from Jonah and accepted it. Then their own king confirmed the message and put changes in place that would rearrange their entire way of life.

"Then God saw their works, that they turned from their evil way; and God relented from the disaster that He had said He would bring upon them, and He did not do it" (Jon. 3:10, NKJV).

Have you ever had a forgiveness experience? Think about a time when you were "in a mess" because of sin in your life. Think of how it changed you. Or how it affected those around you. What does the phrase "Forgive your enemies" mean to you? Have you ever had to forgive someone who harmed you? Whether the hurt was physical or emotional, forgiveness doesn't come easily, does it? When we forgive someone, it changes our relationship with that person, but it also changes our relationship with God. Have you ever chosen *not* to forgive someone? How did that work for you? *That* will also change your relationship with God, and not for the better.

Jonah is out of the fish's belly. He has decided to be obedient and has preached at Nineveh. Any time a whole city repents and turns from their sin, it should please the preacher, right? But not in this case, and the story is far from over!

> But it displeased Jonah exceedingly, and he became angry. So he prayed to the LORD, and said, "Ah, LORD, was not this what I

said when I was still in my country? Therefore I fled previously to Tarshish; for I know that You are a gracious and merciful God, slow to anger and abundant in lovingkindness, One who relents from doing harm. Therefore now, O LORD, please take my life from me, for it is better for me to die than to live!" Then the LORD said, "Is it right for you to be angry?" (Jon. 4:1–4, NKJV)

What's going on here? Why is Jonah so distraught that he would rather die than to see these people saved? He still considered them Israel's enemies! The Ninevites had given up their wicked ways, Jonah hasn't. Perhaps, he is resentful that they were able to do that, and he had not been able to. That would make them "better people" than he is! What does he do, then, with his prejudice against them? He is living under the misconception that God doesn't have enough love for both!

So Jonah went out of the city and sat on the east side of the city. There he made himself a shelter and sat under it in the shade, till he might see what would become of the city. And the LORD God prepared a plant and made it come up over Jonah, that it might be shade for his head to deliver him from his misery. So Jonah was very grateful for the plant. But as morning dawned the next day God prepared a worm, and it so damaged the plant that it withered. And it happened, when the sun arose, that God prepared a vehement east wind; and the sun beat on Jonah's head, so that he grew faint. Then he wished death for himself, and said, "It is better for me to die than to live." (Jon. 4:5–8, NKJV)

So Jonah leaves and finds himself a place to pout. He watches Nineveh from his little place of self-pity. I wonder if he's waiting for them to fail—just waiting for them to slip back into their old ways. Can't you picture him all dejected with his bottom lip sticking out? God gives him comfort even though he was acting like a spoiled brat (to use my grandmother's phrase). Jonah's not stupid. He knew this plant grew at God's command. He also knew it was God that made it wither! Remember the fish picked Jonah up out of the sea at God's command and it was God that told the fish to spew Jonah out onto land! Has he learned nothing? As impatient as we are with Jonah, that's how much love God showed him instead of impatience! Without that bush shading him, Jonah's life was pretty devastating. But, after all, isn't this what Jonah wanted? Hadn't he told God that it was better if he would just die?

> Then God said to Jonah, "Is it right for you to be angry about the plant?" And he said, "It is right for me to be angry, even to death!" But the LORD said, "You have had pity on the plant for which you have not labored, nor made it grow, which came up in a night and perished in a night. And should I not pity Nineveh, that great city, in which are more than one hundred and twenty thousand persons who cannot discern between their right hand and their left—and much livestock?" (Jon. 4:9–11, NKJV)

Jonah hadn't done anything to get himself out of the predicament that he got into by his disobedience. Did he have any right to be concerned? To be angry? Had he worked for any of the food or shelter that his Father had furnished for him? Of course not. God provided all he needed.

Scripture ends before the story does. God has the last word, as He always does. Jonah may have stuck to his guns and died there in the heat and wind, watching Nineveh flourish. He may have repented and continued to be used of God in other cities. He may have repented and lived out his life in peace and quiet. We just don't know.

Think again of Jonah 4:11: "And should I not pity Nineveh, that great city, in which are more than one hundred and twenty thousand persons who cannot discern between their right hand and their left...?"

Think of who you might consider an enemy. And put that name in the place where Nineveh is: Should God not pity _____? How would you answer that question? Are you willing to accept God's unconditional love that embraces all people, even someone who has hurt you?

Chapter 11

Jehoshaphat

> After this the Moabites and Ammonites, and with them some of the Meunites, came against Jehoshaphat for battle. Some men came and told Jehoshaphat, "A great multitude is coming against you from Edom, from beyond the sea; and, behold, they are in Engedi." (2 Chron. 20:1–2, NKJV)

King Jehoshaphat is warned that three of Judah's biggest enemies have joined forces and are now one huge army and they are coming his way...and they are getting close. Fear sent Jehoshaphat to his knees, and in verses 3–4 he commands all his people to fast. Jehoshaphat is king, so his orders are obeyed throughout all of Judah, not just Jerusalem. While they are all fasting, Jehoshaphat assembles them all and prays. In his prayer,

1. he acknowledges who God is,
2. he acknowledges His power and might,
3. he acknowledges that none is able to stand against Him,
4. he reminds God that He had previously driven people out of this land so that the Israelites could inherit and occupy it, and

5.   he thanks God for all of it.

While he is praying, Jehoshaphat is reminding himself of all that he and the Israelites had benefited because of God. Jehoshaphat reminds himself of the refuge they had always found in God, and he declares to God that they will be faithful to the God that is faithful, in all their afflictions. Then Jehoshaphat declares to God that these enemies who are en route to attack are the same tribes that God would not allow Israel to destroy in previous encounters, and Jehoshaphat starts listening to himself and perhaps he has to control his anger. Now they are coming back to haunt them by trying to take back the land God has given them instead of appreciating God for letting them live!

"Oh our God, will you not execute judgment on them? For we are powerless against this great horde that is coming against us. We do not know what to do, but *our eyes are on you*" (2 Chron. 20:12, NKJV [emphasis mine]).

So Jehoshaphat beseeches God to avenge this action, and execute judgment. Then Jehoshaphat does something really human—he cries, "We don't know what to do, but *our eyes are on you*." And he stops…and he waits for an answer…and God answers.

> And the Spirit of the LORD came upon Jahaziel the son of Zechariah, son of Benaiah, son of Jeiel, son of Mattaniah, a Levite of the sons of Asaph, in the midst of the assembly. And he said, "Listen, all Judah and inhabitants of Jerusalem and King Jehoshaphat: Thus says the LORD to you, 'Do not be afraid and do not be dismayed at this great horde, for the battle is not yours but God's. Tomorrow go down against them. Behold,

they will come up by the ascent of Ziz. You will find them at the end of the valley, east of the wilderness of Jeruel. You will not need to fight in this battle. Stand firm, hold your position, and see the salvation of the LORD on your behalf, O Judah and Jerusalem.' Do not be afraid and do not be dismayed. Tomorrow go out against them, and the LORD will be with you." (2 Chron. 20:14–17, NKJV)

God's Holy Spirit speaks through the priest Jahaziel to Jehoshaphat and to all those standing with him in prayer and fasting. And God says, "Fear not...," and God says, "The battle belongs to the Lord."

Did you know that "fear not" or a similar sentiment is in the Bible 365 times? Does that number sound familiar? There is one for every day of the year, and if you are reading this during a leap year, I'm sure God's word is powerful enough you can use one twice! This is the hard part: God says, "Wait and see... do not get in a hurry, do not get ahead of God...tomorrow, go there and watch and wait..." But they weren't idle while they were waiting on God! They were getting ready for battle.

Then Jehoshaphat bowed his head with his face to the ground, and all Judah and the inhabitants of Jerusalem fell down before the LORD, worshiping the LORD. And the Levites, of the Kohathites and the Korahites, stood up to praise the LORD, the God of Israel, with a very loud voice. (2 Chron. 20:18–19, NKJV)

God told them exactly where to find the enemy and He told Jehoshaphat to go there. God's instructions to Jehoshaphat were to go to the mountain, to stand firm, and to watch what the Lord is doing. Watch God step in on your behalf. "Wait and see," not in fear, not in dismay or discouragement or impatience. And then He told them *tomorrow* attack that huge alliance of an enemy...*tomorrow*. Jehoshaphat has already contemplated the size of this army. Back in verse 12, he told the Lord, "For we are powerless against this great horde that is coming against us." That was just before Jehoshaphat said, "We know not what to do but *our eyes are on You.*"

From what I read here, I don't think Jehoshaphat's faith waivered...not even for a moment, because look what he does next. He falls to the ground, and all of the inhabitants follow suit—and they start worshipping the Lord. Their worship grows and they stand (I imagine) with hands raised, praising God loudly! *And God hasn't done anything yet!* At least nothing visible...but they got it! They knew that God is a man of His word and God had just promised them "That the Lord would be with them" and *in fact* that this battle was the Lord's to win. How could they not praise God!

When God gives us a promise we have three things we absolutely must do:

1. We must believe it...100 percent get our heads wrapped around the fact that God promised it, and God never reneges on a promise.
2. We must praise and worship God for His past faithfulness, but also for what He has promised—even before He does it.
3. We must obey... If God says wait and see, you wait and watch expectantly, knowing it's going

to happen. If God says attack, rest assured He will be with you in that battle. And fear not.

> And they rose early in the morning and went out into the wilderness of Tekoa. And when they went out, Jehoshaphat stood and said, "Hear me, Judah and inhabitants of Jerusalem! Believe in the LORD your God, and you will be established; believe his prophets, and you will succeed." And when he had taken counsel with the people, he appointed those who were to sing to the LORD and praise him in holy attire, as they went before the army, and say, "Give thanks to the LORD, for his steadfast love endures forever." (2 Chron. 20:20–21, NKJV)

The next morning Jehoshaphat encourages the people, reminding them to believe in the God they had been following, the God in whom they were established, rooted. He encourages them to remember and believe in the words of the prophets because those words were the words of God. Then Jehoshaphat assigns his people to a specific duty—worshippers so that all the while the battle was raging, God was still being praised for what He had done, what He was doing, and what He would continue to do. For God's steadfast love that endures forever. They were leading the army.

> And when they began to sing and praise, the LORD set an ambush against the men of Ammon, Moab, and Mount Seir, who had come against Judah, so that they were routed (confused). For the men of Ammon and

Moab rose against the inhabitants of Mount Seir, devoting them to destruction, and when they had made an end of the inhabitants of Seir, they all helped to destroy one another. When Judah came to the watchtower of the wilderness, they looked toward the horde, and behold, there were dead bodies lying on the ground; none had escaped. (2 Chron. 20:22–23, NKJV)

Now Jehoshaphat has understood God's orders the previous day to be: "tomorrow go out against them," so his plan was to be obedient and do just that, but while they were praising and worshipping, the Lord wasn't still! (Don't you know God is always working behind the scenes, on our behalf?) The Lord set these armies against each other and they destroyed each other. So when Jehoshaphat and the inhabitants of Judah came to the place God had told them to be, ready to go into battle, they looked down into the valley expecting to see the huge hordes of armies that had been their enemies for years. But what did they see? Dead bodies all around. The battle had indeed belonged to the Lord and God doesn't do anything halfway. None had escaped.

But wait! There's more!

When Jehoshaphat and his people came to take their spoil, they found among them, in great numbers, goods, clothing, and precious things, which they took for themselves until they could carry no more. They were three days in taking the spoil, it was so much. On the fourth day they assembled in the Valley of Beracah, for there they blessed the LORD. Therefore the name of that place has been called the Valley of Beracah [the Valley of Blessing] to this day. Then they returned, every man of Judah and Jerusalem, and Jehoshaphat at their head, returning to Jerusalem with joy, for the LORD had made them rejoice over their enemies. They came to Jerusalem with harps and lyres and trumpets, to the house of the LORD. (2 Chron. 20:25–28, NKJV)

Victors in battles in the Old Testament were always entitled to the plunder that the losers left behind. In this case it took all the inhabitants of Judah three days to transport all the treasures back to Jerusalem. Some of the plunder they obtained from that battle were musical instruments—and they praised the Lord with them in the temple.

"And the fear of God came on all the kingdoms of the countries when they heard that the LORD had fought against the enemies of Israel. So the realm of Jehoshaphat was quiet, for his God gave him rest all around" (2 Chron. 20:29–30, NKJV).

We just read from God's Word that no one escaped this battle. If that's true (and we know it is) who do you think it was that spread that word? The Israelites! The believers! Are you spreading the word of God's victories in your battles? When God shows himself strong in our lives, we *must* share the victory with those around us! Verse 30 tells us that the rest of Jehoshaphat's reign of was quiet and peaceful. Why? Israel's enemies heard about this huge victory. They knew Israel was not strong enough to take on these three huge armies and win! They also knew that Jehovah God, the God of Israel, was mighty and powerful. Israel's enemies were scared, not of Israel but of God.

Jehoshaphat praised God before the battle was ever won. He trusted God enough to believe that what He said He would do would be exactly what would be done. He didn't praise God alone; he enlisted the people as well. That's how much he believed God. Do you believe and trust God enough to praise and thank Him before you see your answer to your prayer? You can! He is trustworthy!

Chapter 12

Jesus: Man of Sorrows

I have three drawings of Jesus hanging on my living room wall at home. One is of Jesus hugging a biker, one is of Jesus praying, and the last one is of Jesus laughing. Although I love them all, I think my favorite one is Jesus laughing, because I like to think of Him as happy. Jesus isn't generally described as happy. He's been called a man of sorrows. When I think of that title, I think of the sufferings He endured on our behalf, the sorrows he bore on the cross for me...for you. Some of those sufferings were physical, some were emotional. All were deeply personal and widely public.

Scripture calls him meek and mild, not a man we would be attracted to (Isa. 53:2). And we know Jesus to be a teacher, always guiding His followers to find the lesson in nearly every event portrayed in the gospels. The book of John, especially, tells us of a man who deeply loves those children that came near Him, or that He healed, but also the adults—Mary, Martha, Lazarus. These are the pictures that show His everyday life, being a sorrowful man, because of hardships that go along with the type of lives people lived in those days. But even more, the *Bible* calls Him a Man of Sorrows:

> He is despised and rejected of men; a Man of
> sorrows, and acquainted with grief; and as it

were a hiding of faces from Him, He being despised, and we esteemed Him not. Surely He has borne our griefs, and carried our sorrows; yet we esteemed Him stricken, smitten of God, and afflicted. (Isa. 53:3–4, NKJV)

Despised and rejected—why do we reject someone? Maybe we're uncomfortable around them because they don't believe the same way we do, or they have different ideas about how to live their lives. The people then *and now* who didn't understand Jesus did that. People can reject Him and go on living as if they never heard of Him. We know that choice won't end well, don't we? But that's what free will is. God gave us *and* them the choice to believe Him or to reject Him. And that's what happened. They "esteemed Him not." They never gave Him a second thought. They went through their lives and never thought about Jesus.

But if you despise someone, you *hate* them. Hate—a strong word, a strong emotion, it makes you grit your teeth just to think about it, doesn't it? It makes your blood boil. Hate is not a passive emotion. You can reject someone quietly. But hate demands action. So when those who despised—hated Jesus, rejected Him, they couldn't just walk away and forget about Him. They had to *do* something. They had spit on Him and rejected Him and insulted Him, and He had just accepted it, mildly, quietly, meekly. They had to do *something*.

Matthew 13:54 tells us about Jesus teaching in the synagogues. Jesus was teaching the Jews. Now remember He was attracting a following of Jews, and the church leaders didn't like that. After all, He was just the son of that carpenter down the street. "What gives Him the right?" they asked. "Besides, how does He even know the things He's teaching?" So of course, the scribes, Pharisees, those who *are* authorized to teach, get word of what's going on and they start watching this Jesus of Nazareth a little more closely. He may become a threat to their own positions of authority.

I imagine that they covertly watched Him and eavesdropped on His teachings. They were probably within earshot when Jesus asked the young man in the synagogue for the scroll and started teaching from Isaiah's prophecies about Himself.

> But He was wounded for our transgressions; He was bruised for our iniquities; the chastisement of our peace was on Him; and with His stripes we ourselves are healed. All we like sheep have gone astray; we have turned, each one to his own way; and Jehovah has laid on Him the iniquity of us all. (Isa. 53:5–6, NKJV)

I wonder if Jesus taught in the first person... "I was wounded for your transgressions... by My stripes you are healed..."

The Jewish leaders were already disgruntled with Jesus. These words were considered blasphemous, but I imagine they were even more explosive to them! In Texas these would have been called "fighting words." So they would have been angrier yet and this would have just added fuel to their fire. In their minds, *they* were the ones who were in charge of these people. *They* had been appointed to deal with their transgressions. *They* were supposed to be the leaders, not this lowly carpenter's son. And it only took a few angry allegations from a few people in positions of authority to start the ball rolling—right to the cross.

> He was oppressed, and He was afflicted; yet He opened not His mouth. He is brought as

a lamb to the slaughter; and as a sheep before its shearers is dumb, so He opened not His mouth. He was taken from prison and from judgment; and who shall declare His generation? For He was cut off out of the land of the living; for the transgression of My people He was stricken. And He put His grave with the wicked, and with a rich one in His death; although He had done no violence, nor was any deceit in His mouth. (Isa. 53:7–9, NKJV)

I doubt the leaders understood what it all meant. They were astute students of the Old Testament Law and the prophets, but there is so much here left to their imaginations. Their experience of men would lead them to realize how impossible it would be for a man to embrace anything like what this prophecy lays out. Even the best of men, in their experience, would never have allowed themselves to be afflicted without saying a word. He would want justice to be known. What innocent man would allow himself to be led to the slaughter like a lamb and never complain, never utter a word to justify himself? Who, in his right mind, would step in and accept thirty-nine lashes with whips laced with broken bones—for someone else's guilt? And even more confusing, how could someone be buried with the wicked when he had done no evil? When he had not even lied? It didn't make any more sense to them then as it does to the world now.

Yet it pleased Jehovah to crush Him; to grieve Him; that He should put forth His soul as a guilt-offering. He shall see His seed, He shall prolong His days, and the will of Jehovah shall prosper in His hand. He shall see the fruit of

the travail of His soul. He shall be fully satisfied. By His knowledge shall My righteous
Servant justify for many; and He shall bear
their iniquities. (Isa. 53:10–11, NKJV)

Romans 6:23 tells us that the wages of sin is death. Our sin demands the penalty be paid and that penalty is death. But God so loved us that He made a way for us to live, in spite of our sin. Because that death sentence had to be carried out, Jesus stepped in and took the penalty that should have been ours.

Isaiah 52:14 states that "Many were horrified at what happened to him. But everyone who saw him was even more horrified because he suffered until he no longer looked human" (CEV).

If any of you have ever seen Mel Gibson's movie, *The Passion of the Christ*,[14] you can probably recall the close-up shot of Jesus's face after the beatings, the flogging, after the crown of thorns had been jammed into his head, so that the blood streamed into his eyes, after He was bludgeoned, tortured, brutalized. They stopped the flogging at thirty-nine lashes, because it was believed that forty would be viewed as barbaric to the public.

Then, with very little skin left on His back, He had to drag His own cross through the streets and up to the hill. Scripture tells us that Simon the Cyrene was enlisted to carry the cross part of the way.

But Jesus, knowing full well He could have removed Himself from the whole situation, chose to stay there on that cross and allow Himself to be nailed barbarically through His hands and through His feet to the wood and hang there until breath left Him. It was no easy physical death. Add the anguish He endured of knowing that His wonderful loving Father God would turn His back on Him.

"My God, my God, why have you forsaken me?" (Matt. 27:46) expresses the extremity of his sorrow. And Jesus, Man of Sorrows, accepted lovingly all of the sin ever committed and ever to be committed. And it's all because "God so loved the world that He gave His only begotten Son that whoever believes in Him should not perish but have everlasting life" (John 3:16). *And all we have to do is not reject Him.* That was the prophecy. Reality appears in the New Testament. The sorrows Jesus actually endured were even worse than prophecy foretold.

Jesus and His friends, the disciples, were almost always together. They got so excited when they watched Him heal people and when the demon left the man! And how they loved to just sit and hear Him talk. His voice was so loving and gentle when He taught them in the stories about seeds and sowers and mustard seeds and branches on vines and such. And feeding all those people! They were witnessing miracles!

But then He started talking about His upcoming death, and they couldn't understand, just as the Scribes and Pharisees hadn't understood the prophecy. And the sorrows became reality.

> [And Jesus prayed] saying, Father, if You are willing, remove this cup from Me. Yet not My will, but Yours be done. And an angel appeared to Him from Heaven, strengthening Him. And being in an agony He prayed more earnestly. And His sweat was as it were great drops of blood falling down to the ground. (Luke 22:42–44, NKJV)

The sorrow Jesus felt just knowing what He was about to do—that He had to do, that He had chosen to do—was so immense that His Father God sent an angel to strengthen Him.

All God and all man—the man-Jesus needed the strength to go through what the God-Jesus had been born to do.

Did you know that the human body really will emit blood through our pores so it appears to be sweating blood? It's called hematidrosis and it occurs under conditions of extreme physical or emotional stress. It causes the nervous system to invoke the "fight or flight" reaction to such an extreme degree that the blood vessels supplying the sweat glands hemorrhage.

Sorrow to the point of sweating blood. What do you think? Is that love? And it's all because "God so loved the world that He gave His only begotten Son that whoever believes in Him should not perish but have everlasting life." And all we have to do is *not* reject Him. All we have to do is say from our hearts, "I believe in you Jesus. Thank you for doing all that for me."

It's been said that that there is a celebration in heaven every time a sinner says that prayer from the heart. Remember the drawing I was telling you about of Jesus laughing? That's what I imagine Jesus does—he rejoices that another heart was changed. That makes Jesus happy. It gives Him a reason to laugh and rejoice and celebrate.

Chapter 13
James—Count It All Joy

James—half-brother of Jesus—he chose to believe that Jesus was more than a brother, but only after Jesus was crucified. Jesus appeared to James after the resurrection. According to 1 Corinthians 15:7, James took on the role of servant, as should we all. Judging from his writings, James understood perhaps better than some what it means to have one's faith tested. He became the leader of the early church in Jerusalem. James was not a stickler for Christian doctrine. His concern was turning the focus of the early church to godly living, emphasizing genuine faith, and urging them to practice practical Christian ethics in their daily living.

"My brothers, count it all joy when you fall into different kinds of temptations, knowing that the trying of your faith works patience" (James 1:2–3, NKJV).

What does James mean by "different types of temptations"? In that day, it may have been greed or jealousy that he was talking about. There have been rumors going round theology for years that James was jealous of Jesus. Today, it could be the same—greed, jealousy, but anything that tempts a person to act in a way that does not please God.

In 1 Peter 5:8, Scripture tells us to "Be sensible and vigilant, because your adversary the Devil walks about like a roaring lion, seeking someone he may devour" (NKJV).

The enemy, the Devil, called our adversary here, is just roaming the earth looking for someone to devour. He knows humans pretty well. He has been confronting and confusing us with his tricks and wiles for generation after generation. He knows your weakness—not from being able to read your mind or hear your thoughts, he can't do that. He watches you. He knows that you have lived your life in search of certain dreams. He has watched you, for example, studying at college to become an architect and he has seen you work hard. Maybe he heard you tell a friend that you'd love to have a position with Huge Architecture Firm in the city. When that job offer comes through, and the pay is great and they offer you a nice apartment to live in and the perks are great, that adversary can work things in your life to keep you too busy to pray about God's plan for you, and you might accept that position, without doing your own research into the firm, without praying.

Satan knows you are a Christian, therefore he wants to destroy your testimony, and he knows that this firm is developing a reputation for shoddy workmanship. Do you see where this is going? The temptations that might lure you away from God's plan for your life are not the same for me, or for your pastor, or for your folks or your friends. But our enemy isn't stupid. He knows what temptation to use on each one of us. And he knows that every one of us struggles with trying to maintain a daily regimen of prayer and communion with God. So he uses the "too busy" trick quite often!

The first part of 1 Peter 5:8 tells us to be sensible and vigilant. Other versions say sober: (1) the obvious definition is to be temperate in the use of liquor, not intoxicated or overpowered, not drunken; (2) not mad or insane, not wild with passion or anger; (3) to be serious, solemn. The word *vigilant* is defined as watchful; circumspect; attentive to discover and avoid danger, or to provide for safety. Diligent means steady in application to business; constant, attentive, industrious; not idle or negligent.

So to "re-word" this passage Peter is saying here: *We must calmly, seriously, carefully watch for our enemy and his tricks, we must never be idle but always attentive to how he might trick us, always being alert to any danger that might be some tactic of our enemy, to draw us out of our place of safety, and steer us down a path that is not God's plan for us.*

This was written by Peter, one of the disciples. Remember Peter? He's the one who fell for our enemy's tricks and denied three times that he knew Jesus after walking with Him and hearing His teachings for three years. If Peter can fall for the wiles of our enemy, what makes us think we won't? No one is exempt!

Think of Judas. Satan knew that Judas was jealous of Jesus. He saw the glint in his eye whenever he put money into the bag and there was a hint of resentment when Judas was asked to pay for something from out of the bag. That was enough for Satan to know how to tempt Judas into accepting thirty pieces of silver for betraying Jesus to the soldiers.

Peter's denial of Jesus ended with Peter being a servant of God who was forgiven and spent the rest of his days serving with the other disciples in ministry. In fact he was even enabled by God to be one of the authors of the New Testament. Not so with Judas. His remorse was immediate and great and there was nothing he could do to undo his betrayal, but even so, he didn't repent.

Going back to our original text, "My brothers, count it all joy when you fall into different kinds of temptations, knowing that the trying of your faith works patience" (James 1:2–3, NKJV).

How can we count it all joy? When my mom was still living, I frequently called on her for some deep sage advice that only a mother can give to her daughter in times of heartbreak.

I remember one of those times, her answer to me was, "Honey, I'm just not sure you are supposed to live that calm quiet life you think you want." It wasn't the answer I was hoping for, but it made me take another look at my life, and more importantly, what God was trying to do in my life! The answer I was hoping for may have allowed me to pursue a career in music when the door opened, but God wanted to use the talents He gave me elsewhere.

I've frequently said that I must be doing something right, because Satan is on the rampage. That's a real simplification, but I think it's true. Maybe we need to think about that. If our lives are going along too smoothly, are we stepping out and truly putting ourselves out there for God?

Returning to our scenario, if you accepted that job offer, you may feel pressured to make compromises along the way. Maybe you would find yourself in a position of having to over-look some of the shortcuts that are being taken. Your integrity might begin to suffer. You may have to subdue your con-science and then deal with the guilt if someone is hurt because of something you approved of that you shouldn't have. But if you hadn't, it could cost you your job...

Instead of considering for one moment a dream job, instead of succumbing to the wiles of the enemy and not pray-ing about what God wants for you, instead of toying with the idea of some small compromise in your walk with God, *be sober and diligent and go forward and count it all joy.*

1. Joy because Jesus is smiling on you when our enemy's tricks are recognized before there has been any compromise on your part.
2. Joy because Satan *is* ticked at you for being the godly Christian man or woman that you are.

3. Joy because you have been obedient to the call of Christ.

4. Joy because by being diligent, you saw the tricks of the enemy in time to thwart them!

And the last phrase of this verse, "...knowing that the trying of your faith works patience." I'm sure you have heard not to pray for patience, right? When we pray for patience, we are asking for afflictions, because that's how we gain patience. But in reality, we should find joy in those afflictions, *because* that's one of the ways God prefects us.

"...We glory in afflictions also, knowing that afflictions work out patience, and patience works out experience, and experience works out hope" (Rom. 5:3–4, NKJV).

Webster's 1828 Dictionary defines *affliction* as "pain, toil, calamity, provocation or other evil, with a calm, unruffled temper; endurance without murmuring or fretfulness. A calm temper which bears evils without murmuring or discontent. The act or quality of waiting long (longsuffering) for justice or expected good without discontent. Perseverance; constancy in labor or exertion. The quality of bearing offenses and injuries without anger or revenge."[12]

Reading through that entire definition was an act of patience! Count it all joy, because these trials that our enemy is attacking us with show our worthiness, because like Job, God sees us as worthy of being tested in our faith. Why would we even want to pursue patience? Because Paul tells us in Galatians 5:22–23 that if certain things are evident in us, the Holy Spirit is in us and one of those things is patience. "The fruit of the Spirit is: love, joy, peace, long-suffering [patience], kindness, goodness, faith, meekness, self-control..."

This evidence indicates the Holy Spirit's presence in our lives. If the Holy Spirit is active in us, then those things are evident in our character—not in perfection but they are there! We are all works in progress. And they will remind us to go to God before we make any decisions that might put us in harm's way.

James says in James 1:2–3, "My brothers, count it all joy when you fall into different kinds of temptations, knowing that the trying of your faith works patience." But look at verse 4: "But let patience have its perfect work, so that you may be perfect and complete, lacking nothing" (NKJV).

Everyone goes through trials and temptations. James acknowledges that those trials are real struggles that we need to endure in order to grow and mature in our faith. Verse 4 assures us that patience will be perfected in us, as will all the qualities listed as fruit of the spirit.

"Blessed is the man who endures temptation, because having been approved, he will receive the crown of life which the Lord has promised to those who love Him" (James 1:12, NKJV).

When we endure those trials and afflictions, and are perfected and matured in our faith, we are promised the crown of life. Count it all joy, because God counts it as joy.

Chapter 14

Prayer: Two-Way Communication

> Then Jesus came with them to a place called
> Gethsemane. And He said to the disciples,
> "Sit here while I go and pray there." And
> He took Peter and the two sons of Zebedee
> with Him, and He began to be sorrowful and
> very heavy. Then He said to them, "My soul
> is exceedingly sorrowful, even to death. Wait
> here and watch with Me." And He went a lit-
> tle further and fell on His face, and prayed,
> saying, "O My Father, if it is possible, let this
> cup pass from Me. Yet not as I will, but as
> You will." (Matt. 26:36–39, NKJV)

We all know the circumstances of this prayer—it was just before
the Cross. We all know the cup Jesus was asking to be passed
from Him. Crucifixion, the most barbaric death imaginable.
Jesus knew it was the purpose for His earthly life. And He knew
that in prayer He would find the strength to do what He was
called to do.

In a general sense, prayer is defined as "the act of asking for
a favor, and particularly with earnestness. In worship, a solemn
address to the Supreme Being, consisting of adoration, or an
expression of our sense of God's glorious perfections, confession

of our sins, supplication for mercy and forgiveness, intercession for blessings on others, and thanksgiving, or an expression of gratitude to God." There is a very important aspect missing from this definition, and that is the fact, simply, that prayer is two-way communication with God. There are many types of prayer but they all fall into two types: individual or solitary prayer, and corporate or public prayer.

We've all prayed what I call crisis prayers. One of my own crisis prayers was prompted by a phone call I received from my father. He was in Illinois and I was in Texas. My brother had been on a ladder with a chain saw, trimming a tree away from the roof of the house. Events never became very clear, but from what I understand, the limb of the tree met very violently with my brother's forehead. He was in emergency surgery at the time I answered the phone. (So as not to keep you in suspense, he came through fine, with what he called a divot in his forehead. Thankfully there was no brain damage.) When I received that call, I was 1,200 miles away. I not only *felt* helpless, I *was* helpless. As the old song goes, "Where could I go but to the Lord?" There was no amount of pacing the floor or worrying that could help my brother. I couldn't be there to support him or my family. I remember plopping in the middle of my bed on my knees, crying out to God. However, I don't actually remember what I said.

We often don't think about the wording of our crisis prayers. God loves it when His people pray, but I think crisis prayers are especially dear to Him, because they just come pouring out from our heart to His. We don't think about their structure. We need help and we know where to go for that help. We know He is able to do *anything*. He is our Abba Father—Daddy God. Jewish people understand very well the concept of Abba Father—the loving, caring *daddy*. He loves us and we know it. So it stands to reason that we would run to Him in our crisis.

Imagine life as a parent, loving your child with all your heart, and not hearing from your son or daughter unless he/she needs help or is in trouble.

"Behold, I stand at the door and knock. If anyone hears My voice and opens the door, I will come in to him and will dine with him and he with Me" (Rev. 3:20, NKJV).

Does this sound like a Savior who wants only to be on speed dial or someone who wants to live always in our hearts and to spend time with us? God hears all of our prayers, whether crisis prayers, or bedtime prayers, or morning devotionals.

In 1963, Robert Boyd Munger wrote a book called *My Heart—Christ's Home*. It's an easy read, if you get a chance to read it, a delightful story. Let me share a portion of it:

> It is difficult for me to think of a higher privilege than to make for Christ a home in my heart, to welcome, to serve, to please and to know Him there. I will never forget the evening I invited Him into my heart. What an entrance He made! It was not a spectacular, emotional thing, but very real, occurring at the very center of my soul. He came into the darkness of my heart and turned on the light. He built a fire in the cold hearth and banished the chill. He started music where there had been stillness and harmony where there had been discord. He filled the emptiness with His own loving fellowship. I have never regretted opening the door to Christ and I never will. After Christ entered my heart, in the joy of that newfound relationship, I said to Him, "Lord, I want this heart of mine to be Yours. I want You to settle down here

and be fully at home. I want You to use it as Your own. Let me show you around and point out some of the features of the home so that You may be more comfortable. I want You to enjoy our time together." He was glad to come and seemed delighted to be given a place in my ordinary little heart.

Getting our heads wrapped around the truth of Christ living in our hearts is difficult for some people, easy for others. There are those who just accept it. As we grow, it becomes obvious that when we accept Jesus into our hearts, it is His choice to move in; all we have to do is allow Him to enter.

When my husband and I moved into the parsonage in Lisbon (June of 2016), there were a dozen or so high school athletes helping to unload. Can you imagine what a mess we would have had if no one had been there to oversee them? Even with my directing them where the boxes and furniture went, there were rooms I couldn't get into because the boxes were deposited just inside the door. Beyond those boxes, the room was empty. This encouraging book is Robert Boyd Munger's portrayal of what a heart can look like if we actively participate in that move of Jesus into our hearts. You've probably heard it said that God is a gentleman and that He won't force Himself on us. When Jesus moves into our hearts, He will only occupy whatever room we allow Him to. To put it bluntly, if we want to continue in our sin, He won't bulldoze it out of our lives. We have to choose to push it out ourselves.

Throughout the Old Testament, the Israelites were taught and trained to pursue and maintain holiness in their lives. The disciples learned from the Master Himself. Sanctified—set apart—made holy. It all comes down to our choice to let Jesus have free access to every room in our hearts. It all comes down to a choice, their choice and ours, to allow Jesus free access to every room of our heart.

If the only time we ever talk to our Father is in those crisis prayers, we are taking advantage of a good and gracious God. Instead, consider spending some time with Him when things are going well in your life. When you are happy, as well as sad about something, share your *entire* life with Him. One of my favorite teachings is on the importance of daily quiet time with the Lord. There are so many aspects of what that might look like for you. If only you will make time for Jesus, you can bet He will have time for you!

> [*My Heart—Christ's Home,* continued] We moved next to the living room. This was a quiet, comfortable room with a warm atmosphere. I liked it. It had a fireplace, sofa, overstuffed chairs, a bookcase and an intimate atmosphere. He also seemed pleased with it. He said, "Indeed, this is a delightful room. Let's come here often. It's secluded and quiet, and we can have good talks and fellowship together." Well, naturally as a new Christian, I was thrilled. I couldn't think of anything I would rather do than have a few minutes alone with Christ in close companionship. He promised, "I will be here every morning early. Meet Me here and we will start the day together." So morning after morning, I would go downstairs to the living room. He would take a book of the Bible from the bookcase, open it and we would read it together. He would unfold to me the wonder of God's saving truth recorded on its pages and make my heart sing as He shared

all He had done for me and would be to me. Those times were wonderful. Through the Bible and His Holy Spirit He would talk to me. In prayer I would respond. So our friendship deepened in these quiet times of personal conversation. However, under the pressure of many responsibilities, little by little, this time began to be shortened. Why, I'm not sure. Somehow I assumed that I was just too busy to give special, regular time to be with Christ. This was not a deliberate decision, you understand, it just seemed to happen that way. Eventually, not only was the period shortened, but I began to miss days now and then, such as during midterms or finals. Matters of urgency demanding my attention were continually crowding out the quiet times with Jesus. Often I would miss two days in a row or more. One morning, I recall rushing down the steps in a hurry to be on my way to an important appointment. As I passed, the door was open. Glancing in, I saw a fire in the fireplace and Jesus sitting there. Suddenly in dismay, it came to me. "He is my guest. I invited Him into my heart! He has come as my Savior and Friend to live with me. Yet here I am, neglecting Him." I stopped and hesitantly went in. With downcast glance, I said, "Master, I am sorry! Have you been here every morning?" "Yes," He replied. "I told you I would be here to meet with you." I was even more ashamed! He had been faithful in spite of my faithlessness. I asked Him to forgive me and He did, as He always does when we acknowledge our failures and want to do the right thing. He said, "The trouble is that you have been thinking of our quiet time, of Bible Study and prayer, as a means for your own spiritual growth. This is true, but you have forgotten that this time means something to Me also. Remember, I love you. At a great cost, I have redeemed you. I value your fellowship. Just to have you look up into My face warms My heart. Don't neglect this hour if only for My sake. Whether or not you want to be with Me, remember I want to be with you. I really love you!"

When we set aside time to just sit with the Lord, it is a time of sweet fellowship, of eagerness to learn and just sit at Jesus's feet. If that time is in the morning, we may be sitting in a quiet corner, with our coffee, our Bible and a notebook. We might start by just a simple prayer of thanksgiving...for the break in the weather, good news from the doctor...or something as simple as a decent night's sleep. This is a popular acronym that may help you when you pray. It puts everything in a respectful order:

> A—Adoration (Openly telling God of our love and adoration for who He is.)
>
> C—Confession (Unconfessed sin in our lives can hinder our prayer.)
>
> T—Thanksgiving (Thanking Him for forgiving us, but also for all He has done for us.)
>
> S—Supplication (Presenting our need, our request. This is not always necessary!)

Jesus taught His disciples how to pray. We know that Jesus sometimes prayed with them. At other times prayed alone, as in this case when Jesus withdrew from all of them, to pray this crisis prayer alone. Just Him and His Abba Father.

One of my recent daily devotional readings says this: "Believer, be much in solitary prayer, especially in times of trial. Family prayer, social prayer, prayer in the Church, will not suffice alone. These are very precious, but the best beaten spice will smoke in your censer in your private devotions, where no ear hears but God's."

When I first married my husband, he introduced me to the motorcycle world. It wasn't long before I was on my own bike and enjoying cross country rides. After one such ride, I shared a praise report at a ladies' Bible study and spoke of God's faithfulness toward me. The heat of the day had made asphalt parking lot very difficult to park a bike in, because the kickstand would sink into the hot asphalt. I was sharing my thankfulness for a safe journey and mentioned that I was grateful that God had worked it out, that just as we were pulling into a restaurant, a car had left a space that was concrete rather than asphalt. A woman at that Bible study, who later became a dear friend of mine, very angrily scoffed that God couldn't care less about my having a parking space. Frequently, I've heard people say, "God's got better things to do than listen to unimportant requests." I disagree. If it's important to us, it's important to God. After all, He is in charge of time, as well as being omnipresent. Time isn't affected by Him listening to our prayers. Everything in "life" connects with the time we spend with Him. The more time we spend with Him, the more things that are important to God become important to us!

In Jesus's crisis prayer, He cries, "Abba Father…take this cup from me…" Robert Boyd Munger goes on to say, "Nothing can forfeit a child's right to a father's protection. Be not afraid to say, 'My Father, hear my cry.'"

Scripture doesn't divulge what Abba Father's specific reply was to this prayer, although we know the outcome. That's what is so personal about prayer. It is a two-way communication with God, but only you hear God's answer to your prayers. The only way someone else will know is if you tell them or if they read your prayer journal. Do I write in a journal every time I pray? Pretty much. If I am driving, and I see an accident, I pray. I don't pull over and grab my journal and write it down. But during my evening, I might write down that I witnessed an accident today, and "Lord, I pray again for the safety of that driver they took away in the ambulance, bless Him or her with your presence, your peace, your strength."

For the most part, when I pull out my journal, I imagine Jesus pulling up a chair beside me. And we talk. There are other times when I feel His nudging in my spirit first, then I will grab my journal and maybe a cup of coffee or tea, and we talk. At times a particular person will come to my mind, and I grab my journal and we talk. Perhaps there are reports on the news that upset me or break my heart, so I grab my journal and we talk. *We* talk. As difficult as it is for me to be quiet, I don't do all the talking! My prayer time has become so much a time of "communion with God" that if I just pray, and say "Amen" and go about my business, I feel like I've hung up on God! I haven't given Him a chance to address what I was presenting to Him, let alone listening for what He wanted me to focus on!

"Call to Me, and I will answer you, and show you great and inscrutable things which you do not know" (Jer. 33:3, NKJV).

Your Bible may use the word *mighty* instead of *inscrutable*. Webster's definition is actually "1. Unsearchable; that which cannot be searched into and understood by inquiry or study. 2. That which cannot be penetrated, discovered or understood by human reason." How exciting that in the Word given way back then God invited us to call on Him so He could tell us about things we don't know and can't search out without Him! The more you know God's Word, the more you'll learn to recognize God's heart. When you know someone very well, you can sense the essence of who they are, coming through their conversation. When you know God's Word, you'll know God's character, His essence. God will never tell you anything out of character or contradictory to His written Word. If God wants to talk to me, and it is my firm belief that He wants to talk to all of us, I don't want to forget a thing He has to say! So I write it down.

God will make Himself heard, if you are listening, when we pray and when we *listen* for God's voice. His answer may come as a feeling that we need to call on someone or do something specific. We make it more difficult than it is. When we have a sense that God is nudging us to do something, we need to test it—by simply taking it back to Scripture. God will never ask you to do something that is against His written word! He will never ask you to sin. He will tell you how much He loves you. He may show you how you could have handled a situation differently, but He will do it lovingly. He may remind you of a verse you had forgotten about, or that you never knew about—a verse that He wants you to apply to a current life situation. He may bring to mind someone who is struggling and needs a friend.

In 1 Samuel 3 it tells the story of Samuel hearing God's call and how he thought it was Eli, who was in the next room. And in verse 10, after hearing the call again, Samuel answers, "Speak, Lord, your servant is listening." That's what we want our response to be, right? If you're like me, however, my own thoughts get in the way! So I've learned a couple of tricks that help me quiet my spirit, which I have shared in this book in a chapter called "Listening for the Shepherd's Voice." You do not *have* to journal. Yet it is so sweet to go back and see how God has answered prayers or changed your heart. It is so nice to see how *you* grow because of meeting with God every day in prayer instead of just in those times of crisis. It truly is inspiring and encouraging to just spend time sitting with the King of kings. It's still called prayer. It's letting God get a word in edgewise in your prayer.

Chapter 15

Mirrors, Jewels, and Masks

When I was in Marine Corps Boot Camp, we were required to go to classes called ID—Image Development. We were taught cleanliness and grooming, how to style our hair, take care of our skin, how to put on our makeup. We were also taught that chickens are plucked and eyebrows are tweezed. Back in the seventies, they'd never heard of waxing! There was an entire week out of that eight-week schedule, that eight hours each day were dedicated to looking at ourselves in a mirror to try to improve what God gave us.

Nowadays, as I dress every morning, I probably look in the mirror a minimum of five to seven times: While I am putting on my makeup, fixing my hair, at least two to three times while I dress, again while I decide which shoes to wear, and if I need a jacket, which one to wear…and one more time just before I walk out the door. The person I see in the mirror is pretty much the same person I've been seeing all my life. Some mornings, I'm still caught off guard as to how much I look like my mom since I started wearing my hair shorter! Several years ago, while I was teaching a Bible study on prayer, I was sharing that we need to spend quality time with the Lord and not just pray on the run—while we're driving to or from work, or while we're putting on our makeup. I said to the group, "Ladies, the only face God wants you to see when you pray is His." Today, I am reminded of that statement almost every time I'm putting on my makeup! I realize now that there is also a flip side.

Who do we see when we look in our mirror? Do we see a single woman? A wife, mother, grandmother? Do we see a student, teacher, secretary, professional? Do we see someone who has been wounded or hardened by life's circumstances? By our own choices? I want you to consider this: Try looking into the mirror and seeing someone God dearly loves dearly—his daughter. You. God wants you to see yourself as God sees you—a saint, a beautiful woman, a princess—a favored daughter of the King. As daughters of the King of kings and Lord of lords, we are rich, because our Father, the King, is rich. How do I know that? Because it's in *the book*. As princesses, we can trust our Father the King to give us what we need to live.

> For every beast of the forest is mine, And the cattle upon a thousand hills. (Ps. 50:10, NKJV)
>
> My God shall supply every need… according to his riches in glory in Christ Jesus. (Phil. 4:19, NKJV)

And Scripture addresses our desires, as well as our needs: "You have given him his heart's desire, and have not withheld the request of his lips. Selah" (Ps. 21:2, NKJV).

It is my belief that those desires are placed in our hearts by our Father God, just so He can make them happen. That's how much our Abba Father—Daddy God—loves us. Our Father delights in giving to us.

> Ask, and it will be given to you; seek, and you will find; knock, and it will be opened to you. For everyone who asks receives, and he who

seeks finds, and to him who knocks it will be opened. Or what man is there among you who, if his son asks for bread, will give him a stone? Or if he asks for a fish, will he give him a serpent? If you then, being evil, know how to give good gifts to your children, how much more will your Father who is in heaven give good things to those who ask Him! (Matt. 7:7–11, NKJV)

What conditions does God put on these verses? Only that we ask. As parents, doesn't it touch our hearts to be able to give something to our children that they really want? It makes us happy that our children know that if they ask, we'll do everything in our power to get it for them. God is no different. Remember, He made us in His image and He is a parent too! We should never give with the motivation of getting something in return, but that is God's additional promise to us in Luke 6:38: "give, and it shall be given unto you; good measure, pressed down, shaken together, running over, shall they give into your bosom. For with the same measure that you use, it will be measured back to you" (NKJV).

We don't have to earn the right to be His daughter—His princess. Just as we cannot earn His love, we can't earn His favor. It is ours, because of our relationship with Him through His Son! As daughters of the King, we need to think of R and R. In the Marine Corps that meant Rest and Recreation, but here it means: Rich and Royal. We need to have the attitude of being rich and royal, because we *are*.

Today Jehovah your God has commanded you to do these statutes and judgments. You therefore shall keep and do them with all your heart and with all your soul. You have today said that Jehovah is your God, and that you would walk in His ways, and keep His statutes and His commandments and His judgments, and listen to His voice. And Jehovah has taken you today to be His peculiar people, as He has promised you, and to keep all His commandments, and to make you high above all nations which He has made, in praise and in name and in honor, and that you may be a holy people to Jehovah your God, even as He has spoken. (Deut. 26:16–19, NKJV)

If you have given your life to Jesus, you have declared that the Lord is your God. You have committed to walk in His ways and obey His voice. When you did that, you became His daughter. You became part of His royal family, you became a princess. You should be wearing a crown!

When you look in your mirror, it's okay to see the woman you are on the outside, but also remember to look for Daddy God's little girl. She's the one who can crawl up on Daddy God's lap any time she wants to, just to feel better about life. She has the right to cry on His shoulder or to tell Him about the injustice or wound she suffered today, or just to rest. *You* are Daddy God's little girl!

When you look in that mirror, do you see a saint or a sinner? That's been an ongoing battle of words for centuries, and we probably won't settle it here, but I challenge you: If you see a sinner in that mirror, think about what God did for you when He sent His Son to die for you on the cross. When God orchestrated His plan of salvation, He made a way for you to leave your sins behind. When you accepted that plan or gift of salvation, your sins were removed from you and placed on Jesus.

That makes you a saint. When that happened, the righteousness of Jesus covered you like a soft blanket and *it still does. That is what* God sees when He looks at you—the righteousness of Christ. A saint. When you look in that mirror, do you see your sin or do you see that that sin has been removed? Do you see Christ's righteousness? Being a saint doesn't mean you are perfect. You are, after all, still human. Being a child of God means we are saints who (occasionally) sin and immediately repent!

God sees you as a sparkling jewel—most of us are still in the rough, but God sees the finished product—the perfect mature daughter that He created. His princess. No two jewels are alike. You are unique—some of you are rubies, some are diamonds, jades, emeralds, sapphires—and you need to know that it is impossible for a ruby to evolve into a sapphire or for an emerald to evolve into a diamond. Can you imagine the chipping away, the grinding and sawing that would take place if a sapphire tried to become a jade? It wouldn't be a pretty sight, would it?

Yet we women often look at someone else and say, "why can't I be like that? I can do what she does, so why am I stuck doing what I'm doing? All I have to do is tell Pastor that I don't want to do this anymore; I want to do something else." Not so. It's called a "calling." God called each of us to be a different jewel—His choice. He's called each of us and gifted each of us to do a specific task. If one of His princesses isn't in the right slot, someone else can't do what God has called *her* to do, and the job isn't being done as God wants it done. That's because (1) He hasn't gifted the person who is in the wrong slot to do that job, and (2) the one He *has* gifted to do that job has no place to perform her calling. That makes for all these unhappy jewels, and God's plan isn't being accomplished. Think about it, ladies. Are you doing what God has called you to do or are you filling a slot you happened to see as needing to be filled? Did you ask God about what task or ministry *He* wanted you to be active in or did you just happen to be there when a vacancy needed to be covered?

"But if any of you lacks wisdom, let him ask of God, who gives to all liberally and with no reproach, and it shall be given to him" (James 1:5, NKJV).

Reproach here means resentment. God will never resent you for asking Him what *He* wants. Have you asked Him which jewel He wants you to be? No one jewel is any more valuable or important as any other jewel. Okay, it's an analogy, but it makes it a little easier to understand, doesn't it? Know that you *are* a jewel. You may not be the jewel you most admire but function as the jewel you were designed to be and make it shine!

Which jewel are you? You and I aren't the same. You're not the same jewel as the woman next door. Even if you and your best friend are both sapphires, no two sapphires are the same! Each jewel is unique. God created them that way, just as He created you that way. After all, what would the world look like with all diamonds and not one topaz in the bunch!

> For I will look on you favorably and make you fruitful, multiply you and confirm My covenant with you. You shall eat the old harvest, and clear out the old because of the new. I will set My tabernacle among you, and My soul shall not abhor you. I will walk among you and be your God, and you shall be My people. I am the LORD your God, who brought you out of the land of Egypt, that you should not be their slaves; I have broken the bands of your yoke and made you walk upright. (Lev. 26:9–13, NKJV)

The women's lib movement of the '60s really did nothing to set us free. God is the one who has broken our yokes, ladies. *He* has set us free. The verse says free from slavery—but that means free from the chains of alcoholism or any other sin that has us bound. We are truly free, free to live, free to dream and to pursue our dreams, free to run or walk, to dance or not dance. We are most certainly free to praise the Daddy God, the Abba Father who promises that we are all His children, His baby girls, His princesses.

Do you feel like a princess? A jewel? I hope so because that's exactly who you are. But if you don't feel like one, consider the possible reasons: (1) Remember that the only way you can become a princess is to accept Jesus as your Savior. Have you done that? There is nothing you can do to earn this royalty. It is a gift from your Daddy God, delivered personally to you by His Son Jesus. (2) If you've already done that and you still don't feel like royalty, you may be buying into the lie that our enemy would love for us to accept—that we aren't good enough. *The truth is, ladies, we aren't good enough.* No one is. It was God's choice to send His Son, Jesus, to the cross. And it was Jesus's choice to die there—for you and for me.

Okay, we've discussed who we see when we look in the mirror. We've talked about how God sees us and how we see ourselves. How do other people see us? Or more to the point, what do we *allow* others to see when they look at us? In an ideal world, other people would see us for who we are—a work in progress.

What do we do about those people who have a wrong picture of who we are?

1. First, let's look at the people—there are those people we know and love. Family and those that we call our friends. Sometimes it hurts that they

may have an imperfect perception of us. If our relationship with those who are in this category is a transparent one, we should be able to talk to this friend or loved one and clarify any misunderstandings or hurt feelings that are spawned by any case of mistaken identity, so to speak.

2. Then there are those people we'll call acquaintances. The line is different for everyone, but after a person has been an acquaintance for a long enough time, they could probably cross over that invisible line into the friendship category, but while they are still "just" acquaintances and you are getting to know each other a little better, there are frequent misconceptions on both sides. If those issues aren't addressed with love and honesty, the relationship ends—it has no chance to grow into a friendship, but instead it falls away into a group we could call "those we tolerate." Be careful who you allow to fall into that group—it's probably not a good idea to let your boss become one of those.

3. In another group, there are people we don't see very often—grocery clerks, mechanics, the guy at the Dollar Store—people who probably know our names because they see our debit card when we pay for our purchases. This is an interesting group to talk about because we might not necessarily give much thought to how they see us. But we should! Scripture tells us in 1 Peter 3:15 to always be ready to give an answer to everyone who asks you the reason for your hope (paraphrased). Okay, picture this: I go to the grocery store five or six times a month. If I am grumpy

and grouchy and maybe even rude, do you think that clerk wants what I have? Is he going to see any hope in me? So why would he want me to explain what he sees? But if I treat him kindly, smile, and be cheerful and encouraging, that person may "want what I've got," namely Jesus!

If we make it our motto in life to represent Christ well, in everything we do and say, to give God the glory for everything good in our life and to openly trust in Him even during the bad things that come to us, everyone who sees us—no matter what category they fall into—will know we are different. Some people are afraid of being different.

When we stand apart (which is what the word *sanctified* means) and live a life that is obviously different from other folks, people sometimes become suspect. But if our lifestyle is consistent—even when we struggle—they can see us as humans who have hope. Then, we can expect the questions: Why doesn't today's economy scare you? How can you be at peace with what's going on in the world? Why aren't you worried about the upcoming election? But the best one of all: How can I have that peace? That's the question we want to always be prepared to answer.

If people have a wrong impression of us, what should we do? Pray and ask God to help you see yourself clearly. If that picture doesn't match up to who you think you are, ask Him to help you understand what matters most—not what others think of you but what God thinks of you. Each situation is different, but if it's a case of being judged by someone, think about this: Matthew 7:1 tells us to "judge not, lest we be judged." It's important that we come alongside our sisters and be strong when they can't be. I pray that each of you have Christian friends who will come alongside you when you stumble. Not just for support, but to gently and lovingly steer you back to where you need to be; for gentle chastisement. I know that isn't always easy to do, but if you pray about it, God will give you the words and the opportunity—to say maybe, "You said something that I don't think you meant"…"the way I understood it, just doesn't sound like who I know you to be." Stating it this way explains an issue, yet doesn't attack the person, and it leaves room for grace. What was stated is actually beside the point, but maybe more importantly, it needed to be a point…

There are three aspects of this question of "Who do I let others see" that I want to address:

#1: **How can I portray to you that I am a good person**, without tooting my own horn, making you feel inferior, bragging on myself, sounding holier than thou, or letting pride ruin any chance of truth in our friendship! A bigger question might be, How important is it that you see me as a "good little Christian," and if it is, why? It all links to the way God created us. He created us with a need to feel loved and accepted. His intention was for us to fill that need with *Him*—fellowship in the garden with Him. When Eve (and Adam) put an end to that plan, we were left with this innate desire to be accepted, and we look everywhere for that acceptance. (This is covered more in the chapter titled "Accepted in the Beloved.")

> Blessed be the God and Father of our Lord Jesus Christ, who has blessed us in Christ with every spiritual blessing in the heavenly places, even as He chose us in Him before the foundation of the world, that we should be holy and blameless before Him. In love He predestined us for adoption as sons through Jesus Christ, according to the purpose of His will, to the praise of his glorious grace, with which He has blessed us in the Beloved. (Eph. 1:3–6, NKJV)

Not only are we accepted, we are *chosen*. There are any number of good books regarding our identity in Christ—our self-worth. The best ones suggest a daily confession that helps us walk in the truth. We cannot live our lives worrying about what other people think of us—keeping in mind that while we *do* want to live our lives in a way that draws people to Christ, we are not to live our lives worrying about what other people think of us. For example, a Bible study that I used to go to recited this: "Because of Christ's redemption, I am a new creation of great value. I am deeply loved, completely forgiven." If I live like I believe that, people will have an honest perspective of who I am.

#2: I am struggling but I don't want you to see that... In today's society, struggle means failure or weakness and if I were really a strong Christian woman, I wouldn't have such a hard time with...getting my children to behave, fighting this addiction, sticking to my budget, whatever you are struggling with!

For several years, my older sister has lovingly made reference to my being a "good little Christian." In my mind, she has a really good picture of me (although it is probably a little unrealistic!) She knows that I am 100 percent human. She knows I stumble, I fall, I struggle, I get back up, and sometimes I just want to give up. She also knows that I know where to go for my strength! Sometimes that's on my knees. Sometimes that's either to her or my other my sister. They will both lead me right back to Jesus!

How can you help me if you don't know I am struggling? How can I come alongside my sister if I don't know she's having problems? I'll bet there isn't a woman alive whose husband/significant other hasn't said to her, "I am not a mind reader!" or "I can't read your mind." Guess what, ladies, God didn't make women mind readers either! The next time someone comes up to you and says, "How are you doing?" be honest with them!

You don't have to tell them all the details, but you can tell them you need some help—a shoulder, a hand, a prayer! And give her a chance to help you through your struggle. Women struggle all the time! Why do we have so much trouble admitting we need help? PRIDE = "Purely Rotten Individualism Doing Evil!" By evil, I am talking about anything our enemy can do to keep us from living the joyful and abundant life God wants us to live. Maybe you think if I know your struggle I will feel obligated to help. And of course you don't want to impose; after all, your problem isn't my problem… Maybe it should be! We are a family, aren't we?

Sometimes we struggle because of what God is doing in our lives. Maybe we are in a season of our lives where God is doing something difficult for us, working on us. I have always enjoyed singing, especially for the Lord. There was a period when I couldn't sing. I lost my voice. That was difficult for me! I tried to be strong about it, but I have to admit to you that I had an occasional pity party. But God kept using me in other areas, and since I am His daughter, He has that right! The point is, sometimes we need a sister to come up to us and just love on us. Other times we just need someone to hear us out.

Several years ago I was teaching women's Sunday school. I was meeting once a week with another elder's wife to help me prepare. Long after I finished that teaching, she and I continued to meet. We chose another book and went through it together, having no idea that we would discover that we had such similar backgrounds and struggles and they were affecting our lives even then! We were able to encourage each other and truly come alongside each other and change the patterns that we had unknowingly been creating in our lives! We developed a beautiful friendship. But even bigger than "us," that meeting started a mentoring program in two churches—older women mentoring younger women. How can we do that if we don't know what the struggles are?

#3: Man, if you knew me you wouldn't want anything to do with me, so I'm really working hard at hiding who I am. There isn't much I haven't done in my life, and I praise God daily that He has forgiven me and delivered me and He uses me, in spite of all the junk I have in my past. I knew when I wrote my first book that certain people would judge me because of it. I knew I would lose some friends, and in some cases, lose the respect I had worked long and hard to earn. But it was as if God gently twisted my arm. I heard that still small voice, telling me why I had to write the book: "Women are wounded, and they need to know you're not perfect either." We can all say, "If you only knew what I did," or, "what I used to be," or, "how I used to live." Even if it was just once, or one thing or one area that we failed at, we want to hide it. About the time I had that book published, someone told me something that has made perfect sense: "What you want to hide in the closet is what God most wants to use to minister to others. How could He use it if you wouldn't be transparent enough in your own life to share it?"

All of these scenarios fall into one general category—how am I doing at keeping up appearances? Or *Is my mask on straight?* Even if your mask is flawless and perfectly straight, there is still a huge problem with it: the fact that you are wearing it at all. It's like Mastercard—we don't leave home without it. When we wear a mask, we don't have to wonder about how others see us, because they see our mask instead of the real us. They never see our true face—not even those we love get to see the full truth of who we are...only a hint. When a little too much truth bleeds through our mask, it just confuses things, because no one ever asks us to reveal more than we are comfortable revealing.

When we wear a mask we convey to others that they too must wear a mask or hide the truth about themselves. We're telling them that the "new creation in Christ" life doesn't really work. That it is better to be unknown or hidden than to risk rejection. When we wear our masks, we teach others to live a guarded life, a life of comparison, envy, jealousy. We teach them to trade authentic weakness, transparency, and vulnerability for the imitation veneer of safety. Our masks deceive us into believing that we can get away with hiding our true selves. In reality, over time, our masks crumble and reveal more of our true faces than we ever intended to let people see. It's expensive to wear masks, to cultivate and curate our image. It's exhausting to always be on guard so that people don't see who we really are!

In the world today, mask-wearing is often more prevalent among Christians than nonbelievers. You see, rather than risk being judged harshly, a nonbeliever will find like-minded people to hang with. Support groups, gangs, Goths—mask wearing is a product of pretending to be something we aren't or hiding who *we think* we are. But for Christians, our pretending may be the result of our sincere desire to "make God look good" by having our act together. Therefore, we cover our dirty laundry and show the world how holy and good we are. *God doesn't need us to make Him look good.* God needs us to be ourselves and let Him clean us up and use us.

What makes us so insecure that we insist on wearing a mask? It may be that we believe we are something we are not. For example, I know I am forgiven, but my life isn't necessarily something other people would forgive. So I ask myself if you still see me as a sinner. Or because I may be having trouble forgiving myself, or accepting forgiveness, therefore, I think you also can't forgive me. I may truly be a "Good Little Christian" but if I don't think you see me that way, I may feel the need to repaint my picture of me, for your benefit.

How many times was God mentioned in that example? How many times was the word *I* used? So what would that entire scenario tell you—it's all about *me* and nothing about *God*. When we transform our thinking into seeing ourselves as God sees us, it's easier to leave our masks at home and let our true faces breathe! Then it's easier to be open and transparent with others in our lives and that frees *them* to be themselves, or transparent! Throw out that mask and let your light shine!

Chapter 16
Sacred Pillars

After finishing early, in the ladies' Bible study, I was leading, I opened the session for general discussion. I was asked how I choose a passage from Scripture to study. I was replying that sometimes it is a person that I am researching, other times it is an event, when I felt the Lord leading me to do a role-playing example. I told the ladies that sometimes, God leads me to what He wants me to study. As I picked up my Bible, God led me randomly to a verse which became a major part of my teachings for the next few years.

> Now when all this was finished, all Israel who were present went out to the cities of Judah and broke the sacred pillars in pieces, cut down the wooden images, and threw down the high places and the altars—from all Judah, Benjamin, Ephraim, and Manasseh—until they had utterly destroyed them all. Then all the children of Israel returned to their own cities, every man to his possession. (2 Chron. 31:1, NKJV)

The Lord faithfully led me to a quick surface explanation of the verse for those present: "We need to look at the 'sacred pillars' in our lives and tear them down!" A sacred pillar is any-thing in our lives that we allow to be above God. This quick example of how God leads opened wide a door that I could not resist going through, at home, later that day...and the next day...and for the week or so, as long as it took me to hear what the Lord wanted me to learn. I share that now with you.

"Now when all this was finished..." Let's stop there a min-ute. All *what* was finished?

Whenever we study our Bibles, it is imperative that we understand the context. One pastor I studied under said you could generally get the true context by reading the twenty verses prior and the twenty after the verse you are looking at. I gen-erally skim the chapter before, and maybe I'll need to go back another to see if something there answers the question God places in my mind. (Inquiring minds want to know) "all what was finished?"

> Hezekiah became king when he was twen-ty-five years old, and he reigned twenty-nine years in Jerusalem. His mother's name was Abijah the daughter of Zechariah. And he did what was right in the sight of the LORD, according to all that his father David had done. In the first year of his reign, in the first month, he opened the doors of the house of the LORD and repaired them. Then he brought in the priests and the Levites, and gathered them in the East Square, and said to them: "Hear me, Levites! Now sanctify yourselves, sanctify the house of the LORD God of your fathers, and carry out the rub-bish from the holy place." (2 Chron. 29:1–5, NKJV)

When we go back a couple of chapters, we see that Hezekiah has become king at age twenty-five, and his first official act is to repair the temple and cleanse it, by calling the priests in, first to sanctify themselves, and then in verse 5, to "carry out the rubbish from the holy place." As a rule, we might do our dusting and vacuuming, our sweeping and mopping on a regular basis, right? Hopefully. But this sounds more like a deep cleaning, doesn't it? Like a spring cleaning. When I was in the Marine Corps, it was called a Field Day: all the furniture was moved; ceilings were dusted; walls were washed down; floors were swept, mopped, waxed and buffed; windows were cleaned inside and out—the whole nine yards. While I was living in Texas, I learned such colorful phrases as "the whole nine yards." I didn't know what it meant, so I asked. It means the whole enchilada. No? Well, that's from Texas too…the whole thing… in this case, it means this cleaning to be done was thorough, complete, inside out, top to bottom.

That raises another question: why was there a need for such a deep thorough cleaning in the temple? The priests were assigned to the maintenance and upkeep, so why was it lacking? That leads us back a bit further in Scripture.

> Ahaz [the previous king] was twenty years old when he became king, and he reigned sixteen years in Jerusalem; and he did not do what was right in the sight of the LORD, as his father David had done. For he walked in the ways of the kings of Israel, and made molded images for the Baals. He burned incense in the Valley of the Son of Hinnom, and burned his children in the fire, according to the abominations of the nations whom the LORD had cast out before the children of Israel. And he

sacrificed and burned incense on the high
places, on the hills, and under every green
tree. (2 Chron. 28:1–5, NKJV)

"…he didn't do what was right in the sight of the Lord."
That right there is enough for me to give King Ahaz a thumbs-down, if I knew nothing else about him. But Scripture goes
on to say "he burned his children in the fire, according to the
abominations of the nations whom the LORD had cast out
before the children of Israel." This is a very brief mention here,
but this is huge! King Ahaz commanded the people to sacri-fice their babies to please the pagan fertility God, in hopes of
having a healthy harvest. This is only one reason God told the
Israelites not to intermarry with these people! Ahaz also took
valuables out of the temple and melted them down to make his
own pagan images to the gods of Baal. Those gods commanded
temple prostitutes to interact with the priests and the people
and Ahaz complied. Without going any deeper, we know why
King Ahaz has been called a wicked and evil king, and why the
temple needed such a deep cleaning. *Those sacrifices were proba-bly made on the altar in the temple.* That's why Hezekiah insisted
on the cleansing of the temple being his first act of reform,
besides the fact that God told him to!

A little history here: Toward the end of King Solomon's
reign, Israel split. The Northern Kingdom remained as Israel
and the Southern Kingdom became known as Judah. Hezekiah
was king of Judah, in Jerusalem. Between King Solomon and
Hezekiah, a span covering 215 years, reigned twelve kings and
one queen—Athaliah. (I call her the Crazy Queen because she
murdered almost the entire royal lineage, her own family, but
that's another story for another day.) Half of those rulers are
described in Scripture as "doing evil in the sight of the Lord—
five kings and Crazy Queen Athaliah. All but one of those

remaining kings "did what was right in the sight of the Lord," but not to the extent of David.

Have you heard the expression two steps forward and one step back? For every two steps toward wickedness and sin that an evil king took, the good kings were only taking one step back toward good, so they weren't gaining ground enough to undo the damage, so the people were being led deeper and deeper into darkness and wickedness and idolatry and sin.

For an example, let's look at King Solomon: wisest and richest of all kings, appointed by God himself as king, over his elder brother, being honored with the humbling job of building the magnificent temple—the one we've been talking about being in such a state of filth and disrepair. King Solomon—the one who was wise enough to fortify Israel's major trade cities to be sure that Israel would never be at the mercy of her enemies. King Solomon—so wise and so rich, and he loved God so much...at least he started out that way. But he was so human. He was susceptible to the beauty of women:

> But King Solomon loved many foreign women, as well as the daughter of Pharaoh: women of the Moabites, Ammonites, Edomites, Sidonians, and Hittites—from the nations of whom the LORD had said to the children of Israel, "You shall not intermarry with them, nor they with you. Surely they will turn away your hearts after their gods." Solomon clung to these in love. And he had seven hundred wives, princesses, and three hundred concubines; and his wives turned away his heart. For it was so, when Solomon was old, that his wives turned his heart after their gods; and his heart was not loyal to the

> LORD his God, as was the heart of his father
> David. For Solomon went after Ashtoreth the
> goddess of the Sidonians, and after Milcom
> the abomination of the Ammonites. Solomon
> did evil in the sight of the LORD, and did
> not fully follow the LORD, as did his father
> David. (1 Kings 11:1–6, NKJV)

Solomon was so totally self-indulgent that even his every-day drinking glass was made of pure gold. The self-indulgence of the king presented a model for his subjects and they emulated King Solomon well. Every king after him—the twelve I mentioned, half good and half bad—contributed toward society's state of wickedness, to bring us to this point where Hezekiah becomes king.

If your Bible has headings, above 2 Chronicles Chapter 30, you might see something like "Hezekiah Keeps Passover" or "Passover Reinstated." If wicked King Ahaz went so far off the deep end, that he would sacrifice children, including his own, he certainly wouldn't have been too concerned about keeping the sacraments of Passover handed down by Jehovah God to Moses! When Hezekiah becomes king, he is trying to reverse that, turn Judah around, back to godliness, but at this point that is no easy accomplishment. He is dealing with people who have totally indulged themselves in selfish human nature, sexual immorality and not just with the temple prostitutes—the epitome of the "all about me" lifestyle. Just like King Solomon, much as we see in today's society.

Passover, as prescribed in Exodus 12, was to be kept every year, as a remembrance of Israel's preservation and deliverance out of Egypt. Their safety and deliverance were not a reward of their own righteousness, but the gift of mercy from God. Passover reminded them of this, and by this ordinance they were taught that all blessings came to them through the shedding and sprinkling of blood. But the people hadn't been faithful in their sacraments, including the sin offerings, because the priests hadn't been. And the priests hadn't been because the kings hadn't been.

Passover was to be held on the fourteenth day of the first month in the temple. But the temple was so not ready (remember it was closed for cleansing) and the priests couldn't even enter it to get rid of the rubbish, until after they themselves had been cleansed and made holy. They had some repenting and cleansing to do. Sometimes obedience to the king is not compatible with obedience to God. God let them know He was not happy about what they were doing:

> Will you steal, murder, commit adultery, swear falsely, burn incense to Baal, and walk after other gods whom you do not know, and then come and stand before Me in this house which is called by My name, and say, "We are delivered to do all these abominations"? (Jer. 7:9–10, NKJV)

When they began obeying the new King Hezekiah, they turned back to the one true God—Jehovah God—and away from the false gods of Baal. Imagine their heartbreak, their mourning…you can't "un-see" what they had seen and in fact took part in that they now realize is an abomination—something morally disgusting to God!

The priests were humbled and re-sanctified, and the temple now cleansed and restored is dedicated back to God and the people are called to Passover—delayed into the second month.

So, all of that—everything since the beginning of this chapter—covers "When all this was finished" and *partially* puts us in the proper context.

I sat in a Beth Moore Bible Study once in which she asked everyone to draw a time line of their lives. The left of the line has a dot depicting birth, and the right has an arrow, indicating life continuing. She asked us to mark events that were important to us. So, for me, it had a cross on my timeline, where I was saved when I was nine years old. I marked when my grandma died, and when I joined the Marine Corps. And when I got married. You get the idea. Then it got a little more difficult.

> Therefore we must give the more earnest heed to the things we have heard, lest we drift away. For if the word spoken through angels proved steadfast, and every transgression and disobedience received a just reward, how shall we escape if we neglect so great a salvation...
> (Heb. 2:1–3a, NKJV)

What did that say? We should guard against neglecting our salvation. I knew nothing about this verse back then! I didn't guard mine and I drifted away. My marriage ended in divorce. So, I marked that on my time line too. I "drifted" for nine years. During those nine years, I was divorced twice more. When I came back to the Lord, I felt so guilty and unworthy. I felt like I could never be quite good enough for God to use me, in all my ugliness, in His beautiful kingdom.

My entire life line at that point was only about a cubit long. (In case you didn't know, a cubit is about twenty and one-half inches long), and when I marked off my nine-year period, it was about half an inch long! As life continues, and my service to God continues, those nine years becomes less and less significant because of what God has done in me since then. What He has done through me and allowed me to do for Him becomes more and more significant in my life and in the lives of those God uses me to help! His grace and mercy and forgiveness, and what God has allowed and enabled me to do makes that period miniscule!

I think of this Passover as similar to my coming back to the Lord. I was so guilty, but I repented and was cleansed and free, starting fresh, refreshed and renewed. All these people came to Passover, the first one in years, they repented and were cleansed, out from under the evil and wickedness, finally under a ruler who was doing what was right in the sight of the Lord, now ready for life changes for the better—a life pleasing to God. So, what was the next step? For me, it was getting back in church, putting God back on the throne of my life, and taking down the things I had put first, ahead of God.

> Now when all this was finished, all Israel who were present went out to the cities of Judah and broke the sacred pillars in pieces, cut down the wooden images, and threw down the high places and the altars—from all Judah, Benjamin, Ephraim, and Manasseh—until they had utterly destroyed them all. Then all the children of Israel returned to their own cities, every man to his possession. (2 Chron. 31:1, NKJV)

They utterly destroyed all of those altars—demolished the sacred pillars—cut down the wooden images that they themselves probably helped erect! They threw down the high places that they had allowed into their lives. Those sacred pillars represented the false idols they had been worshipping. The people who built them hoped that the pagan fertility gods had the power and the desire to give them a bountiful harvest. These altars and wooden images were built to remind the Israelites to put that false god first in their lives. But that is God's place, right? That's the place reserved for the one true living God. He is first, above all, not these false gods. Any time we allow anything or anyone to be first in our lives instead of God, we are falling into idolatry.

So, when Hezekiah became king, the people watched Him, much as we watch a new president when he first takes office. What changes will he make? As king, Hezekiah has the final say so on what is done and not done. They watched as he began re-instructing the people in the ways of Jehovah. They watched as he recalled the priests and led them back to their proper authority—the one true God. Through Hezekiah's reforms and his re-teaching the Israelites of the true God's place in their lives, they understood it. They repented. They tore down all those shrines as if they had had a bulldozer, and they each one returned to his own life and his own possessions.

So, with this Passover, the heads of the families "came back to the Lord," so to speak, and were charged with bringing the reinstated truths home, retraining their wives and children in the ways of the one true God—not Baal.

Chapter 31 continues by telling us that Hezekiah assigned priests to do the burnt offerings, and he himself designated what of his own possessions was to be offered in sacrifice—the lambs, goats, but no children. Another of the reasons the temple had suffered in repair during King Ahaz's reign was because the people were no longer contributing to the welfare and upkeep. In verse 4, King Hezekiah remedies that situation:

Moreover he [King Hezekiah] commanded the people who dwelt in Jerusalem to con-

> tribute support for the priests and the Levites, that they might devote themselves to the Law of the LORD. As soon as the commandment was circulated, the children of Israel brought in abundance the first fruits of grain and wine, oil and honey, and of all the produce of the field; and they brought in abundantly the tithe of everything. And the children of Israel and Judah, who dwelt in the cities of Judah, brought the tithe of oxen and sheep; also the tithe of holy things which were consecrated to the LORD their God they laid in heaps. In the third month they began laying them in heaps, and they finished in the seventh month. (2 Chron. 31: 4–7, NKJV)

Seventeenth Century Bible commentator Matthew Henry had this to say about this passage: "Those who enjoy the benefit of a settled ministry, will not grudge the expense of it."

These renewed Israelites did indeed "get it" and turned from the evil ways that their wicked king had led them into, and obeyed the new king and therefore began obeying God again. Skimming the rest of the chapter, it delineates all the Levites who were the priests and the portion they were given. It takes money to run a ministry—even today!

"And in every work that he [King Hezekiah] began in the service of the house of God, in the law and in the commandment, to seek his God, he did it with all his heart. So he prospered" (2 Chron. 31:21, NKJV).

(By the way, that is our twenty verses after the verse we are looking at. Looks like my mentor was right!)

We never give with the motive of getting back. We give our offerings out of obedience and love for God and the desire to see the gospel spread and the ministry advanced. But that was one of the changes that was needed here. Remember the Passover didn't take place until the second month, and it was in the third month that the people started gathering their offerings. It took them four months to finish bringing them in; such was the abundance that was given out of their generosity. And faith.

We skipped over verses 12–15, but they are important. They tell us that it took sixteen people to organize and oversee the freewill offerings! So this wasn't just the tithes, there were three types of giving here:

1. Tithe by definition as 10% of the increase.
2. First fruits is a declaration of faith. The first field that was harvested was given, in its entirety, as a statement of faith that God was going to bless the remainder of the fields and they would keep that harvest in its entirety.
3. Free will offerings—is whatever above that they wanted to give

The Israelites understood it. They rejoiced in it. They obeyed by faith, knowing that God was going to bless the changes they were making, the changes that would complete the reformation of Israel—the turning away from the previous king's evil ways and returning to God's ways.

Changes aren't always easy to make, even when we do so willingly. When we understand that the change is not just supported by God, but actually commanded by God, we are three-fourths of the way there. God will never tell you to do something He won't enable you to do. When you make a choice to change, especially when it is turning from a sin, God is 100 percent on your side! Nothing is impossible with God!

"But Jesus looked at them and said [And I say now to you], 'With men it is impossible, but not with God; for with God all things are possible'" (Mark 10:27, NKJV).

I sincerely hope you realize that God's word has every answer you need! No matter what you may be going through in your life, your answer is in the Bible!

Is there a sacred pillar that is God asking you to break into pieces? Have you, little by little, put something or someone ahead of God? He is a jealous God, He insists on being first in your life. Is he? If He isn't, you are living in sin. What wooden image have you allowed to be erected that takes your focus away from God? Do you seek Him for his answer to dilemmas in your life or do you pick up your phone to call a friend? God's answer will *always* be better than your friend's. What high place is taking your time away from God? Is the first thing you seek in the morning your Bible or the TV remote?

When Hezekiah led the people to repentance, God heard and answered. He forgave and cleansed. He is the same God now as He was then (Heb. 13:8). Just as these renewed people broke the sacred pillars in pieces, you can do the same thing. Give that sacred pillar to God. Pray this prayer: "Lord God, I give to you this sacred pillar. I break it into pieces as a symbol of removing this idol from my life. I want to honor you and obey you, so I ask you to enable me to eliminate this sacred pillar and turn back to you and put you first. Amen."

Chapter 17

A Tale of Two Nations

If you and I met, it wouldn't take very long at all before you would hear me refer to the Bible as God's love letter—His letter to those He loves. It's a letter full of love and promises. But a promise is only as valuable as the person who makes the promise is trustworthy. In Scripture, God promises that He will do something or be something or provide something. The first promise God made was to Adam and Eve—He gave them a beautiful garden to live in, a garden that supplied all their needs.

When Adam and Eve were assigned their gardening duties, they got to stay cool while they performed them, because there was no need to dress against sunburn, or a rainstorm or hail— in fact, there was no need to dress at all, was there? *All* they had to do was take care of the garden, and God would meet them every day, several times a day, all day long, to fellowship with them and just to love on them, and be loved on—to just flat out let them know how much He loved them. They were, after all, the original "rich and royal." God is absolutely trustworthy.

"God is not a man, that He should lie, Nor a son of man, that He should repent. Has He said, and will He not do? Or has He spoken, and will He not make it good?" (Num. 23:19, NKJV).

God cannot lie. His Word is His bond. A bond is a commitment, guarantee, covenant to be fulfilled at all costs.

8901234567890

The difference between a covenant and a contract is this. They can both be oral or written. But here's the biggest difference: A contract is a binding agreement between two or more parties. If party A does this then party B will do that. But most contracts have a breach of contract clause, which states that if one party doesn't fulfill his end of the agreement, then the other party is released from his responsibility. God doesn't make contracts, He makes covenants. A covenant doesn't have a breach of contract clause. Even if party B—even if *we* don't hold up our end of the bargain—party A—*God*—does. That's who He is—it goes to His character. It goes back to how much He loves us. But why would God promise us anything?

I have a friend in Washington, who is one-quarter Jewish. After her return from a trip to Israel, she told me that the Jewish people were quick to tell her, as I tell you now, we are not God's chosen people. So what promises made to the Hebrew/Israelite nation can we, as Gentiles, claim? Everywhere we go, pastors and Bible teachers try to answer that question by talking about being grafted into Abraham's family, and they say that it is why we can be partakers of these promises. But even that is a bit vague for my satisfaction, so I asked God to clarify the whole thing for me.

> O foolish Galatians! Who has bewitched you that you should not obey the truth, before whose eyes Jesus Christ was clearly portrayed among you as crucified? This only I want to learn from you: Did you receive the Spirit by the works of the law, or by the hearing of faith?—Are you so foolish? Having begun in the Spirit, are you now being made perfect by the flesh? Have you suffered so many things in vain—if indeed it was in vain?

> Therefore He who supplies the Spirit to you
> and works miracles among you, does He do
> it by the works of the law, or by the hear-
> ing of faith? just as Abraham "believed God
> and it was accounted to him for righteous-
> ness." Therefore, know that only those who
> are of faith are sons of Abraham. (Gal. 3:1–7,
> NKJV)

The Apostle Paul's entire theology is based on the prem-
ise that the promises that God made to Abraham are relevant
to *all* who belong to Christ. Remember, everything written in
the Bible—by any author—was inspired by God. Jews are the
chosen people, by flesh and by blood. We (Gentiles) are God's
people by promise. We are grafted into Abraham's family by
God's promise of salvation, the promise God made to Abraham
that He would become the father of nations.

If we are going to accept God's promises, we need to understand just what it was that God *did* through the covenant with
Abraham, to include us non-Jewish folk in His promises.

Let's begin at Galatians 4:22–23:

> For it is written: Abraham had two sons, the
> one out of the slave-woman, and one out of
> the free woman. But, indeed, he out of the
> slave-woman has been born according to
> flesh, and he out of the free woman through
> the promise." (Gal. 4:22–23, NKJV)

Compare that to Genesis 12:1–3:

> And Jehovah said to Abram, Go out of your
> country, and from our kindred, and from

your father's house into a land that I will show you. And I will make you a great nation. And I will bless you and make your name great. And you shall be a blessing. And I will bless those that bless you and curse the one who curses you. And in you shall all families of the earth be blessed. (NKJV)

This is the first mention in Scripture of a covenant to Abram—not *with* but *to* Abram. This is a one-sided covenant— what is God going to do? Make Abram, as Abraham, the father of nations. What does Abram have to do? Believe. That's all, but that's hard to do sometimes isn't it? Apparently, it was for him too. Instead of just believing, Abraham decides to go along with Sarah's plan to take God's promise into her own hands. Don't you feel sorry for Father Abraham? I'm sure Sarah twisted his arm to get him to sleep with her beautiful Egyptian maid... but more on that in a minute. The way I see this, God is telling Abraham that all the families (or nations) of the earth will be blessed or cursed based on how they stand with Abraham. Abraham's friends are God's friends and so they will be blessed. Those who curse Abraham...will not be blessed.

"...which things are symbolic. For these [women] are the two covenants: the one from Mount Sinai which gives birth to bondage, which is Hagar..." (Gal. 4:24, NKJV).

Two mothers:

Hagar	Sarah
Slave woman	Free woman
According to flesh	According to promise

"for this Hagar is Mount Sinai in Arabia, and corresponds to Jerusalem which now is, and is in bondage with her children—but the [new] Jerusalem above is free, which is the mother of us all" (Gal. 4:25–26, NKJV).

Two nations:

Mt. Sinai—Arabia	New Jerusalem
Outside the promised land	Inside the promised land
Children born into slavery	Children born are free
	Our mother!

Abraham understood and cherished the spiritual aspect of this covenant more than he did the possibility of multiplying his physical family or the prosperity and blessings God was pouring out on them. Abraham understood that the promise of salvation that is implied as spiritual blessings in Hebrews Chapters 10–11 extended to *all* nations. Sarah may not have had that clear a picture… Remember "she laughed." Does it help to know that our mother could laugh at herself in her old age? But imagine the frustration for her and the Father of nations to not have a son! In Genesis 16, "Momma Sarah" schemes to fulfill God's promise.

In the culture of that day, sending her slave maid in to her husband's tent was a perfectly legal thing for Sarah to do, and in fact, it was a fairly common practice. But it was not God's will, and God wasn't happy about it. It's my thinking that Sarah probably knew that God wouldn't like it, but after all, everything hinged on Abraham having an heir! Is anyone else a fixer like Momma Sarah?

Think about it—your husband has already told everyone he knows that he's going to be the father of nations, and yet at age ninety-something, he still hasn't had his first child! Wouldn't you step in and help your husband save face? This is one of the Bible's biggest examples of unbelief! And it is a warning not to try to make God's will happen! God is big enough to do it Himself. If He wants your help He'll let you know! And yes it is hard it is to wait on God:

In October 2008 my husband, Hutch, and I found a small farm that we felt was just perfect for us to live "forever and ever amen." After prayer, we decided God thought so too, so we put in an offer. The seller accepted, we applied for financing, and it got approved. We rented out the house we owned, and then found out the seller didn't want to move until after Thanksgiving. On November 5th, our renters moved in the front door of our house as we moved out the back door, ready to stay with friends for the three-week interim.

That fall, as it happens, there was quite a reorganization of lender rules. Lending institutions began getting rather tight with their money. That happened about a week into this process. We got word that our approved lender changed their guidelines and we no longer qualified. We applied elsewhere. Yes, they could do it. Three days later, no they couldn't. Sorry, our guidelines have changed. Third lender, exact same thing. I am a veteran, so someone suggested I check into the VA. So we prayed once more. Our belief was that God was closing all these doors. (I learned years ago that it's easier for God to keep me from going through a door than it is to push me through an open one.) We wanted to be sure it was Him, because I wanted this farm! So we agreed that the Veterans Administration would be the last door we would knock on. We applied. They said yes. But a few days later, I felt myself plummeting into what I feared might be a long and dark depression, fearing the same outcome.

So I called Hutch on my way home from the VA and asked if we could just go somewhere—wherever, I didn't care. I needed to get my mind off it all. Someone had told him about a man who owned an RV dealership a few hours south of us. Apparently, this man had a true love for God and pastors, so we decided to have a look at fifth wheel trailers. One was a bit older, but I fell in love with it. That puzzled me, because I generally plant fairly deep roots. I had lived in a total of eight houses in my entire life, and three of those had been within the five years since Hutch and I got married! Besides the fact that I am horribly claustrophobic! Would God do something like that? Well, it didn't really matter because we were just looking, or so I thought. The very next day, we got the call. You guessed it. VA said no. The final door was closed. We enlisted prayers of several friends who knew our situation by now, and fell to our knees, once more.

We bought the fifth wheel trailer with the money that was now not needed for the down payment on the ranch and with the expert help of our friends, Lyn and Scott, made some repairs to make it livable and moved in…parked in their backyard. Our new plan, which we thought had to be God's plan, was to move the fifth wheel onto the church property where we were pastoring. But delays in getting the power pole erected and septic tank issues led us to again start questioning God as to where He wanted us to go. RV spaces are horribly expensive—even in off season! We asked God if it was not His plan to open another door and *shove us through*!

A pastor in our area told us that his church had complete RV hookups and we were welcomed to stay there at no charge. So on the 12th of January of 2009 that's where we set up our trailer, in Oak Harbor, complete with large dog and two cats and husband and me. My horse had to stay in Day Creek, fifty miles away.

Then in February, just weeks later, the Lord led us to submit our resignation from the church we'd been pastoring for nearly three years. (*Aha! Now* I know why we couldn't get the utilities set up on that church's property for our fifthth wheel! Yes, God wanted us mobile, but He never intended for us to move there!) Have you ever had an "aha moment" with God?

Hutch interviewed for a job as interim pastor and for permanent pastor positions at two small churches. (One told us they wanted someone less conservative. When you realize Hutch's hair was about a foot and a half long then, that shocked us. But God is dealing with human beings here!)

When we wait on God, it doesn't mean we sit and do nothing. In the meantime, we looked for ways to be used of God—teaching, worship team, counseling. Hutch took a job as truck driver and was able to witness to the owner, the dispatcher, and other drivers, as well as those he delivered to. We believed God wanted us mobile (thus the fifth wheel) and we heard nothing different for nearly two years.

How long do we wait on God to fulfill the promises we believe He has made to us? A promise deferred is not a promise forgotten! God does not forget. He does huge things for His children! He hasn't forgotten us and He hasn't forgotten you! He didn't forget Father Abraham and Momma Sarah. As soon as Hagar realized she was pregnant, she started acting superior toward Sarah and the strife began…sin on both sides. The eternal strife began between the freedom God promises us (and that He promised Abraham and Sarah) and the slavery we see represented here by Hagar.

> So Hagar bore Abram a son; and Abram named his son, whom Hagar bore, Ishmael. Abram was eighty-six years old when Hagar bore Ishmael to Abram. (Gen. 16:15–16, NKJV)
>
> He shall be a wild man; His hand shall be against every man, And every man's hand

against him. And he shall dwell in the presence of all his brethren. (Gen. 16:12, NKJV)

Okay, simply put, Ishmael just does not play well with others, he is now the only son of this Father of Nations, and by the time he is fourteen years old, when Isaac is born, he thinks he is pretty hot stuff. Have any of you ever known a cocky teenage boy? Then you understand and we can go on.

Now Abraham was one hundred years old when his son Isaac was born to him. And Sarah said, "God has made me laugh, and all who hear will laugh with me." She also said, "Who would have said to Abraham that Sarah would nurse children? For I have borne him a son in his old age." So the child grew and was weaned. And Abraham made a great feast on the same day that Isaac was weaned. And Sarah saw the son of Hagar the Egyptian, whom she had borne to Abraham, scoffing. (Gen. 21:5–9, NKJV)

On the day Isaac was weaned, Abraham held a big feast. Sarah saw that Abraham's son by Hagar, the Egyptian, was laughing at Isaac. Okay, Sarah won't even call Ishmael by name, Abraham's son by Hagar, and worse yet, this punk kid is laughing at the baby, making fun of the rightful heir! How dare he!

Therefore she said to Abraham, "Cast out this bondwoman and her son; for the son of this bondwoman shall not be heir with my son, namely with Isaac." And the matter was very displeasing in Abraham's sight because of his son. But God said to Abraham, "Do not let it be displeasing in your sight because of the lad or because of your bondwoman. Whatever Sarah has said to you, listen to her voice; for in Isaac your seed shall be called. Yet I will also make a nation of the son of the bondwoman, because he is your seed." (Gen. 21:10–13, NKJV)

Two sons:

Ishmael—a wild donkey	Isaac—a free man
His hand against everyone	All blessings to all nations will come through him
Conflicts with all relatives	The true legitimate heir*

*Those blessings that come through Isaac to all nations are the promises that we are talking about today—the promises we can claim if we are standing on the right side of the cross.

Scripture also talks about two covenants:

Mt. Sinai	New Jerusalem
Slavery—conflict	Freedom
Mosaic covenant law	Abrahamic—grace
God's demands of His people	God's promises to His people—Promise of Salvation

But the law cannot give life. It wasn't meant to. The Mosaic covenant was meant to teach Israel what God expects and demanded of them. It couldn't bring the Israelites to salvation—it only distinguished them from other nation, other peoples—it sanctified them, set them apart.

"Therefore know that only those who are of faith are sons of Abraham. And the Scripture, foreseeing that God would justify the Gentiles by faith, preached the gospel to Abraham beforehand, saying, 'In you all the nations shall be blessed'" (Gal. 3:7–8, NKJV).

Sarah represents freedom—our mother—true heirs. Those who are born of spirit promise, rather than flesh. We are children of promise—free, not slaves.

> Now we, brethren, as Isaac was, are children of promise. But, as he who was born according to the flesh then persecuted him who was born according to the Spirit, even so it is now. Nevertheless what does the Scripture say? "Cast out the bondwoman and her son, for the son of the bondwoman shall not be heir with the son of the freewoman." So then, brethren, we are not children of the bondwoman but of the free." (Gal. 4:28–31, NKJV)

It might be difficult for you to consider Sarah as your mother. (It was easy for me because my mother's name was Sarah.) Think of her, then as your mentor, a godly woman, who presents an example for you to follow. But primarily, think of the freedom she represents. Live in that freedom. Satan would love to keep you in bondage to sin. Don't let him get away with it! Chapter 25 reveals some of the tricks he uses to keep you from enjoying this abundant life God has promised you. Don't fall for them! Live your life in freedom as a child of promise!

Chapter 18

An Army of Women

I don't want you to get the wrong idea of what this "Army of Women" is! But I think it will be easier to give you a brief idea of what it will not be: We will not be issued uniforms, although we will take a step or two closer to receiving our robes of righteousness from our Father in heaven. We will be fed spiritual food to increase our energy levels in our daily walks with God. We will not become militant in our beliefs, but we will become stronger in our beliefs; we will know what we believe and why; we will be diligent in our pursuit of God's best plan for us and for our families for generations to come. We will not be marching in formation, but we will be standing in worship. We will not be broken down so that we become little robots, but we will be decreased so our God can increase in us. We will not be worked to the bone, but we will be asked to be a living sacrifice. And lastly, our faith will be strengthened so we are not afraid of the storm brewing on the horizon of where our nation is heading, but we will be storming the heavens with our sincere love and adoration for a God that is Commander in Chief and is truly worth following.

How many of you realize we are in a battle—for our homes, our families, our children, our country!

President John Adams is noted as a man who had a clear picture of the heartbeat of America. He wrote, "…a woman sets the tone in her home and that tone is carried forth into the country, by her husband and her children."

He was way ahead of his time, because he knew then what we know now: "If Momma ain't happy, nobody's happy!" It is my belief that as women, we are some of God's most powerful weapons in spiritual warfare. That thought puts a whole new meaning to the phrase "walk softly and carry a big stick!" I believe God wants us to look a bit into what I call the camouflaged promise: the way of the warrior—after all, God never calls us to do something He doesn't equip us for, and that, ladies, is a huge promise.

First and foremost, being a warrior means we understand who our Captain is—and that He is leading us from the front ranks. He is fighting right there beside us. Being a warrior means training in the knowledge of who our enemy is, exercising the skills God gives us to fight. It means being tested in endurance, patience, perseverance—and to know when to stand and persist.

Once we understand who our enemy is—not flesh and blood—and know a bit about his tactics or tricks, it's important to stand firm and persist, to stand when no one else is; to keep believing God's promise of victory, even in the face of our own pain. Understand that warfare isn't about quick victory—not like TV—in one hour every battle is all wrapped up and tied with a bow, until the next episode a week later. As a healthy warrior, we need to evaluate our situations:

1. Are we ready for battle—and sometimes God requires us to take His word for that! When we are at our weakest, God can use us. ("Therefore if anyone cleanses himself from the latter, [what is dishonorable] he will be a vessel for honor,

sanctified and useful for the Master, prepared for every good work" [2 Tim. 2:21, NKJV].)

2.   Whether to stay and fight, to stand firm or to leave. Remember, too, that we're evaluating our position—and we do this in the thick of prayer—there are some times when God says, "This is not your battle." ("You will not need to fight in this battle. Position yourselves, stand still and see the salvation of the LORD, who is with you, O Judah and Jerusalem! Do not fear or be dismayed; tomorrow go out against them, for the LORD is with you" [2 Chron. 20:17, NKJV].)

Paul was a warrior for Christ and the Word. He evaluated his predicament every time he was in one and his letters explain a lot of his preparation for battle:

> We give no offense in anything, that our ministry may not be blamed. But in all things we commend ourselves as ministers of God: in much patience, in tribulations, in needs, in distresses, in stripes, in imprisonments, in tumults, in labors, in sleeplessness, in fastings; by purity, by knowledge, by longsuffering, by kindness, by the Holy Spirit, by sincere love, by the word of truth, by the power of God, by the armor of righteousness on the right hand and on the left, by honor and dishonor, by evil report and good report; as deceivers, and yet true.(2 Cor. 6:3–8, NKJV)

When Paul fought his battles, he knew he was in a war. He was running for his life. It never crossed his mind that God might not be with him. In 2 Corinthians 11:33, when Paul was lowered in a basket from a window, to escape capture, he knew he was in a war—just as we need to recognize now, that we are in a war for the very soul of America.

Teacher and biblical scholar Graham Cooke, Morning Star Ministries 27 says "it appears that we are losing" that battle. He believes that "the church doesn't know who she is—that she is schizophrenic—that half the church thinks that God is angry, double-minded and that we are living under God's judgment." He doesn't believe that. I am in agreement with him, in that judgment in this life is not scriptural.

Jesus took all judgment, didn't He? Once and for all for sin—yours, mine, past, present, and future. Was He judged enough? Was He punished enough? Did the Father pour out onto Jesus all His wrath, anger, and indignation until there was none left? If God the Father held any back, Jesus was not judged enough.

Does that line up with Scripture? Between judgment on Christ for us at Calvary and the day of the White Throne Judgment, there is no place for judgment. We are living under grace. God isn't angry. He isn't judging anyone. If anything, I think He might be brokenhearted.

We are the church, aren't we? If women can set the tone in our homes, we can set the tone in our churches. I'm not saying be divisive or undermine your church leadership—I'm saying the church needs to stop being double-minded. And it can start with us, as women warriors of God. We need to stop being of two minds and start understanding what our role is on this earth.

Today's church is defined by what it stands against. Taking a stand against this or that or the other. Yes, we should stand firm on our beliefs, but we should align ourselves firmly with God, and God is defined by what He is for: love, goodness, kindness, reconciliation. God has reconciled the world to Himself, through Christ.

The only way to overcome evil is with good. And we aren't even making a dent. Lack of goodness is the biggest problem in this world. We have allowed our world to become desensitized to the sin around us. Why is evil winning? Because instead of spending our time, money, and energy on being good and spreading God's goodness and love, we find ourselves exhausted by fighting the evil in hand-to-hand combat. The only way to overcome evil is with good.

"To the contrary, 'if your enemy is hungry, feed him; if he is thirsty, give him something to drink; for by so doing you will heap burning coals on his head.' Do not be overcome by evil, but overcome evil with good" (Rom. 12:20–21, NKJV).

When Jesus died on the cross, God removed every obstacle between man and Himself. Every issue, every sin was put on Jesus, to clear the way for us to see what God is really like. And not just us—the not yet believers—those who are hungry. But if we, the church, aren't totally convinced who God is, people can't receive the mercy and grace and the goodness of God. We need to enable people to see God through us, and we need to teach the world that God isn't holding our sins against us. He has nothing against anyone because the most perfect man ever—His Son—already paid the price, and we reap the benefit of it.

The church needs people who are prepared to go to the limits to prove beyond a shadow of a doubt that God is good; to fight with the goodness and kindness of God; to suffer when required; to be persecuted when necessary; to be absolutely clear and confident about who God is to us and what our role is on earth and that God does what He says He'll do, to be absolutely confident that God will back them up in times of crisis, because God promises He will.

Warriors will get extraordinary opportunities to see the hand of God at work. But they are also people who understand that sometimes their faith to fight requires patience, because some situations hang around for a while. And it's not just patience—faith with it—stay strong while we wait, stay determined and focused. It's the fruit of the Spirit in action.

> But the fruit of the Spirit is love, joy, peace, patience, kindness, goodness, faithfulness, gentleness, self-control; against such things there is no law. And those who belong to Christ Jesus have crucified the flesh with its passions and desires. If we live by the Spirit, let us also keep in step with the Spirit. (Gal. 5:22–25, NKJV)

Then we can also fight the battles by the Spirit. Our inheritance in Christ empowers us. Warriors are assured about the heart of God. They don't need everything to be going well or to be reassured at every turn. Warriors don't live in their circumstances; they live in Christ. They live in the promises God has made to them. We know that our circumstance is not our focus—that's not where we live; we live in Christ. It takes discipline to learn that; it takes a few battles—some won and some lost—but every battle is an experience with God. In adversity, warriors have a boldness and courage to stand firm. They may not even realize they have it until it's there. They don't run from a fight.

Warriors know that asking *why* is the wrong question. God won't answer that question. Besides, the answer is always the same—God has a plan. He doesn't always choose to let us in on it. Instead, warriors know that the best questions to ask God, in any circumstance—what does this mean, Lord? How do You want me to respond? What do You want me to do/say/learn?

Warriors aren't looking to be rescued. They know they're in a war. Some days are long and tough. They keep looking to God to protect hem and lead them. When I was in the MC, I went to Basic Training. They taught me certain skills and we practiced them over and over and over again until they were second nature to us. It makes sense, because in the heat of battle, you wouldn't have time to stop and think, "Now what am I going to do?" Warriors have to know ahead of time what their reaction to any given action will be. They cultivate a predetermined response. Daniel and his three friends shared their mutual predetermined responses: we will not bow—our God is big enough to deliver us…but even if He does not…

Warriors put themselves in situations where God has to do something extraordinary. Three men went into the furnace fully trusting in whatever God wanted to do *with* them and *through* them or *to* them! God had to do something extraordinary—he sent a fourth man!

> Jonathan said to the young man who carried his armor, "Come, let us go over to the garrison of these uncircumcised. It may be that the LORD will work for us, for nothing can hinder the LORD from saving by many or by few." And his armor-bearer said to him, "Do all that is in your heart. Do as you wish. Behold, I am with you heart and soul." (1 Sam. 14:6–7, NKJV)

Saul's son, Jonathan, was a warrior. Jonathan, in the midst of being surrounded, says to his armor bearer, "Let's go to the other side. Perhaps the Lord will work for us…let's just see what will happen." Jonathan had a warrior's heart. He was daring and bold.

What if he had missed the signs? No doubt warriors appear to others to look foolish. Jonathan didn't care what the odds were. He could see that they were stacked against them, but didn't look for the easy way out. The way he was looking for was risky and daring, and that's what he wanted.

Warriors are not normal people! God wants people who are willing to look silly, who are willing to take a risk, for His sake. I believe He wants women who are willing to step out in faith, believing every promise He has made to us—to reach a world that is desperately hungry for truth and compassion and love.

God's commanding the Israelites to cross the river Jordan, and circumcise everyone while they were outnumbered by an enemy with better weapons was not logical, in human terms. It doesn't make sense—but God doesn't always make sense in our minds. Neither does it makes sense to send one man who stutters and has no self-confidence to rescue a million people from bondage. God doesn't have to make sense to us! Moses's confronting Pharaoh while God is hardening his heart wasn't logical…but Moses didn't ask why, and God had a plan. God still has a plan! Do you think Moses knew that all those plagues were to show Pharaoh and the Israelites God's awesome and absolute power?

A warrior doesn't go into battle by logic. He goes by trust in His Commander! Gideon was sweeping the threshing room floor when God called him a mighty man of valor. Do you think Gideon felt like a warrior at that moment? Then Gideon's army was reduced by God, based on how they drank their water. Where is the logic in that? But Gideon was still up for a fight after losing 99 percent of his army—that's a true warrior who has faith in his Commanding Officer.

Warriors are not ordinary people. They don't want to walk with God in ordinary ways, no business as usual for them. You won't find them standing in the back. When something difficult happens, they push their way to the front—like Caleb at age eighty-five—"This is my mountain." He wanted that last big fight. He didn't send the army of men he had trained—he fought for his inheritance himself!

Warriors relish the fight. They want to see the power of God—the bigness of God. They don't count how many are out there against them; they don't count what the odds are. They have a passion—a zeal. They're not looking for rescue—they're looking for breakthrough. They know how big our God is and they want to watch Him shine! They defy the circumstances of their own life. They want more of God!

Warriors expect to overcome in situations—because they've already conquered themselves. They aren't prone to fear. They're too busy being fascinated by Jesus to be intimidated by life or circumstances or the enemy. Warriors are not always sensible, reasonable, or rational people—but they're not stupid either, not reckless. They are people who have completely thought out who they're going to be and what they're going to do and they aren't apologizing—they're just doing it.

They're doing what God calls them to do and they're not waiting for the church to wake up. Jesus didn't ask permission of the church leaders—He just did it. He wasn't explaining, He was proclaiming. He was a righteous man doing God's plan.

When something is missing or wrong, warriors look for opportunities to make it right. There is a confidence about them—a single-minded steadfastness—focused. They don't need people to be with them. But if you are going to be with them, you need to be of one mind, one accord. Like Jonathan, David's armor bearer. "Do as you wish. Behold I am with you heart and soul" (1 Samuel 14:7, NKJV).

You have to know what's against you on this level. That's important, because then you know who is for you and what you're going to need to thrive. Warfare is not about surviving, it's about prospering—it's about making the enemy pay, not meekly accepting what he sends against you; it's turning that against him by conquering yourself by being radically loved by God. There is no fear in love!

The enemy you face on any level has to present himself as bigger and stronger than you. It's important that you see this as the tactic that it is, because when he tells you he cannot be beat, you will know not to believe him!

The story of David and Goliath is a true testimony to David's intimacy with the Father. Our intimacy with God should intimidate the enemy. We want to be such warriors that when we wake up, our enemy says, "Oh no, she's up!" Make the enemy tired and weary and depressed—there is a place in the Spirit set aside for us—this is what it means to be in Christ"—to have the heart of an overcomer—the best monster—go into a fight expecting to win and the longer a fight goes on the more you're going to accomplish not less.

If you are hesitant in going into basic training, God says, "It is now—receive your promise." Maybe you feel that you have fought enough battles, or you feel the church has put you out to pasture. But ladies, I would tell you now, God is not done with you yet! If you are a tired warrior, He wants to refresh you and renew you and give you new marching orders—a new promise. If you have floundered around as if you didn't know where to begin, God wants to refocus you and give you new marching orders—a new promise. If you have just been going from battle to battle and are worn out, God wants to refresh you and give you a new fire—a new promise!

"For I know the plans I have for you, declares the LORD, plans for welfare and not for evil, to give you a future and a hope" (Jer. 29:11, NKJV).

Chapter 19

The Blessings of Wisdom

Once upon a time, long, long ago, in a kingdom far, far away, there were two women who had babies at about the same time. One of the babies died. One night the woman who had the living baby laid her baby down for a nap and went into another part of the house. The woman who lost her baby was so brokenhearted that she slipped in and swapped the babies. Now, when the first woman went in to check on her baby, she knew immediately that this was not her baby, and she knew what had happened. She went to confront the woman and of course, found her cuddling with the living baby. Well, something had to be done, she wanted her baby back! So they decided to take it to the king, because they knew he was wise enough to figure it out. That king was Solomon. And he *was* wise enough to straighten it out.

But how did he get that wise? King Solomon was only twenty years old when he became king. He hadn't had time to learn about such things yet.

> "Now, O LORD my God, You have made Your servant king instead of my father David, but I am a little child; I do not know how to go out or come in. And Your servant is in the midst of Your people whom You have chosen,

a great people, too numerous to be numbered or counted. Therefore give to Your servant an understanding heart [wisdom] to judge Your people, that I may discern [use wisdom to see] between good and evil. For who is able to judge this great people of Yours?" The speech pleased the LORD, that Solomon had asked this thing. Then God said to him: "Because you have asked this thing, and have not asked long life for yourself, nor have asked riches for yourself, nor have asked the life of your enemies, but have asked for yourself under-standing to discern justice, behold, I have done according to your words; see, I have given you a wise and understanding heart, so that there has not been anyone like you before you, nor shall any like you arise after you." (1 Kings 3:7–12)

When those two women with one baby stood before Solomon, it was God's wisdom, through Solomon, that brought forth the solution to the problem. (And this is the only time you will ever hear me call a baby a problem!)

And the king said, "Divide the living child in two, and give half to one, and half to the other." Then the woman whose son was living spoke to the king, for she yearned with com-passion for her son; and she said, "O my lord, give her the living child, and by no means kill him!" But the other said, "Let him be neither mine nor yours, but divide him." So the king answered and said, "Give the first woman the

> living child, and by no means kill him; she is
> his mother." (1 Kings 3:25–27)

The very next verse states (1 Kings 3:28), "And all Israel heard of the judgment which the king had rendered; and they feared the king, for they saw that the wisdom of God was in him to administer justice."

All of Israel recognized Solomon's wisdom as being from God. Solomon is the author of three books in the Bible: Proverbs, Ecclesiastes, and the Song of Solomon. Even today, we recognize Solomon's wisdom as being a gift from God.

Let me explain the difference between knowledge and wisdom. I can go to the library and check out all the medical books there and really study all the medical procedures, and instruments and anesthesia and have all that knowledge in my head. But would you want me to take out your appendix? Of course not. Wisdom is putting knowledge into practice. In this case, it is wisdom not to let me practice my knowledge on you!

To paraphrase Proverbs 8:35–36, Solomon says, "For whoever finds [wisdom] finds life, And obtains favor from the LORD; But he who sins against [wisdom] wrongs his own soul; All those who hate [wisdom] love death" (NKJV).

If we find wisdom, we find life and favor from God. But how can you sin against a characteristic? Or a trait? My thinking is this: if we don't seek wisdom, if we don't use wisdom, we could be sinning against wisdom. By not seeking after wisdom, by not using it, by not thinking before we speak or act, those are foolish acts, so to be foolish or to act foolishly would be sinning against wisdom.

One of the Hebrew words for foolish—*mōros*—reminds us of the word moron, right? The Strong's Concordance defines it as "dull or stupid, repeatedly wicked, perverse, heedless, inattentive; careless; negligent, i.e. of safety; thoughtless; unobserving."

It's foolish to not pay attention to wisdom, and by not acting wisely, we are acting like we're stupid, even when we aren't. It's a choice. To think before you act is wisdom. To make wise choices. To just dive in is foolish or folly. Folly is the result of acting on foolishness, rather than acting on wisdom, rather than consulting wisdom first.

"He who sins against [wisdom] wrongs his own soul; All those who hate [wisdom] love death" (Prov. 8:36, NKJV).

So when we "sin against wisdom" or when we choose foolishness over wisdom, we only hurt ourselves and it is our own soul that is wronged.

If we do that repeatedly and make a habit of it, if our lifestyle becomes one of choosing foolishness over wisdom every time, we are choosing death over life. That's why Solomon says those who hate wisdom love death, because by not choosing wisdom, we are choosing death.

Earlier in this chapter, he tells us what it means to choose wisdom:

> Listen, for I [wisdom] will speak of excellent things, And from the opening of my lips will come right things; For my mouth will speak truth; Wickedness is an abomination to my lips. All the words of my mouth are with righteousness; Nothing crooked or perverse is in them. They are all plain to him who understands, And right to those who find knowledge. (Prov. 8:6–9, NKJV)

When I was a kid and had a bad dream, my mother would tell me to think about something pleasant. What is pleasant to a kid? Christmas. As I grew older, I didn't have bad dreams so much. But life has some discouraging things in it. If we dwell on the bad news or whatever it is that makes us sad or discouraged, we become discouraged and depressed, right?

When we use wisdom, we move the focus of our minds off whatever is depressing and on to something pleasant… "whatever things are true, whatever things are noble, whatever things are just, whatever things are pure, whatever things are lovely… meditate on these things" (Phil. 4:8). Focusing our minds on those things is wisdom not folly. Choose wisdom. Use wisdom.

"For wisdom is better than rubies, And all the things one may desire cannot be compared with her. I, wisdom, dwell with prudence, And find out knowledge and discretion" (Prov. 8:11–12, NKJV).

Solomon is actually turning the microphone, so to speak, over to wisdom. "I, wisdom, dwell with prudence"…Prudence: good judgment, common sense, caution." Along with wisdom comes good judgment if we choose wisdom and use wisdom.

Proverbs 8:13–21 lists some of the benefits of having wisdom:

1. The Lord hates pride and arrogance and the evil way and the perverse mouth.
2. Wisdom is counsel, understanding, and strength.
3. By wisdom, kings reign, rulers decree justice, princes rule, and nobles, judges of the earth. It takes wisdom to rule properly.
4. Along with wisdom comes riches and honor, enduring riches and righteousness.
5. The fruit of wisdom is better than gold, why? Because money doesn't last. Wisdom does.
6. Wisdom may cause those who inherit wealth to maintain it, by making *wise* investment decisions…

You see how wisdom works? If you seek wisdom, you will gain it. If you use it, it will be help you. So how do you seek wisdom?

What is the wisest thing you can ever do? Ask for wisdom! That's what Solomon did!

"If any of you lacks wisdom, let him ask of God, who gives to all liberally and without reproach, and it will be given to him. So what is the wisest thing you can ever do? Ask for wisdom! Then chose it and use it!" (James 1:5, NKJV).

> The LORD possessed [wisdom] at the beginning of His way, Before His works of old. [wisdom] has been established from everlasting, From the beginning, before there was ever an earth. When there were no depths [wisdom] was brought forth, When there were no fountains abounding with water. Before the mountains were settled, Before the hills, [wisdom] was brought forth; While as yet He had not made the earth or the fields, Or the primal dust of the world. When He prepared the heavens, [wisdom] was there, When He drew a circle on the face of the deep, When He established the clouds above, When He strengthened the fountains of the deep, When He assigned to the sea its limit, So that the waters would not transgress His command, When He marked out the foundations of the earth, Then [wisdom] was beside Him as a master craftsman; And [wisdom] was daily His delight, Rejoicing always before Him, Rejoicing in His inhabited world, And

my delight was with the sons of men. (Prov. 8:22–31)

Wisdom is a part of God's power. He used it in every aspect of creating this earth for us and it is His Gift to us. Seek it. Ask for it.

For whoever finds wisdom finds life, And obtains favor from the LORD.
—Proverbs 8:35

Chapter 20

The World vs. the Church

I don't know all of what happened in your life in the past week or so, but I can say this: you probably lived in freedom. As Americans, we have more freedoms than pretty much anyone in the world. Think about it. You ate what you wanted, unless you're on a diet. You wore what you wanted, unless you need to go on a diet. You spoke whatever you wanted to speak, with whomever you wanted to speak, without fear that the government would throw you in jail for your faith. The world will always oppose the church, but the church in America has lived in relative freedom for hundreds of years. Knowing that peace in the church is not the norm in the world, let's look at a bit of church history in the book of Acts. After the death of Jesus, the early church has been growing. The disciples and Paul have been pretty much flying under the radar, spreading the gospel. By Chapter 12, things have started to change. Consider these three points:

1. What does the world have to say and what they seek to do?
2. What does the church have to say and what do we do?

3.   What are the results of this confrontation between the world and the church of Jesus Christ?

"Now about that time Herod the king stretched out his hand to harass some from the church. Then he killed James the brother of John with the sword" (Acts 12:1–2, NKJV).

James was the first apostle to be martyred. If you remember, it was James and his brother, John, who had asked Jesus to sit on either side of His throne. In Matthew 20, Jesus responds by telling them that they have no idea of the cup Jesus will have to drink. Jesus ends up telling them that they will drink of the same cup, talking about the suffering for the sake of the gospel, at the hands of the world. That was fulfilled here, when Herod had James beheaded with the sword.

> And because he [Herod] saw that it pleased the Jews, he proceeded further to seize Peter also. Now it was during the Days of Unleavened Bread. So when he had arrested him, he put him in prison, and delivered him to four squads of soldiers to keep him, intending to bring him before the people after Passover. Peter was therefore kept in prison, but constant prayer was offered to God for him by the church. And when Herod was about to bring him out, that night Peter was sleeping, bound with two chains between two soldiers; and the guards before the door were keeping the prison. (Acts 12:3–6, NKJV)

This is not the same Herod that was around at the time of Jesus's birth. That was Herod the Great. Then his son, Herod

Antipas, then came his nephew, Herod Agrippa, who is the one Luke's talking about here. He was only king for three years, being raised under very political times, ruthless in his dealings and lustful for power, self-fulfillment, and self-glorification. Interestingly enough, Herod Agrippa was a devout follower of the Jewish faith, which was why he waited until after Passover week to have Peter executed. In the passage so far, we see that the world and the church are at odds. By the world, I mean those who are not a part of the church of Jesus Christ. Why do the world and the church constantly collide? Are we as the evangelical church that obstinate and difficult? The world seeks to create an avenue for gain unto themselves, regardless of the will of God. On the other hand, the church seeks above all else the will of God, regardless of its earthly gain.

So here we see the world, through the power of a man, an earthly king named Herod, and the Jewish people who agreed with his self-seeking policies. Herod, seeking whatever can bring him political advantage, not only kills James, but after he sees that killing this Christian leader pleases the Jewish people, he starts harassing others and then he goes after the Apostle Peter.

Why? Why is this happening? Being a follower of Jewish law, as well as seeking to please the Jewish people, brought immense persecution on the leaders of the early church. From a practical standpoint, it was probably politically expedient for Herod to put James to death immediately. Herod saw the same threat in allowing the spread of this gospel, as his grandfather saw in Jesus's birth.

Jesus and His gospel didn't fit in with the hope Herod had for his kingdom. He then has Peter thrown in jail. He thinks this will stop the spread of the gospel. Boy was he wrong. Nothing will ever stop the spread of the gospel!

So Herod has Peter arrested and bound and watched by guards. He's going to have this man killed, for his own enjoyment and so his own subjects will be pleased with him, as they were when he had James killed. We should absolutely never live our lives so that others will be pleased with our efforts. Never in a way that we become subject to the demands of the ungodly. Our goal must be to live our lives in a way pleasing to God, by resting in His grace and living a life of humble obedience. Serving the Lord and following His ways will always bring us lasting contentment and joy. A pastor I studied under in Washington used to say it this way: If it pleases you to please God, do as you please.

Point 2: What does the church have to say and what do we do?

The church of Jesus Christ should be willing to suffer for the name of Christ rather than do wrong. We should be willing to endure anything so long as we are in the will of God and He is glorified in it. We are dependent on Him and His sovereignty. We rest in His strength and His promises. The goal of every Christian should be that the glory of God be displayed in our lives, led by the Holy Spirit.

James, their dear beloved brother in the faith, leader of the early church, is killed by the sword by the government. Others are harassed, and then Peter is thrown in jail and just days away from being martyred. Life is pretty bleak, isn't it? What does the church do in the midst of all this?

"Now behold, an angel of the Lord stood by him, and a light shone in the prison; and he struck Peter on the side and raised him up, saying, 'Arise quickly!' And his chains fell off his hands" (Acts 12:7, NKJV).

Say you're Peter, and your faith has landed you in jail, and you're just hours away from death. What do you do? If you're like Peter, you take a nap! He is bound in chains, between two soldiers, in a supposedly impenetrable prison. He knows his time is up, according to the world. And what does he do? He sleeps. He is comfortable in the confidence of God's power! The very fact that I am bound would prevent me from being able to sleep! My Americanized comfort level is so high that I wouldn't be able to sleep. Not to mention the fact that I know that I am about to be put to death. But Peter sleeps. Why? How?

Scripture doesn't tell us that Peter had a special revelation from God that he would be rescued. He just rests in the everyday confidence he has that His Lord is sovereign. He rests in the fact…in the *knowledge* that His Savior is in complete control, whether it is death or life the next day. Is that how you live your life? You have the same Spirit, the same God, working on your behalf as Peter did. Do you have the same confidence? Maybe it will help you, to know that the "Angel of the Lord" mentioned in the scripture above, is an Old Testament visit from the Lord Jesus Christ Himself. Maybe Peter knew that. Scripture doesn't tell us he did, but I'm inclined to believe that might be why Peter was so relaxed that he could sleep.

> Then the angel said to him, "Gird yourself and tie on your sandals"; and so he did. And he said to him, "Put on your garment and follow me." So he went out and followed him, and did not know that what was done by the angel was real, but thought he was seeing a vision. [He was in such a deep sleep that he thought he was dreaming! That's why the angel had to strike him to wake him up!] When they were past the first and the second guard posts, they came to the iron gate that leads to the city, which opened to them of its own accord; and they went out and went

down one street, and immediately the angel departed from him. (Acts 12:8–10, NKJV)

Peter is supernaturally delivered from prison and he's still thinking he's in a dream!

And when Peter had come to himself, he said, "Now I know for certain that the Lord has sent His angel, and has delivered me from the hand of Herod and from all the expectation of the Jewish people." So, when he had considered this, he came to the house of Mary, the mother of John whose surname was Mark, where many were gathered together praying. (Acts 12:11–12, NKJV)

So while Peter is in prison, resting, what is the rest of the church doing?

1. They have put on the full armor of God. (Eph. 6)
2. They have resisted the evil one.
3. They have girded their loins with truth.
4. They have put on the breastplate of righteousness.
5. They have shod their feet with the preparation of the gospel of peace.
6. They have taken up their shield of faith, extinguishing the fiery darts of despair over the loss of James and pending loss of Peter.
7. They have put on their helmets of salvation.
8. They have drawn their swords as they go to God's Word for comfort and strength.

What did they do? They did exactly what they should have. They prepared for battle and started praying. They are praying in the Spirit—they are petitioning the great and mighty God. Their weapons are drawn and they are going to the One who, with one word, spoke all things into existence. The One who will come with a sword—the One who, above all, rules and governs—the One who is Head of the church—the One who will not allow His church to suffer without retribution. This is the One in whom they trust. This trust is the reason Peter can sleep. Peter sleeps, and the church enters into long and fervent prayer. This is how the church of Jesus Christ responds to seemingly uncontrolled peril: we rest in God, we have confidence in Him, and we seek His will in all things.

We don't know why James was killed and Peter wasn't. No doubt the church prayed for both of them. But it is up to God, in His sovereignty, who gets to enter into glorious citizenship first and who stays behind to speak the gospel to lost souls.

> And as Peter knocked at the door of the gate, a girl named Rhoda came to answer. When she recognized Peter's voice, because of her gladness she did not open the gate, but ran in and announced that Peter stood before the gate. But they said to her, "You are beside yourself!" Yet she kept insisting that it was so. So they said, "It is his angel." [Some in those days believed that everyone had their own angel, and that your angel looked like you.] Now Peter continued knocking; and when they opened the door and saw him, they were astonished. But motioning to them with his hand to keep silent, he declared to them how the Lord had brought him out of the prison.

> And he said, "Go, tell these things to James and to the brethren." And he departed and went to another place. Then, as soon as it was day, there was no small stir among the soldiers about what had become of Peter. But when Herod had searched for him and not found him, he examined the guards and commanded that they should be put to death. And he went down from Judea to Caesarea, and stayed there. (Acts 12:13–19)

Meanwhile, back at the prison, Herod sees Peter has disappeared while the guards are sleeping and he has all the guards put to death. The world is always all about self. Nothing can get in the way of "my" demands and "my" pursuit of happiness.

Point 3: What are the results of this confrontation between the bride of Christ and the enemies of Christ?

> Now Herod had been very angry with the people of Tyre and Sidon; but they came to him with one accord, and having made Blastus the king's personal aide their friend, they asked for peace, because their country was supplied with food by the king's country. So on a set day Herod, arrayed in royal apparel, sat on his throne and gave an oration to them. And the people kept shouting, "The voice of a god and not of a man!" Then immediately an angel of the Lord struck him, because he did not give glory to God. And he was eaten by worms and died. But the word of God grew and multiplied. (Acts 12:20–24, NKJV)

What is the result? What is always the result? God is victorious! In this interaction, the result is visible to all those involved! Sometimes the result isn't so visible. Sometimes it looks like the world has the upper hand. But momentary grief for Christians will always result in everlasting glory. Yes, the church will suffer. The church will be hated and persecuted. But Jesus is the Head of the church. It is His church and He takes it very personally when His church is attacked!

In this account, an angel comes down, goes into the prison cell. The guards are fast asleep. They know as well as Herod does that Peter is not going to get out of this one on his own. But there is one thing they haven't counted on: Jesus! Herod is messing with His bride! So He sends His powerful angel, who pokes Peter in the side until he finally wakes up. The chains just fell off! That's the power of Jesus when He comes to the aid of His bride! What is the world going to do with that? Peter watches as the outer gates just swing open. It defies logic. The One who endured the wrath that was meant for us did that! What is the world going to do with *that?*

The disciples are up all night praying that God would intervene and He does. A servant girl recognizes Peter's voice and is so excited that she leaves him standing there outside while she runs to tell the others he is alive and free. But this is what they've been praying for! And they can't believe it! They tell her she's crazy.

Peter is out of prison at the hand of God. God has answered their prayer and they can't believe it! They open the door and see that it is indeed Peter. He tells them his story and tells them to report it all to James, the brother of Jesus, and he leaves to proclaim the gospel, with new fire. Can you blame him? Look what he has just been a part of! This is the same Peter who denied Jesus three times! And Jesus still did this for him! This passage reveals to us that all things are under the power of the creative word of God. God did this in the direct opposition of human, evil leaders, as well as natural cause and effect, all according to God's purposes.

But this passage also reveals what happened to the chief persecutor of the early church. Luke records that Herod dressed up in his pomp and arrogance for the festivities to give an address to the people. When the people call him a god, he says nothing. He does not deny it. His silence is deafening. And because he does not rebuke them for their blasphemy, the one true God strikes him down. God does not share His glory with anyone. This great man Herod was utterly subdued by the Almighty God. He was eaten by worms. The Historian Josephus tells us that Herod laid there for five days as he was being eaten alive by worms.

There are so many lessons that can we take away from this:

1. Knowledge that God is sovereign, all-powerful, full of grace and mercy.
2. Chains are falling off, iron gates are swinging wide.
3. Prayers are being answered.
4. God's enemies are struck down.

There is no power that can match the greatness of our God. And He is the same God now as He was then. There hasn't been a power drain anywhere along the line! We need to live in awareness of Number 1! Full awareness that God is at work in our lives. We are to discipline ourselves to focus on God's gracious actions on our behalf every moment of every day! We are to pray at all times, with expectancy. Why? Because God hears us and answers us. Our prayers will not always be answered the way we expect them to be. God is too gracious for that. Pray, knowing that God will answer your prayers in

His will and His will, will always be accomplished! Live in the knowledge that the church is victorious because of its Head. Jesus Christ has already gained the victory. Be comforted in the power of Christ's eternal victory. Rest assured, nothing will ever stop the spread of the gospel.

Chapter 21

Habakkuk: The Burdened Prophet

Webster's 1828 = BURD'EN, n. burd'n; written also burthen. [L. fero, or porto.] 1. That which is borne or carried; a load. Hence, 2. That which is borne with labor or difficulty; that which is grievous, wearisome or oppressive. 3. A birth. 4. A chord which is to be divided, to perform the intervals of music, when open and undivided, is also called the burden. From Strong's: a burden; specifically tribute, or (abstractly) porterage; figuratively an utterance, chiefly a doom, especially singing; mental, desire:—burden, carry away, prophecy, song, tribute.

"The burden which the Prophet Habakkuk saw" (Hab. 1:1, NKJV).

There are sixteen prophetic books in the Old Testament. Each book opens with something similar to something like this: These are the words of the Lord given to the prophet, or This is the vision... Only two call the Word entrusted to them by the Lord "a burden": Habakkuk and Malachi. Let's see if we can understand why.

> O LORD, how long shall I cry, And You will not hear? Even cry out to You, "Violence!" And You will not save. Why do You show me iniquity, And cause me to see trouble? For plundering and violence are before me; There

is strife, and contention arises. Therefore the law is powerless, And justice never goes forth. For the wicked surround the righteous; Therefore perverse judgment proceeds. (Hab. 1:2–4, NKJV)

These opening verses paint a picture of the wickedness and evil rampant in Habakkuk's world…but this is also a very clear picture of the world today. Prophecy is, by definition, the foretelling of events. Frequently scripture is written depicting life happening in the day of the prophet *and* a future day. Sometimes, the prophet recorded events that were seen only by himself. A good example of this is the apostle John, in the book of Revelation.

Years ago I was in the process of moving from Corpus Christi, Texas to Laredo, three hours away. For a few months we maintained both households, so as furniture began to dwindle in the house in Corpus, my new house in Laredo was slowly being furnished. I would spend the week in Corpus where I was still working, and go to Laredo with a load of furniture, on the weekend, where my former husband was working at his new job. I remember one of those weekends in Laredo. The living room had no furniture in it at all. I took my Bible and lay down in the middle of that living room floor, and started reading the book of Joshua. It was almost as if the Lord had played a DVD for me of Joshua's battles and successes. I thought I had just fallen asleep and dreamed of what I knew was in that book, but when I "awoke" I looked down at the Bible in front of me and I was on page 271…well, that was the last page in Joshua in that Bible. I imagine that is similar to what happened here. God revealed the specific word, through the mind's eye.

This study of Habakkuk was given to me at a time when the world around me was one of violence and evil. The "wicked entrapping the righteous" is exactly what I saw every time I scrolled through Facebook, and viewed friends digging at each other over whose choice of presidential candidates was telling the truth and which one was lying. My stomach churned as I watched the Presidential Candidate Debates…so much so that I stopped watching them, but it wasn't easily ignored. News channels appeared biased in their reporting of events, slanting the news in favor of their preferred candidate. The common opinion had become "the lesser of two evils" more than any election year in recent history. It is my prayer that Christians are at least looking at who God has ordered in the position of president of the United States. It is our Christian and civic duty to vote for the person that *we see* as the most qualified person of integrity for this time in our nation's history. The person that God lays on our hearts. FYI, it is not our duty or our right to coerce others to vote the same way.

> Look among the nations, and watch—be utterly astounded! for I will work a work in your days which you would not believe, though I told it to you. For indeed, I am raising up the Chaldeans, a bitter and hasty nation, which marches through the breadth of the earth to possess dwellings that are not theirs. They are terrible and dreadful; their judgement and their dignity proceed from themselves. Their horses also are swifter than leopards, and are more fierce than evening wolves. their chargers charge ahead; their Calvary come from afar. They fly like the eagle that hastens to eat. They all come for violence; their faces are set like the east wind. They gather captives like sand. They scoff at the kings, and princes are scorned by

them. They deride (laugh at) every stronghold, for they heap up earthen mounds and capture it. Then they sweep on like a wind, and they transgress and commits offenses crediting their power to their god. (Hab. 1:5–11, NKJV)

God's answer is obviously not the answer of expectant hope that this prophet was waiting for: Among the nations—this is not just local rioting anticipated here. This is worldwide. God tells Habakkuk that He Himself is orchestrating all of the dissention and unrest, by raising up the Chaldeans. A bitter, hasty nation—a people who take by force what isn't theirs, a terrible dreadful people, they are known for their evil judgments. Their dignity comes from within themselves and their self-made reputation precedes them. (This description reminds me of the Nazis of World War II.) Their horses, as described here, could represent any of the war equipment and armor. The air here could apply to both airplanes and airwaves—as in media, radio waves. When we apply this to today, the media has a huge part in spreading the dissention, whether between individuals or in misreporting events that feed the political, racial or ethnic frenzy.

The "evening wolves" of verse 8 are fierce because they've been hunting all day with no results. Calvary coming from afar represents allies. These evil Chaldeans are not fighting alone. They gather captives, who become recruits, they enlist accomplices. All of them have violence first and foremost in their minds, with no respect for the leaders of the land or for law enforcement. They sweep through countries like a wind of destruction, and they credit their power to their god—small G—whomever or whatever that god may be at any given moment! Power, greed, lust—you name it. So just from what

Habakkuk has shared with us so far, can you see why he considers this a burden?

> Are You not from everlasting, O Lord my God, my Holy One? We shall not die. O Lord, You have appointed them for judgment; and, Oh Rock, You have marked them for correction. You are of purer eyes than to behold evil, and cannot look on vexation. Why do You look on those who deal treacherously? And hold Your tongue when the wicked devours a person more righteous than he? Why do You make men like the fish of the sea, like creeping things with no ruler over them. (Hab. 1:12–14, NKJV)

The rest of this chapter is Habakkuk continuing to pour out his heart to God. He acknowledges who God is and he understands that God already has these evil people appointed for judgment and marked for correction. He declares that God is too pure to even *look* at this evil going on. Then he questions God: How can You keep silent when the wicked devour a person more righteous than he? (Note: It doesn't say a righteous person; just one a little better that the devourer and he's already described the devourer as wicked, evil, and treacherous.

Matthew Henry's commentary explains it this way: "The prophet complains that God's patience was abused, and because sentence against these evil works and workers was not executed speedily, their hearts were all the more set in them to do evil." Then Habakkuk questions: Why do You make these Chaldeans/modern-day evil people like creeping things that have no ruler...like snakes, serpents...who do we generally describe as a serpent? I'm thinking when the verse says they have no ruler,

since these are like the serpents, we know who their ruler is—
our enemy.

> They take up all of them with a hook; they
> catch them in their net and gather them in
> their dragnet; therefore they rejoice and are
> glad. They sacrifice to their net and burn
> incense to their dragnet; because by them
> their share sumptuous and his food plentiful.
> Shall they therefore empty his net, and con-
> tinue to slay nations. (Hab. 1:15–17, NKJV)

This section is a little easier to understand if you remind
yourself of the phrase "being fishers of men." Evil men are "snag-
ging" what we might call "innocents," as if they are recruiting
them, using them—sacrificing them for their own purposes and
"spitting them out." And they continue through nation after
nation, people after people, with no pity…no conscience…no
feeling that they might be in the wrong…*or* that their evil dealings are totally intentional. Remember that God didn't dictate
the Bible to scribes using chapter and verse numbers. Those
were put there much later, to help us navigate through this tremendous book! Also remember that way back at the beginning
of this, in verse 14, Habakkuk phrased a question to God…
why? And this is why I think *maybe* the chapter break was
placed one verse too early. Habakkuk has asked this question
and is waiting for his answer.

"I will stand on my watch, and set myself on the rampart,
and will watch to see what He will say unto me, and what I shall
answer when I am corrected" (Hab. 2:1, NKJV).

So Habakkuk has asked God why all of this, and God hasn't
answered maybe as quickly as the prophet thought He should
have, so he says, "I will take my stand at my watch-post and sta-

tion myself on the tower, and look out to see what He will say to me, and what I will answer concerning my complaint" (ESV).

The NKJV says "when I am corrected," so Habakkuk already knows he'll be corrected. We know God's thoughts are not our thoughts, and my thought is that just as Habakkuk put to words all the evil he could see, but his thoughts could not include all that God had planned, right? So perhaps he was a bit overly zealous in verbalizing it, maybe out of excitement or fear. Do we ever do that? Do we ever get to listening to ourselves? It feeds our tirade, doesn't it? So I'm thinking maybe *this* is where the chapter break should be, because finally Habakkuk stops to take a breath. And what do you know, God can finally get a word in edge-wise.

"Then the LORD answered me and said: 'Write the vision; make it plain on tablets, so he may run who reads it. For the vision is yet for an appointed time; but at the end it will speak and it will not lie. Though it tarries, wait for it; it will surely come; it will not tarry'" (Hab. 2:2–3, NKJV).

Habakkuk says the Lord answered me, but note that before the Lord answered, He gave very specific instructions as to what Habakkuk was to do with God's answer.

Do you keep a prayer journal? That's what Habakkuk is instructed to do here: write it all down, so that *when* it happens—because this isn't for right this second, but God guarantees that what He is about to share with Habakkuk will happen, and when it happens—these instructions will be needed. Then you can pick up the ball and run with it.

"Behold, his soul is puffed up; it is not upright within him, but the righteous shall live by his faith" (Hab. 2:4, NKJV).

This verse may seem a bit misplaced, but I think God put it where He did, to remind Habakkuk *and us* that just because God chooses to use us in something like this, we can't get all puffed up and prideful about it. But it also reminds *us* that if we live by faith, none of this can cause us to be afraid! Then God gives Habakkuk a stern and detailed warning for those who are not righteous:

> Indeed because he [and this is talking about a wicked person] transgresses by wine, He is a proud man, and he does not stay at home, [an arrogant man who is never at rest]. He enlarges his desire as wide as Sheol; and like death, he cannot be satisfied. He gathers to himself all nations and heaps up for himself all peoples. [like trophies?] Will not all these take up a proverb him, and a taunting riddle for him, and say, "Woe to him who increases what is not his—how long?—and to him who loads himself with many pledges!" Will not your creditors rise up suddenly? Will they not awaken who oppress you? And will you not become their booty? Because you have plundered many nations, all the remnant of the peoples shall plunder you, because of men's and the violence to the earth and the city and all who dwell in them. Woe to him who covets evil gain for his house, that he may set his nest on high, that he may be delivered from the power of disaster. You give shameful counsel to your house, cutting off many peoples; and sin against your soul. For the stone will cry out from the wall, and the beam from the timbers will answer it. Woe to him who builds a town with bloodshed and establishes a city on iniquity! Behold, is it not of the LORD of hosts that peoples labor to

feed the fire, and nations weary themselves in vain? For the earth will be filled with the knowledge of the glory of the LORD as the waters cover the sea. Woe to him who gives drink to his neighbor, pressing him to your bottle, even to make him drunk, that you may gaze on his nakedness! You are filled with shame instead of glory. You also—drink, and be expose as uncircumcised! The cup of the LORD's right hand will turned against you, and utter shame will be on your glory! For the violence done to Lebanon will cover you and the plunder of beasts which made them afraid, because of men's blood and the violence to the land and the city and all who dwell in it. What profit is the image that its maker should carve it, the molded image, a teacher of lies? That the maker of its mold should trust in it. To make mute idols? Woe to him who says to wood, "Awake!" to silent stone, Arise! It shall teach? Behold, it is over-laid with gold and silver, yet in it there is no breath at all. (Hab. 2:5–19, NKJV)

Verse 5–19 is subtitled in my Bible "Woe to the Wicked." God almost itemizes the evils: going out and getting drunk, or getting someone else drunk, so they could be taken advantage of, carousing, hoarding out of never being satisfied, taunting people, going into debt, stealing, plundering, taking what doesn't belong to us, causing blood and violence, envying, plotting ill-gotten gains for yourself and teaching your family that this is the way to get ahead, to be prosperous! And then, quietly slipping into position in verse 20: "But the Lord is in His holy temple. Let all the earth keep silence before Him" (Hab. 2:20, NKJV).

"Be still, and know that I *am* God; I will be exalted among the nations, I will be exalted in the earth!" (Psalm 46:10, NKJV) All the earth is filled with evil and wickedness. But God is still on the throne. Bow before Him in silence. Terrorist attacks are happening when and where we least expect it: But God is still in control. Be still and know. When election is coming up and neither of the candidates look like anything we want for a president, God is still on the throne! God is still God. No matter who is elected president of the United States, God is still God. Jesus is still King.

In verses 1-2 of Chapter 3, Habakkuk acknowledges hearing what God said, and he admits he was afraid. He implores God to revive His work among the people, during this season of adversity. This can be applied to any time there is strife, affliction, or trials in the church, among believers. During such time, we are reminded to remember mercy! He goes on to glorify God's very existence, His glorious appearance, the majesty of Himself and of His creation; He acknowledges the power of God's hand visible in the trembling of the earth and the raging of the seas, God's faithful diligence in placing the moon, sun and stars in their positions, and maintaining them.

In verses 12–13 Habakkuk acknowledges that God went forth for salvation with "his anointed"—which is the Messiah, Son of David, the Christ. Understand that this is the foretelling of something that hasn't happened yet, but as a prophet of God, Habakkuk sees it as if it has. A theophany is a picture of Christ in the Old Testament. It appears here, as if Habakkuk saw God the Father going forth into the plan of salvation with Jesus.

In verses 14–16, Habakkuk explains God's triumph over the wicked Chaldeans, and admits that Habakkuk trembled at the thought of God's wrath and at the sound of God's voice.

The remainder of this chapter is recorded as to the Chief Musician as a psalm, a hymn of faith, a song of rejoicing in victory of what God *has* done *in the future*. God is still on the throne! Bow to Him. The Lord is *still* in His holy temple. Be still and know.

As Christians, we have not been given a spirit of fear (1 Tim. 1:7). It is important that we represent to the world that we are not afraid, even during this time of total chaos in our country—especially in this time, we must show our solid faith in the outcome of this election, because our faith is in the God who is still on the throne, the God who is still in control.

"But the Lord is in His holy temple. Let all the earth keep silence before Him" (Hab. 2:20, NKJV).

Chapter 22

David's Mighty Men

Israel's King David led a powerful army. In 1 Chronicles 11 it tells the story of David's Mighty Men. I'm not going to read it all, but let's look at a few leaders:

1. Jashobeam became chief of the captains because he single-handedly killed three hundred men in one battle, with his spear.

2. Eleazar and his troop (we don't know how many) defended a wide open field and killed the Philistines and he gave credit to the Lord for bringing great victory.

3. When David was hiding from Saul in the cave he longed "for a drink from the well of Bethlehem, outside the gate." The city was surrounded by Philistines camped all around it, but three of David's mighty men loved him so much they broke through the camps and risked their lives to retrieve the water he craved.

4. Abishai, the brother of Joab, lifted up his spear against three hundred men and killed them.

5. Benaiah had killed two lion-like heroes of Moab, killed a lion in a pit, and killed an Egyptian who

was five cubits tall—8'6" tall! David appointed him captain of the guard.

You see the caliber of valor we're dealing with here. All of these mighty men are named in this chapter, and some of their accomplishments are listed here, but I wasn't able to find their names attached to their deeds, anywhere else in scripture. So this is like the Hall of Fame for them—these men were truly mighty men, and they were all in David's army. *God knew their names.* Scripture lists their names only here. Most aren't familiar to us because we don't teach about them other than to call them David's army. But they were important men, and God honored each and every one of them for their part—their obedience to Him in what He called them to do for David. *God knew their names.* Still talking about these same men, 1 Chronicles 12:2 tells us they were Saul's brethren. These men were all from Saul's bloodline and they were fighting *against* Saul.

"...mighty men of valor, men trained for battle, who could handle shield and spear, whose faces were like the faces of lions, and were as swift as gazelles on the mountains" (1 Chron. 12:8, NKJV).

They were mighty, trained, equipped, loyal, and they loved David enough to go to battle *with* him and to go into battle *for* him; they even loved him enough to go get him a drink of water even when it meant going right through the enemy camp. Then came *more* armed, battle-ready men.

And David went out to meet them, and said to them, "If you have come peaceably to me to help me, my heart will be united with you; but if to betray me to my enemies, since there is no wrong in my hands, may the God of our fathers look and bring judgment." Then the

Spirit came upon Amasai, chief of the captains, and he said: "We are yours, O David; We are on your side, O son of Jesse! Peace, peace to you, And peace to your helpers! For your God helps you." So David received them, and made them captains of the troop. (1 Chron. 12:17–18, NKJV)

Sons of Judah	6,800
Sons of Simeon	7,100
Sons of Levi	4,600
Jehoiada	3,700
Sons of Benjamin	3,000
Sons of Ephraim	20,800
Manasseh	18,000
Issachar 200 chiefs plus	50,000
Naphtali	1,000 captains, and 3,700
Danites	28,600
Asher	40,000
Reuben, Gad and Jordan	120,000
David's army totaled	306,300

David didn't recruit these guys. They weren't drafted. They volunteered or enlisted. Then the list continues from the tribes of Israel.

Now these were the numbers of the divisions that were equipped for war, and came to David at Hebron to turn over the kingdom of Saul to him, according to the word of the LORD: of the sons of Judah bearing shield and spear, 6800 armed for war; of the sons of Simeon,

mighty men of valor fit for war, 7100; of the
sons of Levi 4600; Jehoiada, 3700; of the
sons of Benjamin, relatives of Saul, 3000, the
sons of Ephraim 20,800, of the half-tribe of
Manasseh 18,000 designated by name to come
and make David king; the sons of Issachar
200 chiefs, with their tribes: 50,000 expert
in war with all weapons of war, stouthearted
men who could keep ranks; of Naphtali 1000
captains, and 3700 warriors; of the Danites
who could keep battle formation, 28,600;
of Asher, 40,000, of the Reubenites and the
Gadites and the half-tribe of Manasseh, from
the other side of the Jordan, 120,000 armed
for battle with every kind of weapon of war. (1
Chron. 12:23–37, NKJV)

Quite a big army isn't it? And God assigned every one of
them to specific duties. Again they weren't recruited by David,
they came on their own, after hearing of what was happening,
and after God laid it on their hearts that David was His choice
as king and he was under attack. God could have done it with
any number of warriors. David? Maybe not so much. David
was encouraged to see the size of his army, and he needed to
know that these were the men who were loyal and would stay
with him after this battle was over. God always knows not only
what we actually need but what we need to see and hear, in
order for us to stand firm, to be still and know, to let God be
God and to trust him.

Do you have a fairly clear mental picture of David's army?
Now, look at yourselves. What battles have you been through?
What battles have you taken part in on behalf of someone else?
Were you one of "David's mighty men" in someone else's battle?

God knows your name. Every one of you has taken part in a battle that God himself called you to, and you won. Don't for a moment let your enemy convince you that you are not important, that you are not up to the role in whatever battle God calls you to. God knows your name. He knows your accomplishments. And He is smiling on you for being obedient when he called on you.

Many of you have been called to a battle in your church, and you answered the call and you have showed up willing to do your part, armed and ready, just as David's mighty men. God sees you as warriors. The battles David's army won put him in his rightful position as king. This battle that you've won has equipped you for more, prepared you to be ready and strong and equipped to go forward.

David's men knew one important dynamic of being in an army: Once the battle was over, they didn't dwell on it. They gleaned everything they could learn from the battle—what they did right, what they could have done better. They thanked God for the victory and then they moved on. There was always another battle. If they were still focused on what they had just been through, they were endangering themselves and their kingdom.

It fits for us today too. After any spiritual battle, our eyes can't be on God and what God has for us, if we're looking back. It's time to remember the lessons from the battle, but to move forward. It is my belief that as women, we are some of God's most powerful weapons in spiritual warfare. What you have already done proves that here or in your own lives. Remember these thoughts: God knows your name. Just as he knows the names of every one of David's mighty men. He knows what you've already done and He still has more for you to do. He is equipping you every step of the way, just as He did David's army.

Chapter 23

From Fear...to Faith

Experts look at a list of traumatic life events and say a person should avoid going through more than two of these in any five-year period. The list includes the following:[15]

- Death of a loved one
- Marriage
- Divorce
- Major health issue
- Starting a new job, by choice or not
- Moving
- Birth in the immediate family

The five-year period between 1994 and 1999 wasn't the most *peaceful* period in my life:

1. In 1994, I got married.
2. Six weeks later, my mom died.
3. In 1995 I moved to a different city.
4. I started a new job in 1996.
5. In 1997 my dad died.
6. In 1998 I was diagnosed with fibroid cysts in my uterus.
7. In 1999 my doctor found lumps in my breast.

8.   My brother died in 1999.
9.   Also in 1999 my husband left me.
10. I moved again.

The experts tell you not to practice your multitasking with these life events. And I doubled them up within that five-year period. Obviously I didn't have choices in most of these areas.

Item #2 on my list was when my mom died, and when that happened, I decided I wasn't going to go through eternity without seeing her again, so I pulled my "prodigal son" move and came back to the Lord. Thank God that I did because I never could have handled all of these life traumas on my own. To be honest, I couldn't have handled *any* of them without Him.

My emotions were on a roller coaster ride that I was not surviving well. It was during #7—lumps in the breast, that I was so overwhelmed that I needed a team of "warriors" and went to my pastor. Now, I worked for my pastor, so she pretty much knew the ins and outs of my ups and downs. But when that doctor's report came in, I didn't even go home from the doctor's office. I went straight to her office, where she and her husband stopped what they were doing and went into prayer over me.

That was the starting point of some amazing times with the Lord in which He has given me some good words to share. Psalm 61 was the scripture that God led me to during this seriously fearful time in my life. I would find myself starting almost every day reviewing the power of God in this passage. This one I called "From Fear to Faith."

To the choirmaster: with stringed instruments. Of David. Hear my cry, O God, listen to my prayer; from the end of the earth I call to you when my heart is faint. Lead me to the rock that is higher than I, for you have been

my refuge, a strong tower against the enemy.
Let me dwell in your tent forever! Let me take
refuge under the shelter of your wings! Selah.
(Ps. 61:1–4, NKJV)

In these first few verses, David is crying out to God from
fear, "Lord God where are you!" Scripture doesn't tell us the
cause of David's fear, but it really doesn't matter what causes
the fear. When we are afraid, our perspectives can be distorted,
can't they? God gave us imaginations that can go wildly astray
if we let them.

When I was a child and I would have a nightmare, my
mom would always tell me to go back to bed and think about
Christmas…or my birthday, or something pleasant, so I
wouldn't dwell on whatever evil was happening in the nightmare. As an adult, I turn to Philippians 4:5–9:

Let your reasonableness be known to everyone. The Lord is at hand; do not be anxious
about anything, but in everything by prayer
and supplication with thanksgiving let your
requests be made known to God. And the
peace of God, which surpasses all understanding, will guard your hearts and your minds
in Christ Jesus. Finally, brothers, whatever is
true, whatever is honorable, whatever is just,
whatever is pure, whatever is lovely, whatever
is commendable, if there is any excellence,
if there is anything worthy of praise, think
about these things. What you have learned
and received and heard and seen in me—
practice these things, and the God of peace
will be with you. (Phil. 4:5–9, NKJV)

After my pastors prayed over me, I didn't feel any different. If I had gone back to the doctor right then, I couldn't be sure that I was healed. But my next appointment wasn't for another week yet. So during that week, I enlisted others to pray for my healing and I stayed in the Word, reading accounts in the gospels about all the healings Jesus performed…and somewhere, it said, "He healed them all." My peace started returning each time I read them. And I kept thanking Him for healing me, even before I had the doctor's confirmation that I was healed. And when I went in for the second mammogram, the lumps were gone!

There is a word at the end of Psalm 61:4 that we don't always pay much attention to. In fact, frequently when we're reading in the Psalms, we don't even read that word: SELAH. It means "pause and consider." Stop and think about what you just said, David! Pay attention! What did you just write down?

So that's what David did. In the midst of this verbal tirade, he pauses and begins to think about who he is praying to— Jehovah God—the powerful, awesome, amazing, loving God that he serves—the steadfast faithfulness of God. Scripture doesn't tell us how long this pause is, but look at the difference in David's attitude, when we rejoin his story.

> For you, O God, have heard my vows; you have given me the heritage of those who fear your name. Prolong the life of the king; [He's talking about himself here] may his years endure to all generations! May he be enthroned forever before God; appoint steadfast love and faithfulness to watch over him! (Ps. 61:5–7, NKJV)

And then, as if with a sigh of relief, David finishes his prayer, in total faith that his prayer has already been answered:

> So will I ever sing praises to your name, as I perform my vows day after day. (Ps. 61:8, NKJV)
>
> The LORD is my shepherd; I shall not want. He makes me lie down in green pastures. He leads me beside still waters. He restores my soul. He leads me in paths of righteousness for his name's sake. Even though I walk through the valley of the shadow of death, I will fear no evil, for you are with me; your rod and your staff, they comfort me. You prepare a table before me in the presence of my enemies; you anoint my head with oil; my cup overflows. Surely goodness and mercy shall follow me all the days of my life, and I shall dwell in the house of the LORD forever. (Ps. 23, NKJV)

He restores my soul. This phrase explained that even Christians need their souls restored. Maybe you wouldn't think that Christians would get discouraged or depressed. But we have an enemy that roams the earth looking for whom he can destroy! Our souls are attacked daily by issues from inside ourselves—fear, discouragement, depression, sickness, and outside from the world. No matter what causes our souls to crumble, if we pause and consider the God we serve, our soul is restored. It may be a "Selah moment," or a continual effort on our part to make it a "Selah lifestyle." But God can turn our fear into faith, our discouragement into delight, and our sadness into celebration, when we turn to Him to restore our souls.

Chapter 24

It Is Well

Say ye to the righteous, that it shall be well with him.
—Isaiah 3:10 (NKJV)

I quote Charles Spurgeon:

> It is well with the righteous ALWAYS. If it
> had said, "Say ye to the righteous, that it is
> well with him in his prosperity," we must
> have been thankful for so great a boon, for
> prosperity is an hour of peril, and it is a gift
> from heaven to be secured from its snares: or
> if it had been written, "It is well with him
> when under persecution," we must have been
> thankful for so sustaining an assurance, for
> persecution is hard to bear; but when no
> time is mentioned, all time is included. God's
> "shalls" must be understood always in their
> largest sense. From the beginning of the year
> to the end of the year, from the first gathering
> of evening shadows until the day-star shines,
> in all conditions and under all circumstances,
> it shall be well with the righteous. It is so well
> with him that we could not imagine it to be

better, for he is well fed, he feeds upon the flesh and blood of Jesus; he is well clothed, he wears the imputed righteousness of Christ; he is well housed, he dwells in God; he is well married, his soul is knit in bonds of marriage union to Christ; he is well provided for, for the Lord is his Shepherd; he is well endowed, for heaven is his inheritance. It is well with the righteous-well upon divine authority; the mouth of God speaks the comforting assurance. O beloved, if God declares that all is well, ten thousand devils may declare it to be ill, but we laugh them all to scorn. Blessed be God for a faith which enables us to believe God when the creatures contradict him. It is, says the Word, at all times well with thee, thou righteous one; then, beloved, if thou canst not see it, let God's word stand thee instead of sight; yea, believe it on divine authority more confidently than if thine eyes and thy feelings told it to thee. Whom God blesses is blest indeed, and what his lip declares is truth most sure and steadfast.[16]

After reading this devotional one Good Friday morning, my soul was soaring and my heart was pounding! It is well! It is good! Even when my body doesn't agree, I can stand on the promise that it is well! Even when my brain is foggy and unclear, it is well! Even when my memory insists on going on strike, it is still well!

As I have lived my life as a Christian, it has not always felt so. It is way too easy to let our vision be clouded by the "facts" of this earth. For me, the facts say that I have emphysema, so

I have to take one inhaler morning and night, a different one midday, and I carry an emergency inhaler. For me, the fact is that I am allergic to the most common emergency inhaler, so if I don't have an emergency inhaler, and someone else has theirs, I could be thrown into distress.

Not happy facts, but facts that I can live with, because my God has supplied everything I need to keep going, in spite of the facts. He has given me the meds I need, the knowledge that I am restricted from doing certain things—like I can't run a three-minute mile anymore…okay, I never could, but, surprisingly enough, I can still sing! And which is more important to me? Which is more important to God? So, I can honestly say, "It is well."

The facts say that I am lonely, because my son and his family live at one end of the country and I live in another, and he doesn't like to fly and I don't like to fly, so if we ever see each other, someone is most likely driving for twenty hours! But the facts also say that we can talk by phone, email, text and chat, and meet in the middle occasionally. The facts also say that both of my sisters, my nephews, and nieces live fairly close to the middle! So again, I can honestly say, "It is well."

Facts say that I have a lot of junk in my past that I still mourn occasionally. Facts say that most of that junk was caused by my own unwise or selfish decisions. Facts also say that I have repented and been forgiven. Why should I continue to beat myself up? When I choose to keep my eyes on Christ, and remember that he has forgiven me, and in fact He died for me, I can truly and honestly and joyfully say, "It is well!"

> When peace like a river attendeth my way,
> When sorrow like sea billows roll,
> Whatever my lot You have taught me to say,
> It is well it is well with my soul.

But Lord it's for Thee for Thy coming we wait,
The sky not the grave is our goal,
Oh trump of the angel oh voice of the Lord,
Blessed hope blessed rest of my soul.
It is well with my soul.
It is well it is well with my soul.[17]

Whether the facts say I have peace in my life or not or when I feel drowned by the sorrows, the facts remain. I have Jesus in my life. I have God watching over me. I have the Holy Spirit guiding my every step. These facts say, it is well. Not because of anything I have done, except that I accepted Jesus as my Lord and Savior. Not by anything you can do. You may not be physically able to change your circumstances, except that you can accept Jesus as your Lord and Savior and you can trust Him when He says to the righteous: "Say ye to the righteous, that it shall be well with him" (Isa. 3:10. NKJV).

That is you—the righteous means you, if you have given your heart to Jesus. Because when you do that, you live in His righteousness. You can trust that it is well.

Chapter 25

Peace with God through Faith

Therefore, having been justified by faith, we have peace with God through our Lord Jesus Christ, through whom also we have access by faith into this grace in which we stand, and rejoice in hope of the glory of God. And not only that, but we also glory in tribulations, knowing that tribulation produces perseverance; and perseverance, character; and character, hope. Now hope does not disappoint, because the love of God has been poured out in our hearts by the Holy Spirit who was given to us. For when we were still without strength, in due time Christ died for the ungodly. For scarcely for a righteous man will one die; yet perhaps for a good man someone would even dare to die. (Rom. 5:1–7, NKJV)

Lovable or unlovable? I would imagine that everyone here can think of a loved one—friend or family member—who is just easy to love. Lovable. When my husband and I moved to Lisbon, North Dakota, the people in Lisbon met us with open arms, accepted us for who we are, and loved on us. It's easy to love someone who loves us, right? Can you think back in your life and remember someone that was not easy to love? I remember quite a few. I knew a woman who had been divorced for several years and she was in church pretty much every Sunday, sang in the choir, went to missions trips with us, but she was always angry—still very angry with her ex-husband, and with God. She was difficult to love. She grumbled about everything. If you tried to do anything nice for her, she asked what you wanted from her, always looking for an ulterior motive. Some people are just easier to love than others. But Christ tells us to love one another, right? Lovable or not.

"Jesus said to him, You shall love the Lord your God with all your heart, with all your soul, and with all your mind. This is the first and great commandment. And the second is like it: 'You shall love your neighbor as yourself'" (Matt. 22:37–39, NKJV).

We think of our neighbors as those folks who live across the way from us, and on either side and maybe behind us. But the Greek word used here was *plēsion*: defined as a neighbor, that is, fellow (as man, countryman, Christian or friend. We could get into a whole long lesson on who our neighbor is, but the Scriptural intent here is that pretty much everyone is your neighbor! And some of those neighbors aren't so easy to love! But we are commanded to love even those people. And God never tells you to do something that He doesn't enable you to do!

"With man it is impossible, but not with God; for with God all things are possible" (Mark 10:27, NKJV).

God is so compassionate toward us, that He knows how difficult it is for us to love someone who has hurt us. Or who is just mean-spirited, or hard to be around. *And He still expects us to love the unlovable.* But He doesn't expect us to do it alone. He has promised us that it is possible, because anything is possible when we trust Him.

There is a standing joke in the Christian community: "Lord, I am so at peace, I feel your joy in me. Thank you! I haven't bitten off anyone's head this morning. So now I'm going to get out of bed." It's easy to feel peaceful and loving when we don't encounter anyone who threatens to upset that peace, right? But we can so easily upset our own peace, by putting so much pressure on ourselves to do things in our own strength. God doesn't ask us to do that. He asks us to trust Him for our strength and our joy and our peace.

So let's turn things around a little. Do you consider yourself easy to love? Sometimes maybe? Other times, not so much. Maybe, you feel loveable when you are in church, singing with the rest of the folks, enjoying worship service. Maybe you have it in your mind that when you are doing things for God, serving the church, it's easy for God to love you, and when you are not so obedient, He doesn't. That is so not true! God loves us unconditionally—all the time. Remember what we read?

"But God demonstrates His own love toward us, in that while we were still sinners, Christ died for us" (Rom. 5:8, NKJV).

When my son did something as a child that he wasn't supposed to do, I used to tell him, "I love you," but I really don't like what you did. I may not like you very much at this moment, but I still love you. And that's a *human* parent's take on love. God loves us, mightily, no matter what we do. He might not be happy with something we've done: sin, disobedience, rebellion. But He still loves us!

A huge portion of the Bible—all the letters Paul wrote to believers—are love letters from God to you! Even when those believers missed the mark, God still loved them. And He still loves you! God's love, His grace, His mercy are free gifts from Him to us, delivered by Christ Jesus through the cross. We can't do anything to earn those gifts and we can't do anything that would make Him take them back! That's God's love. God wants to meet with you one-on-one. Why do you think He wants to do that? Because He loves you! He wants to spend time with you. Even when you are not so easy to love!

In Ephesians 3, Paul describes himself as less than the least of the saints, and celebrates that "God's grace was given, that I should preach among the Gentiles the unsearchable riches of Christ, and to make all see what is the fellowship of the mystery…" (NKJV).

He's talking about fellowship with Christ Jesus, one-on-one, so that the vast wisdom of God might be made known by the church "according to the eternal purpose which He accomplished in Christ Jesus our Lord, in whom we have boldness and access with confidence through faith in Him" (Eph. 3:12). I call that last verse (verse 12) the A-B-Cs of the gospel: We can *access* God's throne room, the greatness, the very heart of God, with *boldness* and with *confidence*, because Jesus loved us enough to die for us, even when we were sinners—totally unlovable!

Does that tell you how much we are loved by our Heavenly Father? When we approach God in prayer, we don't have to do it sheepishly. He wants us to come to Him with all our cares, boldly and with confidence.

"Therefore, having been justified by faith, we have peace with God through our Lord Jesus Christ, through whom also we have access by faith into this grace in which we stand, and rejoice in hope of the glory of God" (Rom. 5:1–2, NKJV).

Access—there's that word again—in boldness and confidence, because of the love and the grace and the mercy that God gives us through His Son Jesus. If you have felt a little uncomfortable over some of the teachings about hearing God's voice, don't be! If you have a relationship with Jesus Christ, if you have accepted Him as your Lord and Savior, you have the same right to listen for God's voice as I do! You have access to the

One True living God, you can approach Him boldly and with confidence, knowing that He is waiting and wanting to hear your heart, and to share His with you! And when you approach Jehovah God, He has so much more to share with you. Gal. 5:22–23 lists the fruit of the Spirit: love, joy, peace, patience, kindness, goodness, faithfulness, gentleness, self-control. When you spend time one-on-one with the King of kings and Lord of lords, He will develop these traits in you. He will lavish His love on you, so you can share love with others—remember? Love one another? He will flood you with His peace, so that you feel peace inside, so that others around you will feel peace too. You will find yourself displaying more patience in situations that might have upset you before. You will show kindness, gentleness, goodness, because that's what God will be working to develop in you, so you can be kind, gentle, and good.

He works those traits in us to enable us to obey that commandment! How better to "love one another and love your neighbors as yourself" than to share these character traits with people who may not have developed those traits yet? How better to show God's love and to grow in God's love, and to represent Him well with everyone you meet—even those who aren't so loveable?

The verses you read in the beginning of this chapter confirm how much God loves us, through our relationship with His son Jesus Christ. They let us know beyond a shadow of a doubt that God loves us unconditionally and is not mad at us, as some people think. Even when we sin, He still loves us. I include those same verses from the Message.

> By entering through faith into what God
> has always wanted to do for us—set us right
> with him, make us fit for him—we have it
> all together with God because of our Master

Jesus. And that's not all: We throw open our doors to God and discover at the same moment that he has already thrown open his door to us. We find ourselves standing where we always hoped we might stand—out in the wide open spaces of God's grace and glory, standing tall and shouting our praise. There's more to come: We continue to shout our praise even when we're hemmed in with troubles, because we know how troubles can develop passionate patience in us, and how that patience in turn forges the tempered steel of virtue, keeping us alert for whatever God will do next. In alert expectancy such as this, we're never left feeling shortchanged. Quite the contrary—we can't round up enough containers to hold everything God generously pours into our lives through the Holy Spirit! Christ arrives right on time to make this happen. He didn't, and doesn't, wait for us to get ready. He presented himself for this sacrificial death when we were far too weak and rebellious to do anything to get ourselves ready. And even if we hadn't been so weak, we wouldn't have known what to do anyway. We can understand someone dying for a person worth dying for, and we can understand how someone good and noble could inspire us to selfless sacrifice. But God put his love on the line for us by offering his Son in sacrificial death while we were of no use whatever to him. Now that we are set right with God by means of this sacrificial death, the con-

summate blood sacrifice, there is no longer
a question of being at odds with God in any
way. If, when we were at our worst, we were
put on friendly terms with God by the sacrificial death of his Son, now that we're at our
best, just think of how our lives will expand
and deepen by means of his resurrection life!
(Rom 5:1–10 MSG)

There's more to come: We continue to shout our praise
even when we're hemmed in with troubles, because we know
how troubles can develop passionate patience in us, and how
that patience in turn forges the tempered steel of virtue, keeping us alert for whatever God will do next. In alert expectancy
such as this, we're never left feeling shortchanged. Quite the
contrary; we can't round up enough containers to hold everything God generously pours into our lives through the Holy
Spirit! Christ arrives right on time to make this happen. He
didn't, and doesn't, wait for us to get ready. He presented himself for this sacrificial death when we were far too weak and
rebellious to do anything to get ourselves ready. And even if
we hadn't been so weak, we wouldn't have known what to do
anyway. We can understand someone dying for a person worth
dying for, and we can understand how someone good and noble
could inspire us to selfless sacrifice. But God put his love on the
line for us by offering his Son in sacrificial death while we were
of no use whatsoever to him. Now that we are set right with
God by means of this sacrificial death, the consummate blood
sacrifice, there is no longer a question of being at odds with
God in any way. If, when we were at our worst, we were put on
friendly terms with God by the sacrificial death of his Son, now
that we're at our best, just think of how our lives will expand
and deepen by means of his resurrection life!

Somewhere along the way, I started including the phrase "I love you, Lord" or "we love you, Lord" in my prayers. When I think of how very much God loves His children and what He sacrificed in giving His Son for us and what He gives to us every day—the very breath we breathe—how can we not love Him in return?

Chapter 26

An Encouraging Word

During his second missions trip, Paul sent Timothy on a side trip to visit the baby church of Thessalonica to see how they were doing. The Thessalonians were thriving news of their faith had spread throughout much of Macedonia and beyond. The second book of Thessalonians is a letter written to them by Paul after Timothy's visit.

> Paul, Silvanus, and Timothy, to the church of the Thessalonians in God our Father and the Lord Jesus Christ: Grace to you and peace from God our Father and the Lord Jesus Christ. We thank God always for you, brethren, as it is fitting, because your faith grows exceedingly, and the love of every one of you all abounds toward each other... (2 Thess. 1:1–3, NKJV)

This is Paul's greeting to this much loved church and he lets them know that they (Paul, Silas and Timothy) continuously pray for this new little church and that they remember their work in the faith. It's a letter of encouragement.

Can you think of a time when you wrote a real letter? In this electronic age of email and texting, we don't handwrite very often anymore, so let me rephrase my question: Can you remember the last time you encouraged someone, whether by email or text or snail mail? Can you think of a time when you received such correspondence? How did it make you feel?

When I received a card not too long ago, the first thing I see is this small sized envelope that came in the mail. Both my address and the return address were handwritten. And because it wasn't the normal size envelope, before I ever opened it, my mind starts thinking it's a thank-you card for something I did or it's an invitation to something. Either way my mind immediately starts enjoying the process of receiving this card. Anticipation. I think I had it opened before I even got back into the house with it.

And when I opened it the very first words, "My dear sister in the Lord," touched my heart. Much like Paul's greeting to this church, it immediately establishes relationship.

And then the next words, "I just wanted to take a moment..." It acknowledges the fact that we are all busy, but reading between the lines, it immediately told me that I am worth the time someone took and the effort she went to, to write this card. It was a short card. It didn't say a lot, but it spoke volumes. It doesn't take but a moment to do something that means so much by way of encouragement.

With Paul's words in verse 2 he gives thanks to God always for these Thessalonians and then he goes into a brief paragraph honoring them: he remembers their work of faith, their labor of love, and their patience of hope while waiting on Jesus to return.

The card I got did the same thing. "Just wanted to take a moment to let you know how much I appreciate you. All that you do brings me closer in my walk with the Lord."

It went on to give me some specifics that are personal between my sister in Christ and me, but that's what a card of encouragement does. It lifted my spirits. It told me that things I do make a difference in her life.

She had no idea that at the particular moment that I would open that card I had received some bad news, so I was a little discouraged and I needed that pick-me-up. *She* didn't know it, but *God* knew it. God put it on her heart to encourage me. She obeyed. And I received it at the exact moment that God knew I would need that word of encouragement! God is really good at working out things like that!

So I go back to my first question: Can you think of a time when you wrote or texted or emailed someone just to encourage them? Think about someone that you might need to encourage. I watch people. Before services start or before Bible study starts or afterward, as we are on our way out the door, I see my church family encourage each other and love on each other. When was the last time you "took a moment" and wrote a kind thought down on a card or texted it on your phone or wrote an email? When was the last time you sent a note of encouragement to someone?

Paul's letter goes on in great detail as to why these Thessalonians are so important to him:

> ➤ In verse 6, "you became followers of us and [more importantly] of the Lord."
> ➤ In verse 7, "you became examples to all in Macedonia and Achaiah who believe."
> ➤ In verse 8, "From you the word of the Lord has sounded forth not only in Macedonia and Achaiah but also in every place. Your faith toward God has gone out so we do not need to say anything."

> ➤ In verse 9, "for they themselves declare concerning us how you turned to God from idols to serve the living and true God"
> ➤ verse 10, "to wait in hope for His Son from heaven." Rom 5:10 (MSG)

How do you think the Thessalonians reacted to those words? It had to have excited them, don't you think, to know that Paul, their mentor, was hearing about how well they had understood his teachings and were acting on them. Remember he is the founder of that church. How proud he is of them! How nice to know that! How encouraging to hear that they were doing good!

About a year ago, there was a post on my Facebook account with a picture of a woman I immediately recognized. She was my grade school music teacher and the post announced her ninetieth birthday. It listed an address and requested as many birthday cards be sent as she had students that were reading that post. I don't remember how many she received, but can you imagine her delight at even receiving ten to twelve cards from students that she taught fifty years prior?

I am a sucker for sentiment. But I don't think I'm the only one. I think Paul was too, because so many of his letters are just that—sentimental and encouraging and instructing love letters. I would go so far as to say that he was loving them with God's love *and* his own.

It only takes a moment. It doesn't take a lot of effort and it doesn't take a lot of thought. I would encourage you this afternoon to jot down a thought of encouragement with someone in mind. It doesn't have to be a pretty card or elegant stationery, and yes, it can be on your computer or a text on your phone. Something as simple as "Thank you for touching my life" will mean so much to someone who is discouraged. And if you can't think of anyone, ask God who you need to encourage. And do it. And if you are the one receiving one of those letters of encouragement, enjoy.

Chapter 27

The Armor of God for Women

I joined the USMC after one semester of college that didn't go the way I thought it should. I wasn't unhappy at home. I wasn't running from anything. I just needed to go forward in life. After I got to Basic Training—that's the official name for Boot Camp—I learned that there were a lot of girls who were there because they *weren't* happy at home or because they *were* running from something.

In those days ('70s), it was a common occurrence for men and women who got in trouble with the law to be given a choice: four years in the Marine Corps or jail time. And more often than not, it worked out well, because the bullies soon learned that they couldn't get their own way by bullying the drill instructors or other marines! The DIs (drill instructors) were the tough, seasoned marines, both women and men, who were in charge of teaching us twenty-five to thirty green recruits how to be marines, how to act as a team, and how to work together to serve our country and its people. They taught us all about the Uniform Code of Military Justice—the dos and don'ts of military life; they taught us how to wear our uniform, shine our boots, iron our uniforms, how to eat. They taught us everything from how and who to salute to how to fold our socks and underwear! After eight weeks of boot camp, we thought we knew it all!

Although male marines are also taught tactical warfare and weaponry, women were not until the mid-1980s. No karate or anything. And I never had a problem with that, because, I knew I wasn't going to go into battle. Those days women didn't. I was going to be stationed in an office somewhere. There were never going to be battles in the office, right? Wrong! (Although I didn't know it then.)

Danger was something I didn't even think about then. I was young, and the young are invincible. I was a Christian, but Marine Corps life didn't leave time for much except Sunday morning worship. Our time was theirs to control. The Marine Corps didn't teach us anything about the Bible, let alone Ephesians 6, or the Armor of God. They made us sing the Lord's Prayer every night at lights out. I hadn't thought about or been taught anything about spiritual warfare.

Spiritual warfare is a "Christianese" term we use for the battles that we go through, but can't see…the battles in the Spiritual realm. You can't see them, but you can feel them and you can be beat up by them, if you aren't prepared…if you don't know what armor and weapons are available to you for those spiritual battles.

What my being a woman marine changed first was the world's view of who I was. Some were surprised that as a shy young "Daddy's girl," I would leave the safety and protection of my very sheltered childhood. Some were impressed that I would do something so bold, so patriotic. Some were proud—my daddy was proud, my mom was scared. But other reactions weren't so positive: What type of woman would join the Marine Corps? There were assumptions and wise-cracks about my sexuality.

Other changes in my life changed me—I had a choice to eat for free in the Chow Hall (where the food wasn't all that great and you ate what they served whether you liked it or not) or to go eat at the enlisted men's club where I could order off the menu. But it wasn't free, and you had to go into the bar area to order your drink, even pop or coffee. That's where I heard more innuendo and crude remarks. Even in the office I was assigned to, I was constantly exposed to foul language by both men and women. Out from under the solid love and protection of my father, there was no trustworthy protection there—no one I could trust to be on "my side" of any verbal wounds or emotional hurts. For me, it was time to "get tough." All these things resulted in desensitizing me to the gentle nudging of the Holy Spirit that I had once felt so strongly. I started building walls around my heart to protect myself against the verbal and emotional attacks from outsiders.

Like I said, the Marine Corps didn't teach me anything about Ephesians 6. So when the spiritual warfare hit, I felt totally alone and on my own. If I had known about the armor available to me even back then, I might not have made quite so many mistakes along the way. Because I lost those battles, I gave in to my enemy and eventually the battles stopped.

I hope this chapter will touch your heart and will serve several purposes for you:

1. To ease any guilt you may still be dealing with over past failures or battles lost.
2. To give you new strength for today, tomorrow, and every day going forward.
3. To help you equip not just your daughters (although that's the place to start) but your daughters-in-law, your moms and mothers-in-law, your sisters and sisters-in-Christ, for every woman in your life—to face the battles in their lives—expected and unexpected—and to come out victorious!

God is all-knowing. He knew when you asked Him into your heart as your Lord and Savior that you would encounter a few battles along the way! The first several verses in Ephesians set us up to being obedient to God and respectful of each other, including our bosses and those in authority over us. These are things that must be settled, in our hearts and minds, before the armor of God is truly effective for us. Those, and being caring of those less fortunate to us, being willing to serve mankind as we serve God.

"And you, masters, do the same things to them, giving up threatening, knowing that your own Master also is in heaven, and there is no partiality with Him. Finally, my brethren, be strong in the Lord and in the power of His might" (Eph. 6:9–10, NKJV).

We've already established the fact that the armor we're talking about is the armor of God—these are figurative in that they are not physical items of clothing that we put on. God has inspired Paul here to give us a visual picture of what He has supplied for us to not only survive the battles but to thrive and grow through them, with minimal battle scars!

> Put on the whole armor of God, that you may be able to stand against the wiles of the devil. For we do not wrestle against flesh and blood, but against principalities, against powers, against the rulers of the darkness of this age, against spiritual hosts of wickedness in the heavenly places. (Eph. 6:11–12, NKJV)

We don't want to glorify our enemy or give him too much credit, but Scripture is telling us not to underestimate him either. The word *wiles* in the Greek is *methodeia*—travesty, (trickery):—wile, lie in wait. Methodical—as in a planned ambush—not just happenstance.

Our enemy is sneaky and he has been at it for a while, so he knows all the tricks that will get our goat. He knows to attack when you're tired, busy, distracted, or sick. And he knows what will keep your mind off of what God wants your mind on—Him and living the victorious Christian life. Therefore, God has devised not only the battle plan for us but also the exact uniform we need to wear in this army of God.

"Therefore take up the whole armor of God, that you may be able to withstand in the evil day, and having done all, to stand" (Eph. 6:13, NKJV).

There is an evil day coming. But there is evil in every day! So we need the whole armor, not just part of it. And we need to make the conscious effort to put it on by reading or praying through these verses every morning.

"Stand therefore, having girded your waist with truth, having put on the breastplate of righteousness, and having shod your feet with the preparation of the gospel of peace" (Eph. 6:14–15, NKJV).

First, we put on the defensive pieces of armor—your uniform:

1. The truth of the Word of God—when you know the truth you cannot easily be fooled by Satan's schemes and lies.

2. The breastplate of righteousness is only yours when you have given your life to Jesus because it is His righteousness that we are putting on, not our own.

3. Then think of the shoes you would want to wear going into battle—combat boots. Solid, sturdy, well-fitting. You sure wouldn't want to go into

battle with flip-flops on, and you won't want running shoes, because guess what—we're not going to be running! The combat boots represent our preparation (again) in the word, knowing the gospel of peace. In the middle of battle, we must be prepared and be ready for peace, watching for it, working toward it.

"Above all, taking the shield of faith with which you will be able to quench all the fiery darts of the wicked one" (Eph. 6:16, NKJV).

4. The shield of faith—I've heard different versions of how the shields David's army used were made, but I like the one I was taught years ago by a pastor in Texas. They built frames of wood and covered them with layers of animal hides. Then the shields were put in the river to soak up water, so when the fiery darts or flaming arrows hit them, they would immediately be extinguished.

    When the group I was with learned about this, we started doing something that would immediately remind us of this. What sounds do you hear when a lit match gets dropped into water? *Tsst.* And every time we sensed our enemy firing those flaming arrows at us, we'd make the sound "tsst." Fire went out—no harm done. It just made us think more about what was going on in the spiritual realm. And the armor that we were wearing! Remember the spiritual warfare I mentioned earlier? This spiritual realm is where it all happens. You don't see it, but you feel it and you know it's there!

"And take the helmet of salvation, and the sword of the Spirit, which is the word of God" (Eph. 6:17).

5.   The helmet of salvation, as the Arabic version renders it, represents either "the helmet of the Savior," or the salvation itself. That helmet is a protection for our minds (against false teachings or verbal attacks) but it is also a piece of armor that helps us to lift our heads, to keep our heads up, in times of difficulty, affliction, and distress. This is the last item of defensive armor that God gives us, but it is one of the most important. The Marine Corps issued helmets to protect us from physical damage. They taught us how to use a gas mask in the event that chemical warfare broke out. They taught us where the bunkers were to hide. Our training was lacking in anything offensive...anything to charge with! They never taught us how to fight! God's armor leaves nothing out!

6.   The Sword of the Spirit is our only offensive or attacking weapon of warfare. Would you pick up an M16 rifle and go into battle with no training? Neither do we want to go into a spiritual battle without training either. God doesn't leave us ill-quipped! He has given us everything we need to protect ourselves, but He has also given us this magnificent sword that we can count on to carry into battle.

But we can't expect it to do the work for us unless we are trained in it! We have to know what's in here to stand up against our enemy, the devil! Do you know what this Word says?

> You will not need to fight in this battle. Position yourselves, stand still and see the salvation of the LORD, who is with you, O Judah and Jerusalem! Do not fear or be dismayed. (2 Chron. 20:17, NKJV)
>
> Therefore submit to God. Resist the devil and he will flee from you. (James 4:7, NKJV)

Those are just two verses in here that should give you strength to fight whatever battle comes your way! They are two of my favorites! But we have to practice with our weapon to get good with it.

And then lastly, prayer: "praying always with all prayer and supplication in the Spirit, being watchful to this end with all perseverance and supplication for all the saints" (Eph. 6:18).

These are things that we have heard about or learned about on the surface, for years—probably since the day we became a Christian. We learned them and we adhered to them, we stuck like glue to them...for a while... and then things start going pretty well, so we forget about those battles that we face every day. But trust me! The battles don't stop. If they have, you're doing something wrong. Because Satan doesn't stop attacking, unless you're not going forward with the Lord. That's why the battles stopped when I was in the Marine Corps. I stopped moving forward with the Lord.

His attacks step up; they are the strongest when you take your daughter, your daughters-in-law—all those girls I was talking about earlier—when you take them by the hand and lead them forward into God's Word—into God's plan for their lives. That's when the battle gets stepped up because Satan knows he's losing you! And He's losing all those women that you're taking with you!

Here are our marching orders: Let God be God in your lives. Don't *worry* about what Satan is doing, be *prepared*. As long as you keep your eyes on God and are *watchful* and *prepared* every single day with the armor of God that He provides for us, then Satan has no power whatsoever in your life! It is my prayer that you are alongside me in the army of women that God calls, to make His declarations of truth whenever He asks us to speak, to act as He commands, to serve whenever and wherever He sends us. But we can't serve him properly unless we are prepared. That preparation starts with God's armor, and it is a perfect fit.

Chapter 28

All about Angels

I want to take you on an in-depth tour of the scriptural truth of angels and also to share some angel encounters. The word angel simply means messenger or agent. Angels are God's messengers. The Bible clearly teaches the existence of angels, not as a race reproducing themselves, but as a "company" created to minister to the heirs of salvation. Who are the heirs of salvation? Anyone who has accepted God's gift of salvation!

There are two classes of angels, elect and fallen, and man is forbidden to worship either.

The elect—These are the good angels, the ones who remained loyal to God and did not follow Lucifer.

I charge you before God and the Lord Jesus Christ and the elect angels that you observe these things without prejudice, doing nothing with partiality (1 Timothy 5:21, NKJV).

Fallen angels—One-third of heaven's angels fell to the sin of self-will. In reality, they didn't fall; they chose to rebel, which caused them to be cast out of heaven with Lucifer.

"For if God did not spare the angels who sinned, but cast them down to hell and delivered them into chains of darkness, to be reserved for judgment" (2 Peter 2:4, NKJV).

We are talking about the fallen here. God showed no partiality toward the angels who chose to sin. They were not required to follow Lucifer (or Satan). There was still a place for them in heaven.

> And the angels who did not keep their proper domain, but left their own abode, He has reserved in everlasting chains under darkness for the judgment of the great day; Yet Michael the archangel, in contending with the devil, when he disputed about the body of Moses, dared not bring against him a reviling accusation, but said, 'The Lord rebuke you!' (Jude 1:6, 9, NKJV).

Even the angels don't have the authority to rebuke our enemy, only Jesus does.

> And war broke out in heaven: Michael and his angels fought with the dragon and the dragon and his angels fought, but they did not prevail, nor was a place found for them in heaven any longer. So the great dragon was cast out, that serpent of old, called the Devil and Satan, who deceives the whole world; he was cast to the earth, and his angels were cast out with him (Revelation 12:7–9, NKJV).

Let's get a glimpse of an environment like that of angels. Ptolemy Tompkins shared this story in his book Proof of Angels:

A few years ago I took my stepdaughter Evie snorkeling for the first time. She was eight and though she'd put on a face mask before, she'd never had a chance to look below the waves in an area that was really populated with sea life. We were in the Bahamas, floating in the water by what looked like a pretty humdrum chunk of rock. Evie pushed and fumbled with her mask, getting the water out of it and blowing through her snorkel so she could breathe. When she was finally comfortable with her equipment, she lowered her head beneath the water. Kabook! The reef was swarming with fish—parrot fish, triggerfish, and swarms of little black and yellow sergeant majors that were all around her, investigating her completely without her knowledge. I'll never forget the look in her eyes when she brought her head back out of the water and the uncontrollable smile that formed around the snorkel in her mouth. She had thought she was bobbing about by a barren rock, when in fact she had been immersed in a whole other universe of color and light and life. Imagine the world, changed in an instant from a place of fear and uncertainty and emptiness to a place of wonder and beauty and overwhelming number of beings, invisible but present, all the same.

Think of this as a picture of the spiritual realm. We can't see it, but it's there. Angels, and fallen angels or spirits are around us at any particular moment. We can't see the spiritual realm because we don't have the right equipment, but we don't have the right equipment because God is the one who can enable us to see it, and He knows when we are ready to see and when we are not! Consider the story of Balaam:

> Now the donkey saw the Angel of the LORD standing in the way with His drawn sword in His hand, and the donkey turned aside out of the way and went into the field. So Balaam struck the donkey to turn her back onto the road. Then the Angel of the LORD stood in a narrow path between the vineyards, with

a wall on this side and a wall on that side. And when the donkey saw the Angel of the LORD, she pushed herself against the wall and crushed Balaam's foot against the wall; so he struck her again. Then the Angel of the LORD went further, and stood in a narrow place where there was no way to turn either to the right hand or to the left. And when the donkey saw the Angel of the LORD, she lay down under Balaam; so Balaam's anger was aroused, and he struck the donkey with his staff. Then the LORD opened the mouth of the donkey, and she said to Balaam, "What have I done to you, that you have struck me these three times?" And Balaam said to the donkey, "Because you have abused me. I wish there were a sword in my hand, for now I would kill you!" So the donkey said to Balaam, "Am I not your donkey on which you have ridden, ever since I became yours, to this day? Was I ever disposed to do this to you?" And he said, "No." Then the LORD opened Balaam's eyes, and he saw the Angel of the LORD standing in the way with His drawn sword in His hand; and he bowed his head and fell flat on his face. (Numbers 22:23–31, NKJV)

Imagine a helmet like the ones the old-fashioned divers used to wear: one that covers the entire head like a fishbowl. Then imagine that this helmet is made of magical glass-like substance, one so thin and unobtrusive, that it lets just about everything through. It never gets dirty, never gets wet, and is absolutely transparent to light and penetrable by air. Essentially, it's as if this helmet isn't there at all. Except it is. And the one thing this helmet blocks out—the one thing it keeps the person wearing it from experiencing—is the spiritual world. Everything else gets past it. But that one thing—that singular, all-important part of the world, without which the world isn't really the full, complete world at all, but only half of it—doesn't make it through. What kind of world do we see when looking through these magical, spirit-filled helmets? We would see a world in which the earth is just above the earth, where good things happen and bad things happen, where there is happiness and sorrow, where people are born and people die. Yet somehow, none of this seems to mean all that much. We see a world in which everything is relative and essentially insignificant.

I think this is a fair analogy of the spiritual realm. When we learn about angels, we must acknowledge the presence of a spiritual realm that we cannot see. If you are a sci-fi buff, you might have heard of the phrase "parallel universe." The spiritual realm is similar in thought but real and happening right here, right now, right beside us, simultaneously, and we can't see it or hear it, unless God wants us to. Balaam didn't see it, until God opened his eyes and allowed him to.

I won't say this is where the angels live, because scripturally, angels live in heaven. I will tell you that I believe this spiritual realm, the one that is simultaneous to the one we live in, is where the angels may sometimes "hang out." They roam the earth, worshipping God, waiting for God's commands to go to the aid of one of His children…one of us.

Churches today don't frequently address the doctrine of angels for several reasons:

1.   It is an intense and sometimes passionate subject that requires in-depth and time-consuming

study of the Scriptures to enable accurate and adequate teachings on the subject. In reality, if all that the Bible reveals about angels were known and accepted, much of this unbelief, fear, and undue adoration would be eliminated.

2. Disbelief of the Sadducees in Scripture, in the very existence of angels.

    "For Sadducees say that there is no resurrection—and no angel or spirit; but the Pharisees confess both. Then there arose a loud outcry. And the scribes of the Pharisees' party arose and protested, saying, 'We find no evil in this man; but if a spirit or an angel has spoken to him, let us not fight against God'" (Acts 23:8–9, NKJV).

3. Fear of the unseen spiritual realm of spirit beings, which is also rarely taught.

4. Undue attention and worship of the angels. Scripture warns us not to worship them. "Let no one cheat you of your reward, taking delight in false humility and worship of angels, intruding into those things which he has not seen, vainly puffed up by his fleshly mind." (Colossians 2:18, NKJV)

Angels are a unit. Think of the government or hierarchy of the angels as similar to a military company. Scripture tells us that the Lord Jesus is the captain of the host—that means the captain of the army of angels.

> So He [the Angel of the Lord] said, 'No, but as Commander of the army of the LORD I have now come.' And Joshua fell on his face to the earth and worshiped, and said to Him,

'What does my Lord say to His servant?'
(Joshua 5:14, NKJV).

An Angel Encounter: The Traveling Companion (from
"Angels Among Us"):

John F., a pastor, was traveling alone from
Wyoming to his new pastorate in New Jersey.
This journey was the most sorrowful of his
life. His beloved wife had gone spiritually
adrift and ended their marriage in order to
take up with a same sex companion. Fifteen
years of marriage and service together turned
to dust. Never had life seemed so desolate
and lonely. Pastor John had to move to a
completely new area away from the pain and
loss, away from the consternation of grieving
church members who felt as helpless in the
face of this tragedy as he did.

Knowing the journey was long, Pastor
John wanted to cover as many miles as he
could each day. He prayed for comfort, and
it came. From time to time, as he crossed
the vast expanse of his beloved Wyoming, he
felt the sustaining presence of a diving being
with him. He was able to look forward to the
future with some hope.

As John came toward the eastern end of
Wyoming, he felt very tired. He saw a sign
indicating that a motel and diner lay seventeen miles ahead in Bushnell, Nebraska.
"That's where I'll stop," he decided. I'll spend
the night. If only I can hold out until then.

I'm so tired, he thought. "Oh, Lord, be with me," he prayed. Moments later, John fell asleep at the wheel.

The next thing he knew, a voice called to him, "Wake up, John." Startled, he looked ahead and saw himself cruising along at the allowed speed. His hands were firmly on the wheel. Immediately, to the right, a sign appeared that read: Bushnell Exit 1/2 Mile. By now, John was really awake. It struck him. "I've been asleep for the past fifteen miles or so. Thank you, Lord, for preserving my life."

Pulling off at the next exit, John went to the nearest gas station. Two attendants were sitting outside, smoking and chatting on this summer's night. Ambling over the car a few moments later, one filled the tank while the other washed the car windows. Learning from the attendant where the nearest motel was, John paid him and said goodnight.

"Wait just a minute, sir," the attendant said, concern written on his face. "Where is the other fellow that was with you?"

"What fellow?" John asked.

"You know that young blond guy that was sitting next to you in the passenger seat. My partner and I both saw him as you drove in."

John knew that they had seen his angel, while he himself was only dimly and sporadically aware of his presence. But how could he explain this to the puzzled attendants.

"Oh, he's my traveling companion," said John. "Sometimes you can see him, and sometimes he's invisible."

"Oh, I see. Sure, mister, sure. You have a good night, now." The attendant uneasily backed away. But John just smiled. He knew who was in the seat beside him.

The Hebrew translation of the Bible states that there are twelve archangels, which corresponds to the number of tribes in Israel, indicating to the Jews, a royal number for government. However, canonized Scripture only names three archangels.

Let me explain canonized Scripture. In AD 397, at one of the councils of Nicaea, Roman Emperor Constantine and the church leaders reviewed the books of the Bible book-by-book. They decided which ones would be considered "official scripture" and which would not be included. This was not a decision of which books were good and which were not or which were true and which were not. Much of it was because they could not determine definite authorship, and therefore the validity of the books could not be authenticated. The books that were excluded as canon are called the Apocrypha and are still included in the Catholic version of the Bible. They are First and Second Maccabees, Judith, Tobit, Baruch, Sirach, and Wisdom, with additions to the books of Esther and Daniel. As far as I can determine, much of the content of the Apocrypha includes more history, more graphic portrayals of Israel's battles, etc.

Those books mention twelve archangels, but their names coincide with the names of God. For example, the angel Raphael was called the healing angel. The name of God Jehovah Rapha means the God who heals. That might be one reason God allowed the canonization of Scripture to include only three: Lucifer, Michael, and Gabriel, each of whom had charge of one-third of the angels of heaven. (We know that God shares His glory with no one—not even angels.)

Lucifer—His name means day star, light-bearer, or son of the morning. He is seen as the archangel who was leader of worship at the throne of God but, through pride and rebellion, fell from this position and one-third of the created angels chose to go with him. That's where the term fallen angels comes from.

How you are fallen from heaven, O Lucifer, son of the morning! How you are cut down to the ground, you who weakened the nations! For you have said in your heart: 'I will ascend into heaven, I will exalt my throne above the stars of God; I will also sit on the mount of the congregation on the farthest sides of the north; I will ascend above the heights of the clouds, I will be like the Most High' (Isaiah 14:12–14, NKJV).

Michael—His name means "who is like God." He is known as the chief prince of Israel, and his activities are always connected with warfare. There are only four times in Scripture when he is mentioned by name:

But I will tell you what is noted in the Scripture of Truth. No one upholds me against these, except Michael your prince. (Daniel 10:21, NKJV)

> At that time Michael shall stand up, the great prince who stands watch over the sons of your people; And there shall be a time of trouble, Such as never was since there was a nation, Even to that time. And at that time your people shall be delivered, everyone who is found written in the book. (Daniel 12:1, NKJV)

> Yet Michael the archangel, in contending with the devil, when he disputed about the body of Moses, dared not bring against him

a reviling accusation, but said, "The Lord rebuke you!" (Jude 1:9, NKJV)

And war broke out in heaven: Michael and his angels fought with the dragon; and the dragon and his angels fought, but they did not prevail, nor was a place found for them in heaven any longer. (Revelation 12:7–8, NKJV)

Gabriel—His name means "strength of God" and is generally accepted as the prophetic angel. He appeared to Daniel twice; Zachariah, John the Baptist's father; Mary, mother of Jesus; each time involving the Messianic revelation.

And I heard a man's voice between the banks of the Ulai, who called, and said, "Gabriel, make this man understand the vision." So he came near where I stood, and when he came I was afraid and fell on my face; but he said to me, "Understand, son of man, that the vision refers to the time of the end." Now, as he was speaking with me, I was in a deep sleep with my face to the ground; but he touched me, and stood me upright. And he said, "Look, I am making known to you what shall happen in the latter time of the indignation; for at the appointed time the end shall be." (Daniel 8:16–19, NKJV)

Therefore I was left alone when I saw this great vision, and no strength remained in me; for my vigor was turned to frailty in me, and

I retained no strength. Yet I heard the sound of his words; and while I heard the sound of his words I was in a deep sleep on my face, with my face to the ground. Suddenly, a hand touched me, which made me tremble on my knees and on the palms of my hands. And he said to me, "O Daniel, man greatly beloved, understand the words that I speak to you, and stand upright, for I have now been sent to you." While he was speaking this word to me, I stood trembling. (Daniel 10:8–11, NKJV)

And the angel answered and said to him, "I am Gabriel, who stands in the presence of God, and was sent to speak to you and bring you these glad tidings. Now in the sixth month the angel Gabriel was sent by God to a city of Galilee named Nazareth. (Luke 1:19, 26, NKJV)

Let's look at an angel encounter—"The Man who couldn't Be Killed":

Does God still send angels to protect His people as He did in Bible times? During the revolutionary period a few years ago in an African country that is still in political tur- moil, Mike Pearson served as pastor in a large district situated in the midst of the conflict. Three times a week he had to drive on the main highway where the traffic was sparse because of guerilla activity. Anybody who traveled that way was subject to being killed without cause. But Pastor Mike was faithful, and several times a week for about two years he drove along this road as he fulfilled his pastoral duties. Finally, the day came when the two sides declared a truce, and a shaky peace returned to that African country. One day Pastor Mike had some official business to conduct at a government office. After completing his errand, he came out of the building and was astonished to be greeted by a tall man in military dress, with bandoleers and grenades attached to his uniform. With a genial smile the soldier said to the Pastor Pearson, "Sir, I'd like to shake your hand." Pastor Mike is a friendly person, but this approach from such a stranger took him by surprise, so he answered, "Oh, why would you like to do that?" The soldier replied, "I'd like to shake the hand of the man we could not kill." Pastor Mike said, "Please explain." "Did you not travel on the main highway every Monday, Wednesday, and Thursday, and pass the midpoint at about 10:00 AM on those days in your Brown Toyota wagon?" "Yes," Pastor Mike answered, his curiosity rising. "Well, sir, on seven different occasions my fellow guards and I tried to kill you. Our plan was to shoot you as you drove by. Each time you came along, we had you clearly in sight from our post in the bush, but our guns refused to work when we pressed the triggers. As soon as you drove out of our range, our guns would work again. We carefully tested our AK 47s before and after your passing through that way, and they worked flawlessly. But they simply would not fire when we directed them at you. It could only have been a spirit or an angel that kept our guns from working. So that's why I'd like to shake your hand. God is on your side—or you are on his!"

If we wore that magical helmet, we would see and hear the angels (both elect and fallen) that roam the earth. Then we could perhaps understand better that there is a realm besides the physical one in which we live. If you're familiar with the series of movies of The Matrix, you can get a glimpse of there being two realms operating simultaneously, but even the moviemakers couldn't carry it off completely, and the analogy eventually falls apart. The difference is there is no magical helmet we can put on to see or hear the spiritual realm. That realm is there, whether we can see it or not. Much like the air we breathe, we can't see or hear it but we know it is there. What we accept by faith now—that there is a spiritual realm—we'll understand when we are in heaven and can see it all.

This angel encounter has been quoted from Angels on Assignment by Jennifer LeClaire:

We hiked up the Smokey Mountains far higher than my friend had told me we were headed. When we arrived, I was absolutely exhausted and wanted nothing more than to lie down and sleep. Of course, we had to set up the tent first. Since I knew nothing about putting up tents, I assisted as best I could, while my friend did most of the work. Of course, I figured it served her right since she had told me we were hiking a mile up the mountain, and it was surely ten miles or more by this point.

After the tent was set up, and the fire going, she informed me that we had to do one more thing before we settled in for the night—we had to hang the bag of food we carried up the mountain on that bear pole. That's right. I said bear pole. She explained with intensity, that if we left food out in the camp, hungry bears might invade the site and devour us, along with the trail mix.

My friend climbed the pole and hung the food at the top, and we finally closed the zipper on the tent. The nightmare of my day was over. When the sun rose, I felt like I had been in the wilderness for forty days, like Jesus.

After that stretch of time, the Bible says He was hungry. I was not only hungry, I was starving. I was going after that trail mix with a vengeance, or at least I tried to. I couldn't get it down from that bear pole.

I finally woke up my friend and politely suggested that she shimmy up that pole and retrieve said trail mix. She shimmied all right, but the knot she tied in the rope was so tight that she couldn't loosen it. She hemmed and hawed, while I just about went into travail. My flesh was crying out to the living God for sustenance, and it was looking like we would die on the mountain from starvation.

Long story short, my friend got hold of a camping knife and set out to cut the cord and set the trail mix free. It was a brilliant idea that was poorly executed. Instead of cutting the knot, she cut the bag. Trail mix went flying everywhere. In that moment, all I could think about was the bears coming down into our camp that night, seeking whom they might devour. Since I have more fat on my body tan she did, I was sure they would devour me first.

When night fell again, I was hungry, sore, tired, and scared, not to mention cold. It was freezing up in those mountains. I closed the zipper on the tent and lay my head down on the pillow in complete darkness. There was no moonlight nor a star in the sky. The only available light was the flickering flames on the fire in the center of our camp. I wondered, for a moment, if we had descended into hell.

Determined to make the best of it, I bundled myself up as tightly as I could and started counting sheep in my head. I heard the wrestling noise that I was sure originated from a bear outside the tent. I was certain it was a grizzly scavenging for the M&M's and nuts that were scattered to and fro. I'm not sure why I unzipped the tent door and poked my head outside. I don't know what I thought I would do if I saw a bear. I guess all the fasting had gone to my head.

What I saw was something darker than the blackest shade of black lunge toward me with vicious force. It scared me half to death, and I screamed. My body flew to the back of the tent, then I froze. Speechless. Finally, I managed to utter one word, "Bear!"

My friend didn't believe me. She decided to take a look for herself. I feared for her life, but was still frozen like an ice sculpture, so I watched in silent terror as she looked out the tent doors. I was sure she had sealed my fate. She stuck her head out for what seemed to be an eternity, when suddenly, I heard her exclaim, "Wow! Wow! Wow!"

Somewhat annoyed, I said, "What?"

Her only response, "Wow!"

Especially annoyed at this point, I replied, "What?"

She then informed me that three were giant angels—one on either side of the tent, with swords drawn. They were protecting us. They were angels of protection. God had opened her eyes and allowed her to see into the spiritual realm.

"He [Jesus] is the image of the invisible God, the firstborn over all creation. For by Him all things were created that are in heaven and that are on earth, visible and invisible, whether thrones or dominions or principalities or powers. All things were created through Him and for Him" (Colossians 1:15–16, NKJV).

These verses establish that the angels were created. They are not born and they cannot die. The creation of heaven and earth and the hosts thereof was completed in Genesis 2:1. God is not creating any more hosts, so the angels are a stationery number.

The angels operate in a hierarchy or order of the angels—that's what it means by "thrones, dominions, and principalities." Generally, we think of dominions and principalities as the evil or fallen angels, which is simply a counterfeit of God's kingdom. They can be either, but as these verses assure us, they are all still under the authority of God. He has allowed Satan to be in control of one-third of them, for the time being! We know how that will end!

> For in Him dwells all the fullness of the Godhead bodily; and you are complete in Him, who is the head of all principality and power. (Colossians 2:9–10, NKJV)
>
> Having disarmed principalities and powers, He made a public spectacle of them, triumphing over them in it. (Colossians 2:15, NKJV)

Christ has subdued our enemies by His death on the cross. A complete victory was achieved so that everything is in subjection to Him, and we have nothing to fear.

These next two passages remind us that we are not to fear the evil forces, that Jesus has already defeated them for us. Even when we feel we are being attacked by people (flesh and blood), we are not— it is the principalities, powers, rulers of the darkness of this age, and the spiritual hosts of wickedness or fallen angels that are attacking us—and again, Jesus has already defeated them all!

> For I am persuaded that neither death nor life, nor angels nor principalities nor powers, nor things present nor things to come, nor height nor depth, nor any other created thing, shall be able to separate us from the love of God which is in Christ Jesus our Lord. (Romans 8:38–39, NKJV)

> For we do not wrestle against flesh and blood, but against principalities, against powers, against the rulers of the darkness of this age, against spiritual hosts of wickedness in the heavenly places. (Ephesians 6:12, NKJV)

Another angel encounter: This is taken from "Angels Among Us—The Mystery of the Silver Dollar":

> Many years ago, about 1896 or 1897, a Christian man—who sold books and Bibles door to door—was walking down Market Street in San Francisco when a stranger stopped him and asked him why he didn't take his Bibles and books to a certain valley beyond Sacramento. The bookseller explained that he had never heard of the valley but would be glad to go when he could find the time. Then the stranger bade him goodbye and disappeared into the crowd.
> That's strange, the man thought to himself. I wonder why that man spoke to me.

How did he know my business? And why is he interested in that particular valley? I must try to go to that valley someday.

But the busy days and weeks slipped by, and the bookseller didn't go. Yet somehow, he couldn't forget what the stranger had said. Every now and then, a voice seemed to say to him, "Go to that valley."

At last, he felt he could wait no longer, so he set forth on his journey, taking his Bibles and other books with him. It was a long and tiring trip, for there were no autos in those days—part of the way he went by train, part on horseback, part on foot. Coming to a wide river, which had not been bridged, he wondered how he was going to get to the other side. As he waited at the water's edge, a man appeared in a rowboat and asked him if he wished to cross.

"I surely do," said the bookseller. "How much will you charge to take me over?"

"A dollar," replied the man with the boat, and the bookseller agreed.

On the way across, the bookseller opened his purse and brought out a silver dollar. It was the only one he had, and having time on his hands, he looked at it with more than usual care. It was a new coin, bright from the mint, but marred by a scratch on the eagle. The date on the coin was 1896. Arriving at the other side, he gave the boatman the silver dollar and bade him goodbye.

"Be sure you call on the first cottage you come to up the Valley," called the boatman as he turned the boat back to the River.

"I will," replied the bookseller, wondering what this might mean and what he would find there. Soon, he caught site of a cottage on a hillside, about a mile ahead, and walked briskly toward it. To his surprise, as he drew near the cottage, the front door opened, and three children started running down the hill to meet him.

"Did you bring her Bible?" they cried. "Did you bring our Bible?"

"Your Bible!" he exclaimed. "What do you mean? How do you know I have Bibles?"

"Oh," they cried, "we've all been praying for a Bible, but mother didn't have the money until today. But God sent her the money, so we felt sure he would send us the Bible soon."

By this time, they were at the house, and the mother came out—all flushed and excited—waiting to tell her story of what had happened.

"It's true," she said. "We have wanted a Bible for so long. We've been praying for one for many months, but somehow could never afford it. Then this afternoon, just after we prayed again, a voice seemed to say to me, "Go look out the front door." So I opened the door, and there, lying on the ground was a silver dollar. It seemed so wonderful that I felt sure that God had sent it, and that the

Bible would come so soon! Sir, does your Bible cost a dollar?"

"It does," he said. "Just a dollar."

Opening his case, he took out a Bible and handed it to the mother, who in return passed over to him the dollar she had found outside her front door that very afternoon. Now it was the bookseller's turn to be astonished.

Something about the silver dollar arrested his attention. It was newly minted but had a scratch on the eagle. And the date was 1896!

"Is something wrong with it?" the mother asked anxiously.

"No, no," he said. "But, madame, this is the identical dollar I gave to the boatman this very afternoon, less than half an hour ago!"

"What boatman?" she asked.

"The one at the ferry."

"But there is no ferry," she said. "Never has been as long as I've been here."

"But he just brought me across the river this very afternoon and told me to come to this cottage, and I gave him this very same silver dollar!"

So they talked on, going over it all again, and again marveling at how God works his wonders to perform.

The mystery of that silver dollar will perhaps never be solved, but both bookseller and that godly woman were convinced, as I am, that God was in this thing. He knew of the longing of that dear mother and her children to read His Word, and in His own wonderful way, He made it possible for them to receive it.

Let's close with another angel encounter:

On a bitterly cold day in January 1940, the car taking the Thomas family into London crept along the slippery road. In spite of constant movement, the windshield wipers could not keep the windshield clear of the snow that was falling thick and fast. Several times Pastor Thomas stopped the car and brushed the snow away. It was nearly dark when the family finally reached the railway station where they would take the train to the channel port of Folkestone. From there they would cross to France. The Thomas family had been home for a year from Kenya, in East Africa. During that fateful year, England and the empire had been plunged into the horrors of World War II. Although no bombs had yet fallen on Britain, many ships have been sunk in the waters surrounding the island. Because of the dangers of sea travel, the returning missionary family decided to go from France to Italy by train, then take a neutral ship to the East African port of Mombasa. Pastor and Mrs. Thomas and their four sons, ranging in age from three to thirteen, stood in the pitch blackness of the railway station, holding on to their suitcases, waiting for the train to come. The blackout was a serious matter in those days.

Civil authorities allowed no lights of any kind that might be seen from the air. The Thomas family heard, rather than saw, the coaches as they came to a stop in front of them. Tightly holding hands, the Thomas's boarded the train. Five hundred soldiers also got on. The doors slammed, the guard blew his whistle, and the train slowly pulled out of the station. How strange it felt to be riding along in the blackness of night! Conversations were going on all around them, but they could not see a single soul. Some of the soldiers were singing, some were cursing the war that had taken them from their homes and families. The minutes seemed to pass slowly as the rails clicked off the miles. Noses pressed against the window, the Thomas boys could see no friendly lights from farmhouses, nor from any of the villages they passed through. Even the ground, though covered with snow, could hardly be seen in the gloom. After what seemed like hours, the train began to slow down as it neared the Seacoast where the steamer was waiting to take them across the English Channel to France. Once again, Pastor Thomas reminded the boys to keep together, hold hands, and follow him. The train stopped, and hundreds of passengers poured onto the platform, the Thomas family among them. But where were they to go? An icy wind blew around them as they stood, bewildered. Suddenly, a tall man appeared out of the darkness. "Follow me," he said. "I know where you must go." Down the platform they followed his dimly visible form. He led them through a dark room into another that was well-lighted. For a few minutes all they could do was blink, the lights were so bright. Then they saw that this was the room where officials would examine their passports and luggage. They turned to look at their guide and saw that he was a tall man dressed in a heavy brown overcoat. The man led them to a table where an officer sat ready to inspect their passports. The officer asked whether Thomas was carrying any letters. During the war, military officials would very carefully inspect all letters leaving or entering England to see that they contained no important information that might help the enemy. Pastor Thomas admitted he was carrying some letters, and at the request of the officer he laid them on the table. The letters had been written by former missionaries in Kenya, and Pastor Thomas was carrying them to African people whom the missionaries had known. They were all written in Luo, an African language. This is very serious indeed because, no one in that room could read and translate the letters except Pastor Thomas himself, and the officer said that he could not accept Pastor Thomas' word. Just then the man in the brown coat spoke up. "These are missionaries," he said. "I know them, and I know that there is nothing in those letters dangerous to our country." "Very well," said the officer, "we will let them pass." Pastor Thomas looked at the stranger in surprise. Where had this man ever known the Thomas family? When had he read those letters? It was very mysterious. Pastor Thomas expressed his gratitude to him. The man did not answer, but proceeded to help them out of another difficulty. All over the room, customs officers were examining luggage. They were taking no chances. One of the officials came to Pastor Thomas and indicated that he wanted the luggage opened for inspection. Pastor Thomas had not expected this. Ordinarily, British subjects traveling in peacetime did not have their luggage inspected when going from one part of the empire to another. Knowing this, and not stopping to think of the difference wartime might make, he had strapped up his suitcases very thoroughly. The idea of opening them all now filled him with dismay. The man in the brown coat spoke up again. "These people are missionaries," he told the inspector. "I can vouch for their luggage. It does not contain anything prohibited by law." "Very well," said the officer briskly, and motioned them toward the door leading to the gangplank. A few minutes later the family had climbed aboard the ship. Dim lights burned here and there in the long corridors. One of the stewards came to meet them. He explained that the soldiers had taken almost all the beds on

board, but he did have a few places for the
ladies. He asked Mrs. Thomas to follow him.
Mrs. Thomas shook her head. "No, I am not
going to be separated from my husband. If
this ship is going to be torpedoed, the whole
family will go down together." Seeing she was
determined to stay with her husband and their
boys, the steward shrugged his shoulders and
went on his way. Almost instinctively, Pastor
Thomas turned to the man in the brown
coat. For the third time, he did not fail them.
"I know a place for you," he said. "It is not an
ideal place for a missionary family to sleep,
but at least you will not be disturbed." He led
them to the ship's bar. It was after midnight,
and the bar was closed. Around the room by
the walls were leather-padded benches. On
these, the family could lie down and rest for
the remainder of the night. Pastor Thomas
pushed the suitcases one by one under the
benches. Then he turned to thank the tall
stranger once more for all his kindness. But
he was gone! Stepping quickly into the hall,
Pastor Thomas looked up and down the passage. He could see no sign of the man. He
went to the top of the gangplank and asked
the officers there whether they had seen the
man in the brown overcoat. "There wasn't
anyone like that on the boat tonight," they
replied. If there had been we would have
seen him. Yet Pastor Thomas knew there had
been such a man, for he had talked with him.
But now he had disappeared into the night.

He returned to the bar room and reported to his family. "It must have been an angel," said Mrs. Thomas softly. (The Stranger in the Brown Overcoat)

Chapter 29

More about Angels

Angels were created by God and for God's pleasure. There was a specific number created. Only God knows how many He created, but they are innumerable. They are as myriad as the stars of light. Jesus spoke of legions of angels in Matthew 26:53, "Or do you think that I cannot now pray to My Father, and He will provide Me with more than twelve legions of angels?" (NKJV).

In military terms, a legion is ten thousand. So in this verse, Jesus is saying that He could have called one hundred twenty thousand angels to come to His rescue! It was His choice to die on that cross for you! (Do you have any doubt how much Jesus loves you?)

Angels are limited and dependent. They cannot do anything other than what God instructs and empowers them to do, but they were created with freewill—the ability to make their own choices.

Angelic beings are God's messengers, but they are not God's only messengers; Isaiah, Haggai, and other prophets are also messengers of God:

> I am the LORD, that is My name; And My glory I will not give to another, Nor My praise to carved images. Behold, the former things have come to pass, And new things I declare;

Before they spring forth I tell you of them.
(Isaiah 42:8–9, NKJV)

Who is blind but My servant, Or deaf as My messenger whom I send? Who is blind as he who is perfect, And blind as the LORD's servant? (Isaiah 42:19, NKJV)

Then Haggai, the LORD's messenger, spoke the LORD's message to the people, saying, "I am with you, says the LORD." (Haggai 1:13, NKJV)

John the Baptist was spoken of as the messenger of the Lord in Malachi 2:7, and Jesus Christ himself is spoken of as the Messenger of the covenant in Malachi 3:1.

For the lips of a priest should keep knowledge, And people should seek the law from his mouth; For he is the messenger of the LORD of hosts. (Malachi 2:7, NKJV)

"Behold, I send My messenger, And he will prepare the way before Me. And the Lord, whom you seek, Will suddenly come to His temple, Even the Messenger of the covenant, In whom you delight. Behold, He is coming," Says the LORD of hosts. (Malachi 3:1, NKJV)

Although these men were not angels, they, too were messengers.

The ministry and function of angels, is primarily twofold: worship and service (acting as a messenger is service).

> But to which of the angels has He ever said: "Sit at my right hand, till I make your enemies your footstool." Are they not all ministering spirits sent forth to minister for those who will inherit salvation? (Hebrews 1:13–14, NKJV)

> Bless the LORD, you His angels, who excel in strength, who do His word, Heeding the voice of His word. Bless the LORD, all you His hosts, you ministers of His, who do His pleasure. (Psalms 103:20–21, NKJV)

David was said to have written Psalm 103:20–21 while in the Spirit. The word bless means to praise or worship the Lord. David is telling the angels to praise the Lord, and he reminds them that they minister to do His pleasure.

Jesus said that the angels of God ascend and descend upon the Son of man, who is the fulfillment of Jacob's ladder. Thus, they minister to those who, like Jacob, are the heirs of salvation.

> And He said to him, "Most assuredly, I say to you, hereafter you shall see heaven open, and the angels of God ascending and descending upon the Son of Man." (John 1:51, NKJV)

> Now Jacob went out from Beersheba and went toward Haran. So he came to a certain place and stayed there all night, because the sun had set. And he took one of the stones

of that place and put it at his head, and he lay down in that place to sleep. Then he dreamed, and behold, a ladder was set up on the earth, and its top reached to heaven; and there the angels of God were ascending and descending on it. (Genesis 28:10–12, NKJV)

Then Jacob awoke from his sleep and said, "Surely the LORD is in this place, and I did not know it." And he was afraid and said, "How awesome is this place! This is none other than the house of God, and this is the gate of heaven!" Then Jacob rose early in the morning, and took the stone that he had put at his head, set it up as a pillar, and poured oil on top of it. And he called the name of that place Bethel; but the name of that city had been Luz previously. (Genesis 28:16–19, NKJV)

When Jacob comes to this place that he will name Bethel (after he has his famous dream of angels ascending and descending the ladder) he says, "How awesome is this place." For the Jews, building a ladder to heaven was presumptuous and could lead only to the kind of outcome that the builders of the Tower of Babel suffered.

For humans to make any power-based claims upon the spiritual world, means asking to be reduced to confusion, for our understanding of the world is provided by God. So it is then that Jacob's ladder was not a ladder built up to heaven from earth, but let down by God, from heaven to earth.

Billy Graham's book holds a treasure of information about angels. This is one story he shares:

A celebrated Philadelphia neurologist had gone to bed after an exceptionally tiring day. Suddenly he was awakened by someone knocking at his door. Opening it he found a little girl, poorly dressed and deeply upset. She told him her mother was very sick and asked him if he would please come with her. It was a bitterly cold snowy night, but though he was bone tired, the doctor dressed and followed the girl. As the Readers Digest reports the story, he found the mother desperately ill with pneumonia. After arranging for medical care he complemented the sick woman on the intelligence and persistence of her little daughter. The woman looked at him strangely and then said, "My daughter died a month ago." She added, her shoes and coat are in the clothes closet there. Amazed and perplexed, the doctor went to the closet and opened the door. There hung the very coat worn by the little girl who had brought him to tend to her mother. It was warm and dry and could not have possibly been out in the wintery night. Could the doctor have been called in the hour of desperate need by an angel who appeared is this woman's young daughter? Was this the work of God's angels on behalf of the sick woman? [22]

I am not about to say that the little girl that ran to the doctor for help was not an angel. God can do that. He is sovereign. I do not think God sent the little girl back to her mother. As much as we would be comforted thinking that our departed loved ones are angels, Scripture doesn't support that. They are "like the angels," in that they are residents of heaven with the angels (Matthew 22:30).

While all denominations believe in angels, both fallen and elect, not all believe in guardian angels. Roman Catholics and Church of Jesus Christ of Latter Day Saints (Mormons) believe in guardian angels, while most evangelical Christians do not. The term evangelical Christian has arrived on the media scene more and more prominently in recent times. My quick definition would be those who believe in a "born-again experience." They are distinct from "mainline Christians" by these five points:

1. Evangelicals point to a specific, personal conversion experience in which they are "born again" or "saved."

2. Evangelicals believe in the Bible as God's inspired Word to humankind, perfect in truth in the original language.

3. Evangelicals believe the work of Jesus Christ on the cross, through His death and resurrection, is the only source of forgiveness of sins, that salvation is through faith alone. They believe in doing "good works" in grateful response to that pardon, not as earning it.

4. Evangelical Christians are generally strongly motivated to share the gospel either one-on-one or through organized missions. Emphasis is placed on the Great Commission's call to share with the world, the Christian message of salva-

tion through Christ, and to be publicly baptized as a confession of faith.

5.   Most evangelicals, though not all, believe there will be a rapture in the end times, in which the church will be caught up with Christ either before, during, or after the Great Tribulation.

So with their faith in the Bible and Jesus, Evangelical Christians are similar to other Christian denominations, even bearing some of the same names. But their unique interpretations of Christianity make them a distinct worldwide movement, emphasizing the born-again experience, the infallibility of the Bible, salvation through faith in Jesus alone, the need to evangelize or spread the message, and the rapture of the Church in the end times.

Take heed that you do not despise one of these little ones, for I say to you that in heaven their angels always see the face of My Father who is in heaven (Matthew 18:10, NKJV).

The term guardian angel is not used anywhere in Scripture, although the position is described in the verse above, without specifically calling them that. I tend to disbelieve, however, that there is one guardian angel assigned to one person. If I am in trouble and God sends an angel to assist me, I can trust that that one angel is equipped to do whatever God wants to be done in my defense. I am also assured in the fact that God knows when it is necessary to send hundreds of His huge warring angels! However, God is not restricted, as far as I can see, to only assigning a certain angel, who has been tagged "Karen's guardian angel," to help me! It's humans who have dubbed them guardian angels, and in reality, that fits the task that God has given them, even if He didn't name them as such.

I take exception, however, to the drawings or images that have arrived on scene, lovely as they may be, that depict angels as beautiful women with long blond hair and huge wings. Although they are frequently spoken of as masculine and the names listed in Scripture are considered masculine by society, my research finds them to be genderless.

> Jesus answered and said to them, 'You are mistaken, not knowing the Scriptures nor the power of God. For in the resurrection they neither marry nor are given in marriage, but are like angels of God in heaven' (Matthew 22:29–30, NKJV).

In the days in which this passage was written, gender was very clearly defined. Men married and women were given in marriage, thus the differentiation in the verse. Angels are neither men (they neither marry) nor women (given in marriage), but are like the angels: they don't have male/female urges and desires to marry; they don't get hungry or thirsty. If we could see them, we would never catch them having a snack or in the middle of a nap!

> Psalm 91:11 says, "He shall give his angels charge over you to keep you in all your ways" (NKJV).

This perhaps is the most famous angel verse in the Bible. Partly because it comes from the ninety-first Psalm, which God's people have treasured for thousands of years, but also because Satan tried to make deceptive use of this verse when tempting

Jesus in the wilderness. He wanted the Savior to presume on God's protective care by jumping off the pinnacle of the temple, and thereby challenge his Father to give Him a safe landing.

Jesus would never allow Himself to be lured into such a dare. Not only did Satan misapply this verse when presenting it to Jesus as an excuse for recklessly endangering His life, but he also misquoted it. Satan omitted the words "in all your ways." God will keep us safe and secure when our ways harmonize with His ways.

Here's another angel encounter—"A Tall American Angel":

> Nick and Claudia Parks, a couple from Lincoln, Nebraska, signed up to serve as English teachers in the city in northern China. During their first tour of duty they taught at the provincial university and lived in a "Foreign Expert Building" where they could be kept under the ever watchful eyes of officialdom. Between university students in the daytime and government workers in the evening, Nick and Claudia taught about five hundred students each week. In this city of six million, there are fewer than fifty Americans at any one time. On Thanksgiving Day, 1993, Nick and Claudia were scheduled to start class with a new group of students. The classroom assigned for their use was cold and bleak. Sharp Siberian winds knifed through the loosely hinged windows to kill whatever warmth might accumulate from the people gathered in the room. Claudia tells the rest of her story in her own words: "In class, after enrolling and designating English

names to this diverse group, I decided to tell a story and test our students' listening comprehension. I told them the story of Pollyanna. They loved the idea of learning to play the "Glad Game" and to hunt for something to be glad about in every situation. We were glad that putting smiles on our faces, even here in China, could melt frozen hearts and smooth the way for us to make forever friends. 'Dear Jesus,' I prayed, 'please give us a sign that you are in this place and that you still care for us.' For the last half of our class we had "free talk." The students really liked that time. We divided the class into two sections.

I moved my group to the top part of the room. The students circled closely around each of us so we could talk and listen together. Below and to my left I could hear them asking Nick questions about his Christianity and if he really believed and accepted Jesus as his personal savior. I was proud of him for speaking boldly about his faith even though he recognized the danger. This is not America. Religious freedom is different here from the way it is in our homeland, but questions of the heart need to be answered. My group talked about other things. They asked me to sing for them, so I taught them "Over the River and through the Woods "and "Jesus Loves the Little Children." I thought of our new granddaughter and the Thanksgiving celebrations going on back home. Meanwhile, our three Communist guards looked on with stony faces, and I became concerned over our boldness in talking about Jesus. Suddenly, an older man dressed in the soldier's overcoat stepped very close to my face and asked, "Who is that tall American-looking boy that always goes everywhere with you when you go out?" There are no Americans anywhere in the area where we live. We could see Nick in our classroom, so I knew the boy he asked about wasn't my husband. I couldn't think of whom he might mean. And then the question went around the circle with others asking the same thing. In various levels of English and in sometimes difficult to understand accents, many of them asked, "Yes, who is that tall American boy that goes with you? We have seen him with you as you walk from class to class and when you are headed out the campus gates to go shopping." I had no answer. Any boys who go with us in China look very Chinese, and most of them are short! I came home from class still wondering, but as I awoke this morning the answer came to me. Many years ago when I was just a little girl I remember my Auntie Ruth teaching me the good news of Psalm 34:7. I prayed, "Oh, thank you, God, for the best Thanksgiving ever!" I'm not sure just what a guardian angel looks like, but I feel convinced that mine looks like a tall American boy and has been seen by many Chinese eyes. And I believe that God provided a tall American boy to hold the door open for the entrance of gospel light in China.

Angels are immortal. Because they were created and not born, angels are not subject to physical death, as man is. They do, however, take on human form or appearance. Angels are a not a race but a created company of beings, comparable to a military company. Angels were created before man, and Hebrews 2:6–9 tells us that man was created a little lower than the angels.

> But one testified in a certain place, saying: "What is man that You are mindful of him, or that You take care of him? You have made him a little lower than the angels. You have crowned Him with glory and honor, and set Him over the works of Your hands. You have put all things in subjection under His feet." For in that He put all in subjection under him, He left nothing that is not put under him. But now we do not yet see all things put under him. But we see Jesus, who was made a little lower than the angels, for the suffering of death crowned with glory and honor, that He, by the grace of God, might taste death for everyone. (Hebrews 2:6–9, NKJV)

Yes, that verse does say all men were created a little lower than the angels—that includes Jesus, However, read on.

> God, who at various times and in various ways spoke in time past to the fathers by the prophets, has in these last days spoken to us by His Son, whom He has appointed heir of all things, through whom also He made the worlds; who being the brightness of His glory and the express image of His person,

and upholding all things by the word of His power, when He had by Himself purged our sins, sat down at the right hand of the Majesty on high, having become so much better than the angels, as He has by inheritance obtained a more excellent name than they. (Hebrews 1:1–4, NKJV)

Angels are superior to man but inferior to God. The very fact that some angels sinned shows they all have the power of choice and could either choose to do God's will or to follow self-will.

Angels have personalities. Just as God is a person having all the attributes and qualities of personality, so are the angels. They are not mere good and evil influences. They are real beings, with real personalities, having intelligence and will. Though they have their own character, they are not glorified human beings.

The Spirit Himself bears witness with our spirit that we are children of God, and if children, then heirs—heirs of God and joint heirs with Christ, if indeed we suffer with Him, that we may also be glorified together. (Romans 8:16–17, NKJV).

These verses confirm that we—redeemed sinners, joint heirs with Christ—will be glorified. That means these bodies will be changed when we get to heaven—we will have glorified bodies. It does not mean that we will become angels. Again, I refer to Matthew 22:29–30: "Jesus answered and said to them, 'You are mistaken, not knowing the Scriptures nor the power of God. For in the resurrection they neither marry nor are given in marriage, but are like angels of God in heaven'" (NKJV).

Jesus is talking about the brothers who died, leaving the widow to the next brother, and so on. They asked who she would be married to in heaven. And Jesus's answer included that the deceased men would only be "like the angels."

An angel encounter that Dr. Billy Graham shared in his book entitled Angels: [21]

> The Reverend John G Paton, pioneer missionary in the New Hebrides Islands told a thrilling story involving the protective care of angels. Hostile natives surrounded his mission headquarters one night intent on burning the Patons out and killing them. John Paton and his wife prayed all during that terror-filled night that God would deliver them. When daylight came they were amazed to see that, unaccountably, the attackers had left. They thanked God for delivering them. A year later the chief of the tribe was converted to Jesus Christ and Mr. Paton, remembering what had happened, asked the chief what had kept him and his men from burning down the house and killing them. The chief replied in surprise, who were all those men you had with you there? The missionary answered there were no men, just my wife and I. The chief argued that they had seen many men standing guard, hundreds of big men in shining garments and broad swords in their hands. They seemed to circle the mission station so that the natives were afraid to attack. Only then did Mr. Paton realize that God had sent his angels to protect them. The chief agreed there could be no other explanation. Could it be that God had sent a Legion

of angels to protect His servants, whose lives were in danger?

Angels are the most singularly potent and overwhelming representatives of the world that we don't see—the spiritual half of the world, that so many today pretend doesn't exist at all. Angels are created beings that often appear to people in trouble, people to whom life as they know it is about to become too much for them to cope with successfully. Angels, by definition (messengers) manifest when God assigns or commands them to. Scripture does not give me the authority to give orders to angels. It does, however, give me the authority to use the name of Jesus Christ! So in His name, I can call on them. (Remember, Satan is a fallen angel. This means, in the name of Jesus, I can command him to flee!)

If you remember earlier, I compared the hierarchy of angels to a military unit. Satan has copied Jesus's order of the angels. I mentioned that dominions and principalities usually refer to the evil or fallen angels. It is simply a counterfeit of God's kingdom. The reason I return to this is because we need to remember that we have an enemy and that enemy has his own army.

Today, more and more attention is being brought to the evil or demonic side of the spiritual realm, in very subtle ways. One of the TV shows I loved to watch as a teenager was Bewitched. It was just a subtle transition to influence me (and millions of others like me) to accept witchcraft. It was done as a comedy, but there is nothing funny about the magic that was done by warlocks and witches. Harry Potter and The Good Witch are examples of the entertainment industry presenting to the public whatever it takes to desensitize us to the evil influences of the spiritual realm.

As incongruous as it sounds, the first war ever fought was by angels in heaven. John writes in the book of Revelation, "War broke out in heaven: Michael and his angels fought against the dragon; and the dragon and his angels fought, but they did not prevail, nor was a place found for them in heaven any longer" (Revelation 12:7–8, NKJV).

How did heaven become the first battlefield? It all began with Lucifer, the highest-ranking angel who defected because of pride over his vast abilities and power. Ezekiel 28:6–8 and Isaiah 14:12–14 tell the story. Egotism, hunger for power, jealousy over his subordination to the Godhead and especially to Jesus, the cocreator of the universe with His Father and the Holy Spirit—all these factors combined to promote rebellion in Lucifer's heart.

It did not have to be that way. Physically and mentally, Lucifer was created to be perfect. God gave him a flawless education. Heaven's laws were reasonable then as they are now. Living conditions were perfect—no poverty, sickness, disease, iniquity, harsh rule, unreasonable requirements, or arbitrary exercise of power on God's part. One thing God would not do was to create His intelligent beings to give Him preprogrammed loyalty and praise. Instead, he endowed angels with powers to grow mentally and morally and to exercise freedom of choice. True, all were created to harmonize naturally with God's character and will, but this desire to obey was to be sustained voluntarily by each being, rather than maintained by coercion. Plainly put, any being at any time could choose to disobey God and strike out on a path of independence. Never would God give any provocation to that, not even by being uncommunicative about the goodness of His ways and laws. God has always been generously self-revealing, always willing to communicate with His creatures.

When Lucifer rebelled, God did not leave him or the angels in the dark about the terrible consequences that would follow his departure from the right path. Lucifer had launched an elaborate campaign to misrepresent God to the angels. One can readily deduce from his brash ranting recorded in Isaiah 14 that his complaints included allegations of tyranny on God's part, unfairness in His law, and suppression of their personal liberty. The fact that he was able to ensnare of third of the angels, all of whom knew what God is really like, should warn us that Satan's powers of deception are very great indeed. It should also convince us that we need to fully trust God and submit to His grace and authority if we want to be rescued from the horrible effects of sin and rebellion!

Scripture tells us that God does not change (Hebrews 13:8). Therefore, we can safely assume that prior to open warfare in heaven, God did everything within the reach of His infinite love and wisdom to call Lucifer back from his subversive alienation. I believe the loyal angels, undoubtedly, did all they could to dissuade Lucifer and his angel followers from their growing moral madness. Each angel was free to choose masters—Lucifer or Christ. As Lucifer's defiance mounted, his charges grew more strident and desperate. He forced a showdown. Then war erupted in heaven.

The arch-rebel and his followers were cast out. You might wonder why God didn't simply destroy Satan, once his hostility to truth and love became so apparent. We must remember that sin was a new factor in the universe. Not even the loyal angels could fully conceive of its final effects. And since God's trustworthiness had been called into question by Satan, I believe the Lord deemed it wisest to allow this adversary to act out his plans in full so that everyone—human and angel alike—could trace the course of sin from its seemingly innocuous beginnings to its truly devastating end. That is why Paul identifies this planet as the theater of the universe, viewed by angels and men (1 Corinthians 4:9). By seeing Satan fully exhibit his character and purposes, all could see beyond question that no justification can be found for disobedience to God and no good results can come of it. Thus, the universe is rendered sin-proof.

Angels are known by various titles. Just as various titles and names of God are used to declare various aspects of God's nature, being, and ministry, so are the designations by which the angels are known:

> Watchers or watchmen. Angels behold this earth as a theatre, they are ever awake.
>
> I saw in the visions of my head while on my bed, and there was a watcher, a holy one, coming down from heaven. (Daniel 4:13, NKJV)
>
> I have set watchmen on your walls, O Jerusalem; They shall never hold their peace day or night. You who make mention of the LORD, do not keep silent. (Isaiah 62:6, NKJV)
>
> Ministering spirits. They are the servants of the creator. Angels, though intermediaries,

are not mediators. There is only one mediator between God and man, the man Christ Jesus.

But to which of the angels has He ever said: "Sit at my right hand, till I make your enemies your footstool?" Are they not all ministering spirits sent forth to minister for those who will inherit salvation? (Hebrews 1:13–14, NKJV)

Bless the LORD, all you His hosts, you ministers of His, who do His pleasure. (Psalm 103:21, NKJV)

Flames of fire. Significant of the holiness of God upon them. Fire is the symbol of divine holiness and burning against sin. "Who makes His angels spirits, His ministers a flame of fire" (Psalms 104:4, NKJV).

The elect. The angels who refused to follow Satan are now the elect angels

For if God did not spare the angels who sinned, but cast them down to hell and delivered them into chains of darkness, to be reserved for judgment. (2 Peter 2:4, NKJV)

And the angels who did not keep their proper domain, but left their own abode, He has reserved in everlasting chains under darkness for the judgment of the great day. (Jude 1:6, NKJV)

Sons of God. It is generally accepted that it is angels that are referred to as the "sons of God" in Job 1:6, "Now there was a day when the sons of God came to present themselves before the LORD, and Satan also came among them" (NKJV).

Morning stars. Angels are as stars of light. Lucifer was the day star before his fall. He became a falling angel when he sinned against God.

When the morning stars sang together, and all the sons of God shouted for joy? (Job 38:7, NKJV)

How you are fallen from heaven, O Lucifer, son of the morning! How you are cut down to the ground, you who weakened the nations! (Isaiah 14:12, NKJV)

Princes. Angels are designated as princes over the various nations. Satan is spoken of as being a prince over the world system and also as having his princes over the nation. They are also called principalities.

But the prince of the kingdom of Persia withstood me twenty-one days; and behold, Michael, one of the chief princes, came to help me, for I had been left alone there with the kings of Persia. (Daniel 10:13, NKJV)

Then he said, "Do you know why I have come to you? And now I must return to fight with the prince of Persia; and when I have gone forth, indeed the prince of Greece will come. But I will tell you what is noted in the Scripture of Truth. No one upholds me against these, except Michael your prince." (Daniel 10:20–21, NKJV)

At that time Michael shall stand up, The great prince who stands watch over the sons of your people; And there shall be a time of trouble, Such as never was since there was a nation, Even to that time. And at that time your people shall be delivered, Every one who is found written in the book. (Daniel 12:1, NKJV)

Thrones, dominions, and powers. Thrones are symbolic of the rulership of certain angels in God's order. Dominions speak of lordships or spheres of influence as under the Lord of Angels, Jesus Christ. Powers speak of authorities or administration, which God has given to various angels (Colossians 1:16 [above]).

Look again at Colossians 2:15: "Having disarmed principalities and powers, He made a public spectacle of them, triumphing over them in it."

No matter what "titles" you come across, especially for the fallen angels (or demons), we remember our assurance from these verses in Romans: "For I am persuaded that neither death nor life, nor angels nor principalities nor powers, nor things present nor things to come, nor height nor depth, nor any other created thing, shall be able to separate us from the love of God which is in Christ Jesus our Lord" (Romans 8:38–39, NKJV)

Chapter 30

Even More About Angels

Both the Old and New Testaments give abundant evidence of angelic appearances in ministry to the saints. The Old Testament is replete with angelic ministrations to the heirs of salvation, as well as ministering the judgment of God upon the willful and rebellious who refuse to respond to God's dealings. These are just some examples:

1. An angel ministered to Hagar and Ishmael.

   And He said, "Hagar, Sarai's maid, where have you come from, and where are you going?" She said, "I am fleeing from the presence of my mistress Sarai." The Angel of the LORD said to her, "Return to your mistress, and submit yourself under her hand." Then the Angel of the LORD said to her, "I will multiply your descendants exceedingly, so that they shall not be counted for multitude." (Genesis 16:8–10)

   And God heard the voice of the lad. Then the angel of God called to Hagar out of heaven, and said to her, "What ails you, Hagar? Fear not, for God has heard the voice of the lad where he is." (Genesis 21:17, NKJV)

2.   Three angels visited Abraham and Sarah.

Then the LORD appeared to him [Abraham] by the terebinth trees of Mamre, as he was sitting in the tent door in the heat of the day. So he lifted his eyes and looked, and behold, three men were standing by him; and when he saw them, he ran from the tent door to meet them, and bowed himself to the ground, and said, "My Lord, if I have now found favor in Your sight, do not pass on by Your servant. Please let a little water be brought, and wash your feet, and rest yourselves under the tree. And I will bring a morsel of bread, that you may refresh your hearts. After that you may pass by, inasmuch as you have come to your servant." They said, "Do as you have said." So Abraham hurried into the tent to Sarah and said, "Quickly, make ready three measures of fine meal; knead it and make cakes." And Abraham ran to the herd, took a tender and good calf, gave it to a young man, and he hastened to prepare it. So he took butter and milk and the calf which he had prepared, and set it before them; and he stood by them under the tree as they ate. Then they said to him, "Where is Sarah your wife?" So he said, "Here, in the tent." (Genesis 18:1–9, NKJV)

3.   Two angels rescued Lot out of Sodom from the fire and brimstone.

Now the two angels came to Sodom in the evening, and Lot was sitting in the gate of Sodom. When Lot saw them, he rose to meet them, and he bowed himself with his face toward the ground. And he said, "Here now, my lords, please turn in to your servant's house and spend the night, and wash your feet; then you may rise early and go on your way." And they said, "No, but we will spend the night in the open square." But he insisted strongly; so they turned in to him and entered his house. Then he made them a feast, and baked unleavened bread, and they ate. Now before they lay down, the men of the city, the men of Sodom, both old and young, all the people from every quarter, surrounded the house. And they called to Lot and said to him, "Where are the men who came to you tonight? Bring them out to us that we may know them carnally." So Lot went out to them through the doorway, shut the door behind him, and said, "Please, my brethren, do not do so wickedly! See now, I have two daughters who have not known a man; please, let me bring them out to you, and you may do to them as you wish; only do nothing to these men, since this is the reason they have come under the shadow of my roof." And they said, "Stand back!" Then they said, "This one came in to stay here, and he keeps acting as a judge; now we will deal worse with you than with them." So they pressed hard against the man Lot, and came near to break down the door. But the men reached out their hands and pulled Lot into the house with them, and shut the door. And they struck the men who were at the doorway of the house with blindness, both small and great, so that they became weary trying to find the door. Then the men said to Lot,

"Have you anyone else here? Son-in-law, your sons, your daughters, and whomever you have in the city—take them out of this place! For we will destroy this place, because the outcry against them has grown great before the face of the LORD, and the LORD has sent us to destroy it." So Lot went out and spoke to his sons-in-law, who had married his daughters, and said, "Get up, get out of this place; for the LORD will destroy this city!" But to his sons-in-law he seemed to be joking. When the morning dawned, the angels urged Lot to hurry, saying, "Arise, take your wife and your two daughters who are here, lest you be consumed in the punishment of the city." And while he lingered, the men took hold of his hand, his wife's hand, and the hands of his two daughters, the LORD being merciful to him, and they brought him out and set him outside the city. So it came to pass, when they had brought them outside, that he said, "Escape for your life! Do not look behind you nor stay anywhere in the plain. Escape to the mountains, lest you be destroyed." Then Lot said to them, "Please, no, my lords! Indeed now, your servant has found favor in your sight, and you have increased your mercy which you have shown me by saving my life; but I cannot escape to the mountains, lest some evil overtake me and I die. See now, this city is near enough to flee to, and it is a little one; please let me escape there [is it not a little one?] and my soul shall live." And he said to him, "See, I have favored you concerning this thing also, in that I will not overthrow this city for which you have spoken. Hurry, escape there. For I cannot do anything until you arrive there." Therefore the name of the city was called Zoar. The sun had risen upon the earth when Lot entered Zoar. Then the LORD rained brimstone and fire on Sodom and Gomorrah, from the LORD out of the heavens. (Genesis 19:1–24, NKJV)

4. The Angel of the Lord called to Abraham to spare Isaac, his only begotten son, and offer a ram in his stead.

But the Angel of the LORD called to him from heaven and said, "Abraham, Abraham!" So he said, "Here I am." And He said, "Do not lay your hand on the lad, or do anything to him; for now I know that you fear God, since you have not withheld your son, your only son, from Me." Then Abraham lifted his eyes and looked, and there behind him was a ram caught in a thicket by its horns. So Abraham went and took the ram, and offered it up for a burnt offering instead of his son. And Abraham called the name of the place, The-LORD-Will-Provide; as it is said to this day, "In the Mount of the LORD it shall be provided." Then the Angel of the LORD called to Abraham a second time out of heaven. (Genesis 22:11–15, NKJV)

5. Jacob experienced the ministry of angels throughout his life. Genesis chapters 28, 31, 32, 48.

6.   The angel of the covenant wrestled with Jacob and changed his name to Israel.

Then Jacob was left alone; and a Man wrestled with him until the breaking of day. Now when He saw that He did not prevail against him, He touched the socket of his hip; and the socket of Jacob's hip was out of joint as He wrestled with him. And He said, "Let Me go, for the day breaks." But he said, "I will not let You go unless You bless me!" So He said to him, "What is your name?" He said, "Jacob." And He said, "Your name shall no longer be called Jacob, but Israel; for you have struggled with God and with men, and have prevailed." Then Jacob asked, saying, "Tell me Your name, I pray." And He said, "Why is it that you ask about My name?" And He blessed him there. So Jacob called the name of the place Peniel: "For I have seen God face to face, and my life is preserved." Just as he crossed over Penuel the sun rose on him, and he limped on his hip. Therefore to this day the children of Israel do not eat the muscle that shrank, which is on the hip socket, because He touched the socket of Jacob's hip in the muscle that shrank. (Genesis 32:24)

Yes, he struggled with the Angel and prevailed; He wept, and sought favor from Him. He found Him in Bethel, And there He spoke to us. (Hosiah 12:4, NKJV)

The angel of the covenant is another name for the angel of the Lord. Both are theophoric appearances of Jesus.

7. Moses received the revelation of the name of God from the angel of the Lord in the burning bush.

And the Angel of the LORD appeared to him in a flame of fire from the midst of a bush. So he looked, and behold, the bush was burning with fire, but the bush was not consumed. Then Moses said, "I will now turn aside and see this great sight, why the bush does not burn." So when the LORD saw that he turned aside to look, God called to him from the midst of the bush and said, "Moses, Moses!" And he said, "Here I am." Then He said, "Do not draw near this place. Take your sandals off your feet, for the place where you stand is holy ground." (Exodus 3:2–5, NKJV)

8. Angels were involved in the giving of the law to Moses at Sinai.

This Moses whom they rejected, saying, "who made you a ruler and a judge?" is the one God sent to be a ruler and a deliverer by the hand of the Angel who appeared to him in the bush. (Acts 7:35)

This is he who was in the congregation in the wilderness with the Angel who spoke to him on Mount Sinai, and with our fathers, the one who received the living oracles to give to us. (Acts 7:38)

Which of the prophets did your fathers not persecute? And they killed those who foretold the coming of the Just One, of whom you now have become the betrayers and murderers. (Act 7:52)

Who have received the law by the direction of angels and have not kept it. (Acts 7:53)

What purpose then does the law serve? It was added because of transgressions, till the Seed should come to whom the promise was made; and it was appointed through angels by the hand of a mediator. (Galatians 3:19)

For if the word spoken through angels proved steadfast, and every transgression and disobedience received a just reward. (Hebrews 2:2, NKJV)

9. The angel of His presence (again, another name for the angel of the Lord) went before Israel to lead and guide them in the pillars of cloud and of fire.

And the Angel of God, who went before the camp of Israel, moved and went behind them; and the pillar of cloud went from before them and stood behind them. So it came between the camp of the Egyptians and the camp of Israel. Thus it was a cloud and darkness to the one, and it gave light by night to the other, so that the one did not come near the other all that night. Then Moses stretched out his hand over the sea; and the LORD caused the sea to go back by a strong east wind all that night, and made the sea into dry land, and the waters were divided. So the children of Israel went into the midst of the sea on the dry ground, and the waters were a wall to them on their right hand and on their left. And the Egyptians pursued and went after them into the midst of the sea, all Pharaoh's horses, his chariots, and his horsemen. Now it came to pass, in the morning watch, that the LORD looked down upon the army of the Egyptians through the pillar of fire and cloud, and He troubled the army of the Egyptians. (Exodus 14:19–24, NKJV)

10.   An angel reproved Israel for their compromise and idolatry among the Canaanites.

Then the Angel of the LORD came up from Gilgal to Bochim, and said: "I led you up from Egypt and brought you to the land of which I swore to your fathers; and I said, 'I will never break My covenant with you. And you shall make no covenant with the inhabitants of this land; you shall tear down their altars.' But you have not obeyed My voice. Why have you done this? Therefore I also said, 'I will not drive them out before you; but they shall be thorns in your side, and their gods shall be a snare to you.'" So it was, when the Angel of the LORD spoke these words to all the children of Israel, that the people lifted up their voices and wept. (Judge 2:1–4, NKJV)

11.   An angel uttered a curse on those who did not help the Lord in the battle against Israel's enemies.

'Curse Meroz,' said the angel of the LORD, 'Curse its inhabitants bitterly, Because they did not come to the help of the LORD, To the help of the LORD against the mighty'(Judges 5:23, NKJV).

12. The angel of the Lord encamps around them that fear Him.

The angel of the LORD encamps all around those who fear Him, And delivers them. These verses are together here, to make a point: The Lord curses those who did not help Israel in battle. But on the flip side, He encamps around all who revere Him (Psalms 34:7, NKJV).

The New Testament also contains many references to angelic ministry. These are seen in the life of the Lord Jesus in the Gospels, then in the early church in the book of Acts and the epistles, and then it consummates in the book of Revelation.

In the ministry of the Lord Jesus:

1. Angels ministered to Jesus in His birth. An angel spoke to Mary in Luke 1:26–38:

Now in the sixth month the angel Gabriel was sent by God to a city of Galilee named Nazareth, to a virgin betrothed to a man whose name was Joseph, of the house of David. The virgin's name was Mary. And having come in, the angel said to her, "Rejoice, highly favored one, the Lord is with you; blessed are you among women!" But when she saw him, she was troubled at his saying, and considered what manner of greeting this was. Then the angel said to her, "Do not be afraid, Mary, for you have found favor with God. And behold, you will conceive in your womb and bring forth a Son, and shall call His name JESUS. He will be great, and will be called the Son of the Highest; and the Lord God will give Him the throne of His father David.

And He will reign over the house of Jacob forever, and of His kingdom there will be no end."
Then Mary said to the angel, "How can this
be, since I do not know a man?" And the angel
answered and said to her, "The Holy Spirit will
come upon you, and the power of the Highest
will overshadow you; therefore, also, that Holy
One who is to be born will be called the Son
of God. Now indeed, Elizabeth your relative has
also conceived a son in her old age; and this is
now the sixth month for her who was called barren. For with God nothing will be impossible."
Then Mary said, "Behold the maidservant of the
Lord! Let it be to me according to your word."
And the angel departed from her.

Also in Matthew 1:20–23:

But while he thought about these things,
behold, an angel of the Lord appeared to him in
a dream, saying, "Joseph, son of David, do not
be afraid to take to you Mary your wife, for that
which is conceived in her is of the Holy Spirit.
And she will bring forth a Son, and you shall
call His name JESUS, for He will save His people from their sins." So all this was done that it
might be fulfilled which was spoken by the Lord
through the prophet, saying: "Behold, the virgin
shall be with child and bear a Son, and they shall
call His name Immanuel," which is translated,
"God with us."

And to Joseph in Matthew 1:20–21 above,
and in Matthew 2:13, "Now when they had
departed, behold, an angel of the Lord appeared
to Joseph in a dream, saying, 'Arise, take the

young Child and His mother, flee to Egypt, and stay there until I bring you word; for Herod will seek the young Child to destroy Him'" (NKJV).

In a recent teaching of this example, a fire drill sounded. A staff member popped her head in the door and told us it was just a drill and we needn't evacuate the building. Moments later we read Matthew 2:19, "Now when Herod was dead, behold, an angel of the Lord appeared in a dream to Joseph in Egypt." That's when she the staff member stepped back in and said it was all clear. The Holy Spirit gave us the perfect example!

2. An angel spoke to the shepherds in Luke 2:13, "And suddenly there was with the angel a multitude of the heavenly host praising God and saying: 'Glory to God in the highest, And on earth peace, goodwill toward men!' So it was, when the angels had gone away from them into heaven, that the shepherds said to one another, 'Let us now go to Bethlehem and see this thing that has come to pass, which the Lord has made known to us'"' (NKJV).

3. Angels ministered to Christ after his temptation in Matthew 4:11, "Then the devil left Him, and behold, angels came and ministered to Him." And in Matthew 1:13, "And He was there in the wilderness forty days, tempted by Satan, and was with the wild beasts; and the angels ministered to Him" (NKJV).

4. Angels ascended and descended upon the Son of Man in ministry. "And He said to him, 'Most assuredly, I say to you, hereafter you shall see heaven open, and the angels of God ascending and descending upon the Son of Man'" (John 1:51, NKJV).

5. An angel strengthened Christ inwardly in Gethsemane. Twelve legions of angels were available if he requested help. "And He was withdrawn from them about a stone's throw, and He knelt down and prayed, saying, 'Father, if it is Your will, take this cup away from Me; nevertheless not My will, but Yours, be done.' Then an angel appeared to Him from heaven, strengthening Him" (Luke 22:41–43). And in Matthew 26:53, "Or do you think that I cannot now pray to My Father, and He will provide Me with more than twelve legions of angels?" (Luke 22:41–43, NKJV).

6. Two angels were seen in his empty tomb after the resurrection. An angel rolled the stone away to let the disciples into the tomb.

   And behold, there was a great earthquake; for an angel of the Lord descended from heaven, and came and rolled back the stone from the door, and sat on it. His countenance was like lightning, and his clothing as white as snow. And the guards shook for fear of him, and became like dead men. But the angel answered and said to the women, "Do not be afraid, for I know that you seek Jesus who was crucified. He is not here; for He is risen, as He said. Come, see the place where the Lord lay. And go quickly and tell His disciples that He is risen from the dead, and indeed He is going before you into Galilee; there you will see Him. Behold, I have told you." (Matthew 28:2–7, NKJV)

7. The angels were also outside His empty tomb. "And she saw two angels in white sitting, one at the head and the other at the feet, where the body of Jesus had lain" (John 20:12, NKJV)

Angels will attend Christ in his second coming.

They will gather the elect and separate the wicked from them.

For the Son of Man will come in the glory of His Father with His angels, and then He will reward each according to his works (Matthew 16:27).

When the Son of Man comes in His glory, and all the holy angels with Him, then He will sit on the throne of His glory. (Matthew 25:31)

The Son of Man will send out His angels, and they will gather out of His kingdom all things that offend, and those who practice lawlessness, and will cast them into the furnace of fire. There will be wailing and gnashing of teeth. Then the righteous will shine forth as the sun in the kingdom of their Father. He who has ears to hear, let him hear! (Matthew 13:41–43)

For the Lord Himself will descend from heaven with a shout, with the voice of an archangel, and with the trumpet of God. And the dead in Christ will rise first. (1 Thessalonians 4:16)

And to give you who are troubled rest with us when the Lord Jesus is revealed from heaven with His mighty angels. In flaming fire taking vengeance on those who do not know God, and on those who do not obey the gospel of our Lord Jesus Christ. (2 Thessalonians 1:7–8, NKJV)

God's angels were instrumental in the early church:

1. An angel opened the prison doors to release the apostles to witness.

   But at night an angel of the Lord opened the prison doors and brought them out, and said (Acts 5:19, NKJV).

2. Phillip was sent by an angel to the desert to witness to the Ethiopian.

   Now an angel of the Lord spoke to Philip, saying, 'Arise and go toward the south along the road which goes down from Jerusalem to Gaza.' This is desert (Acts 8:26, NKJV).

3. An angel instructed Cornelius to send for Peter to hear the words of the gospel.

   Send therefore to Joppa and call Simon here, whose surname is Peter. He is lodging in the house of Simon, a tanner, by the sea. When he comes, he will speak to you. So I sent to you immediately, and you have done well to come. Now therefore, we are all present before God,

NO STRINGS ATTACHED

to hear all the things commanded you by God. (Acts 10:32–33, NKJV).

4.   An angel rescued Peter out of prison the night before he was to be slain.

Peter was therefore kept in prison, but constant prayer was offered to God for him by the church. And when Herod was about to bring him out, that night Peter was sleeping, bound with two chains between two soldiers; and the guards before the door were keeping the prison. Now behold, an angel of the Lord stood by him, and a light shone in the prison; and he struck Peter on the side and raised him up, saying, "Arise quickly!" And his chains fell off his hands. Then the angel said to him, "Gird yourself and tie on your sandals"; and so he did. And he said to him, "Put on your garment and follow me." So he went out and followed him, and did not know that what was done by the angel was real, but thought he was seeing a vision. When they were past the first and the second guard posts, they came to the iron gate that leads to the city, which opened to them of its own accord; and they went out and went down one street, and immediately the angel departed from him. And when Peter had come to himself, he said, "Now I know for certain that the Lord has sent His angel, and has delivered me from the hand of Herod and from all the expectation of the Jewish people." (Acts 12:5–11, NKJV)

5.   Herod was smitten dead by an angel for his pride.

    And he called for two centurions, saying, 'Prepare two hundred soldiers, seventy horsemen, and two hundred spearmen to go to Caesarea at the third hour of the night' (Acts 23:23, NKJV).

6.   Paul experienced the presence of the angel in the storm on his way to Rome.

    For there stood by me this night an angel of the God to whom I belong and whom I serve (Acts 27:23, NKJV).

7.   Angelic spirits are round about the church as believers gather to worship Christ.

    But you have come to Mount Zion and to the city of the living God, the heavenly Jerusalem, to an innumerable company of angels, to the general assembly and church of the firstborn who are registered in heaven, to God the Judge of all, to the spirits of just men made perfect, to Jesus the Mediator of the new covenant, and to the blood of sprinkling that speaks better things than that of Abel. (Hebrews 12:22–23)

    For this reason the woman ought to have a symbol of authority on her head, because of the angels. (1 Corinthians 11:10)

    For I think that God has displayed us, the apostles, last, as men condemned to death; for we have been made a spectacle to the world, both to angels and to men. (1 Corinthians 4:9)

To me, who am less than the least of all the saints, this grace was given, that I should preach among the Gentiles the unsearchable riches of Christ, and to make all see what is the fellowship of the mystery, which from the beginning of the ages has been hidden in God who created all things through Jesus Christ, to the intent that now the manifold wisdom of God might be made known by the church to the principalities and powers in the heavenly places. (Ephesians 3:8–10)

I charge you before God and the Lord Jesus Christ and the elect angels that you observe these things without prejudice, doing nothing with partiality. (1 Timothy 5:21, NKJV)

The Angels and the Gospel

Peter tells us that the angels desire to investigate the mystery of our great salvation as foretold by the Old Testament prophets.

Of this salvation the prophets have inquired and searched carefully, who prophesied of the grace that would come to you, searching what, or what manner of time, the Spirit of Christ who was in them was indicating when He testified beforehand the sufferings of Christ and the glories that would follow. To them it was revealed that, not to themselves, but to us they were ministering the things which now have been reported to you through those who have preached the gospel to you by the Holy

Spirit sent from heaven—things which angels desire to look into. (1 Peter 1:10–12, NKJV)

The angels are never permitted to preach the gospel to sinners. However, God did use the angels to make special announcements relative to the gospel:

1. The angel could not preach the gospel to the Ethiopian but did tell Peter where to go in the desert so he could preach it.

   Now an angel of the Lord spoke to Philip, saying, 'Arise and go toward the south along the road which goes down from Jerusalem to Gaza.' This is desert (Acts 8:26, NKJV).

2. The Archangel Gabriel announced the birth of Messiah's forerunner to Zacharias.

   There was in the days of Herod, the king of Judea, a certain priest named Zacharias, of the division of Abijah. His wife was of the daughters of Aaron, and her name was Elizabeth. And they were both righteous before God, walking in all the commandments and ordinances of the Lord blameless. But they had no child, because Elizabeth was barren, and they were both well advanced in years. So it was, that while he was serving as priest before God in the order of his division, according to the custom of the priesthood, his lot fell to burn incense when he went into the temple of the Lord. And the whole multitude of the people was praying outside at the hour of incense. Then an angel of the Lord appeared to him, standing on the right side of the altar of incense. And when Zacharias saw him, he was troubled, and fear fell upon him. But the angel said to him, "Do not be afraid, Zacharias, for your prayer is heard; and your wife Elizabeth will bear you a son, and you shall call his name John. And you will have joy and gladness, and many will rejoice at his birth. For he will be great in the sight of the Lord, and shall drink neither wine nor strong drink. He will also be filled with the Holy Spirit, even from his mother's womb. And he will turn many of the children of Israel to the Lord their God. He will also go before Him in the spirit and power of Elijah, 'to turn the hearts of the fathers to the children,' and the disobedient to the wisdom of the just, to make ready a people prepared for the Lord." And Zacharias said to the angel, "How shall I know this? For I am an old man, and my wife is well advanced in years." And the angel answered and said to him, "I am Gabriel, who stands in the presence of God, and was sent to speak to you and bring you these glad tidings. But behold, you will be mute and not able to speak until the day these things take place, because you did not believe my words which will be fulfilled in their own time." And the people waited for Zacharias, and marveled that he lingered so long in the temple. But when he came out, he could not speak to them; and they perceived that he had seen a vision in the temple, for he beckoned to them and remained speechless. So it was, as soon as the days of his service were completed, that he departed to his own house. Now after those days his wife Elizabeth conceived; and she hid herself five months, saying, "Thus the Lord has dealt with me, in the days when He looked on me, to take away my reproach among people." (Luke 1:5–25, NKJV)

3.   The Archangel Gabriel also announced to the Virgin Mary, the birth of the Christ child, and gave her the name for the baby, Jesus.

Now in the sixth month the angel Gabriel was sent by God to a city of Galilee named Nazareth, to a virgin betrothed to a man whose name was Joseph, of the house of David. The virgin's name was Mary. And having come in, the angel said to her, "Rejoice, highly favored one, the Lord is with you; blessed are you among women!" But when she saw him, she was troubled at his saying, and considered what manner of greeting this was. Then the angel said to her, "Do not be afraid, Mary, for you have found favor with God. And behold, you will conceive in your womb and bring forth a Son, and shall call His name JESUS. He will be great, and will be called the Son of the Highest; and the Lord God will give Him the throne of His father David. And He will reign over the house of Jacob forever, and of His kingdom there will be no end." Then Mary said to the angel, "How can this be, since I do not know a man?" And the angel answered and said to her, "The Holy Spirit will come upon you, and the power of the Highest will overshadow you; therefore, also,

that Holy One who is to be born will be called
the Son of God." (Luke 1:26–35, NKJV)

As an aside: In light of these last two passages, both Zacharias and Mary were given news
by Gabriel that spoke of a miracle. Zacharias is
told that his wife will have a baby and his name
will be John. In verse 18, his reply is, "How
will I know, I and my wife are old." In verse 19,
we're told that he is immediately struck mute,
because of his unbelief. Mary's news, also from
Gabriel, is that she will conceive and have a son
and his name will be Jesus. Her reply, in verse
34, is, "How can this be, as I am a virgin?"
Gabriel explains patiently to her, how it will
happen, and she says, "Be it as you say." Two
birth announcements, two responses, totally different reactions—why? "I and my wife are old"
as opposed to "I am a virgin." Both questions are
totally logical—physical conditions should have
prevented these births from happening, unless
you bring God into the picture. So why were
they answered so differently? I see three answers:
Compare the two people. Zacharias is a priest
and elderly man (as he admits himself), who has
been around a while. He has learned, formally in
the synagogue and by everyday life experience,
who God is and how He works. He is a priest,
which means he should have a deep understanding of how to act and react on the presence of an
archangel! Mary, on the other hand, is a young
girl. She was not learned in the ways of the Lord,
other than observation—God was to be feared
and obeyed. They weren't taught anything from

the synagogue. So the first answer would be the difference in status. He should know better. She is an innocent. Next issue is attitude. Zacharias's attitude in posing his question comes across as disrespectful, scoffing, and even disbelief, while Mary's is truly a question of curiosity, respectful excitement, and open wonder. In my opinion, the major issue, as it often is in Scripture, is motive. In Zacharias, I sense a feeling of pride. "Look at me. God sent His archangel to bring me a message." As if he is anxious to go brag to his buddies. With Mary, there is nothing but awe! Excitement! There is no sense of "all about me" in her mind.

4. Joseph was told by an angel of the incarnation of the Christ child in his espoused wife, Mary.

Now the birth of Jesus Christ was as follows: After His mother Mary was betrothed to Joseph, before they came together, she was found with child of the Holy Spirit. Then Joseph her husband, being a just man, and not wanting to make her a public example, was minded to put her away secretly. But while he thought about these things, behold, an angel of the Lord appeared to him in a dream, saying, "Joseph, son of David, do not be afraid to take to you Mary your wife, for that which is conceived in her is of the Holy Spirit. And she will bring forth a Son, and you shall call His name JESUS, for He will save His people from their sins." So all this was done that it might be fulfilled which was spoken by the Lord through the prophet, saying: "Behold, the

Virgin shall be with child, and bear a son, and they shall call His name Immanuel," which is translated, "God with us." Then Joseph, being aroused from sleep, did as the angel of the Lord commanded him and took to him his wife, and did not know her till she had brought forth her firstborn Son. And he called His name JESUS. (Matthew 1:18–25, NKJV)

5. Gabriel gave Daniel the skill to understand what he was about to tell him.

Now while I was speaking, praying, and confessing my sin and the sin of my people Israel, and presenting my supplication before the LORD my God for the holy mountain of my God, yes, while I was speaking in prayer, the man Gabriel, whom I had seen in the vision at the beginning, being caused to fly swiftly, reached me about the time of the evening offering. And he informed me, and talked with me, and said, "O Daniel, I have now come forth to give you skill to understand." (Daniel 9:20–22, NKJV)

6. Gabriel had also foretold to Daniel the notable seventy-week prophecy, which involved the coming of the Messiah and his crucifixion.

Seventy weeks are determined For your people and for your holy city, To finish the transgression, To make an end of sins, To make reconciliation for iniquity, To bring in everlasting righteousness, To seal up vision and prophecy, And to anoint the Most Holy. "Know therefore and understand, That from the going forth of the command to restore and build Jerusalem Until Messiah the Prince, There shall be seven weeks and sixty-two weeks; The street shall be built again, and the wall, Even in troublesome times." And after the sixty-two weeks Messiah shall be cut off, but not for Himself; And the people of the prince who is to come Shall destroy the city and the sanctuary. The end of it shall be with a flood, And till the end of the war desolations are determined. Then he shall confirm a covenant with many for one week; But in the middle of the week He shall bring an end to sacrifice and offering. And on the wing of abominations shall be one who makes desolate, Even until the consummation, which is determined, Is poured out on the desolate. (Daniel 9:24–27, NKJV)

7.   The shepherds in the field heard the angelic announcement of the birth of Jesus and the heavenly host worshipping God. The angel announced the good tidings that the Savior had been born. "Then the angel said to them, 'Do not be afraid, for behold, I bring you good tidings of great joy which will be to all people. For there is born to you this day in the city of David a Savior, who is Christ the Lord'" (Luke 2:10–11, NKJV).

8.   It was an angel who appeared to Cornelius to send for Peter who would give him "words whereby he could be saved."

There was a certain man in Caesarea called Cornelius, a centurion of what was called the

Italian Regiment, a devout man and one who feared God with all his household, who gave alms generously to the people, and prayed to God always. About the ninth hour of the day he saw clearly in a vision an angel of God coming in and saying to him, "Cornelius!" And when he observed him, he was afraid, and said, "What is it, lord?" So he said to him, "Your prayers and your alms have come up for a memorial before God. Act 10:1-4

And they said, "Cornelius the centurion, a just man, one who fears God and has a good reputation among all the nation of the Jews, was divinely instructed by a holy angel to summon you to his house, and to hear words from you." (Acts 10:22)

While Peter was still speaking these words, the Holy Spirit fell upon all those who heard the word. And those of the circumcision who believed were astonished, as many as came with Peter, because the gift of the Holy Spirit had been poured out on the Gentiles also. (Acts 10:44–45)

And he told us how he had seen an angel standing in his house, who said to him, "Send men to Joppa, and call for Simon whose surname is Peter, who will tell you words by which you and all your household will be saved." (Acts 11:13–14, NKJV)

9.   It was an angel who told Paul that he would testify before Caesar at Rome.

> For there stood by me this night an angel of the God to whom I belong and whom I serve, saying, 'Do not be afraid, Paul; you must be brought before Caesar; and indeed God has granted you all those who sail with you' (Acts 27:23–24, NKJV)

Angels may give the announcements pertaining to the good tidings, but redeemed sinners must preach it. Thus, the burden of the gospel is upon those who are redeemed from sin. That's us, folks!

Angels in the Book of Revelation

The book of Revelation reveals an active involvement of angels prior to, as well as at the second coming of Christ. I mention several but certainly not all:

1. Innumerable angels worship God and the lamb.

    Then I looked, and I heard the voice of many angels around the throne, the living creatures, and the elders; and the number of them was ten thousand times ten thousand, and thousands of thousands, saying with a loud voice: 'Worthy is the Lamb who was slain to receive power and riches and wisdom, And strength and honor and glory and blessing!' (Revelation 5:11–12, NKJV).

2. Four angels restrain the winds of judgment blowing up on the earth until the sealing of God's servants.

    After these things I saw four angels standing at the four corners of the earth, holding the four winds of the earth, that the wind should not blow on the earth, on the sea, or on any tree (Revelation 7:1, NKJV).

3. Seven angels sound seven trumpets of judgment (Revelation 8:2–12).

4. Michael and his elect angels engage in war with Satan and his fallen angels and cast them out.

    And war broke out in heaven: Michael and his angels fought with the dragon; and the dragon and his angels fought, but they did not prevail, nor was a place found for them in heaven any longer. So the great dragon was cast out, that serpent of old, called the Devil and Satan, who deceives the whole world; he was cast to the earth, and his angels were cast out with him. Then I heard a loud voice saying in heaven, 'Now salvation, and strength, and the kingdom of our God, and the power of His Christ have come, for the accuser of our brethren, who accused them before our God day and night, has been cast down' (Revelation 12:7–10, NKJV).

5. An angel announces the fall of Babylon.

    And another angel followed, saying, 'Babylon is fallen, is fallen, that great city, because she has made all nations drink of the wine of the wrath of her fornication' (Revelation 14:8, NKJV).

6. An angel announces the everlasting gospel of judgment, warning the earth-dwellers not to take the mark of the beast.

Then I saw another angel flying in the midst of heaven, having the everlasting gospel to preach to those who dwell on the earth to every nation, tribe, tongue, and people. (Revelation 14:6)

Then a third angel followed them, saying with a loud voice, "If anyone worships the beast and his image, and receives his mark on his forehead or on his hand." (Revelation 14:9, NKJV)

7. The wicked are to be tormented in the presence of the lamb and the holy angels, whose mercy in ministry they have spurned.

He himself shall also drink of the wine of the wrath of God, which is poured out full strength into the cup of His indignation. He shall be tormented with fire and brimstone in the presence of the holy angels and in the presence of the Lamb (Revelation 14:10, NKJV).

The angels will be associated with Christ in the gathering of the redeemed of the earth at His second coming.

For the Son of Man will come in the glory of His Father with His angels, and then He will reward each according to his works. (Matthew 16:27 NKJV)

And He will send His angels with a great sound of a trumpet, and they will gather together His elect from the four winds, from one end of heaven to the other. (Matthew 24:31 NKJV)

But of that day and hour no one knows, not even the angels of heaven, but My Father only. (Matthew 24:36 NKJV)

For whoever is ashamed of Me and My words in this adulterous and sinful generation, of him the Son of Man also will be ashamed when He comes in the glory of His Father with the holy angels. (Matthew 8:38 NKJV)

And then He will send His angels, and gather together His elect from the four winds, from the farthest part of earth to the farthest part of heaven. (Matthew 13:27 NKJV)

And to give you who are troubled rest with us when the Lord Jesus is revealed from heaven with His mighty angels. (2 Thessalonians 1:6–7, NKJV)

There is much angelic activity in the New Testament times, and Scripture seems to indicate that the church can expect much more in these last days leading up to the second coming of Christ. Eternity alone will reveal how much ministry angels will have rendered to the redeemed of all ages.

I have a very dear Christian friend who shared these encounters with me.

She was driving with her four children, two of whom were in car seats, on a busy highway, when the van she was driving overheated and caught fire. Through her prayers, she drove the vehicle to the side of the road, flung the door open, and she sent the two older girls to the median with her most serious motherly command to stay put. As she frantically reached for one of the car seats, they miraculously released and popped open. Grabbing her precious babies, she ran toward the grass just as the vehicle blew up behind her. As she ran toward the median, she realized there was only one child standing there waiting for her! She looked up and saw Amanda screaming in terror, running down the middle of Highway 6! She also saw a man come out of nowhere, picking up the frightened child and bringing her back, comforting her all the way. He had no car, and there was no place he could have come from. Police and fire department came, along with the ambulance to check everyone out. No injuries. When she turned to thank the man that saved her daughter, he was nowhere to be seen. She asked the policeman nearby; he hadn't seen anyone. She asked another and another; there was no one who had seen anyone!

Was he an angel? You will never convince her he wasn't. I'm inclined to agree!

One of those kids in the car seat grew to be a young man seeking God's own heart. He was dozing in the front seat, again with his mom driving. This time three of her grandchildren were buckled in the back seat, when a semi–tractor trailer flew past them on the interstate. In the ice and snow, her car went into a spin from the wind draft. This godly woman knew where her help comes from and started calling Him. "Jesus, Jesus, Jesus!" Her son awoke to a slow motion video of her car spinning between the other vehicles, never striking even one. Her car landed nose-first in the snow in an eight-foot embankment. Jason later said, "Mom, I knew something was wrong when I heard you calling on Jesus!" The first responders were called, and because of a recent knee replacement, my friend wasn't able to get out of the car. The snow bank partially blocked Jason's door, and suddenly there was a stranger there, helping Jason to remain calm. EMTs came and got her and the grandbabies out of the car. My friend was chilling, so the EMTs covered her with a sheet to help keep her warm. When Jason looked over and saw this, his reaction was panic, thinking his mom had not survived the accident. The stranger softly spoke to him, "She is not dead. It is not her time yet. She has a lot to do yet." Jason ran over to her and found that she was indeed alive. When Jason turned happily to thank him, the stranger was gone. Again, no one else remembered seeing him, just Jason and his mom. And I have it on good authority (my own) that she has indeed accomplished a lot for the kingdom of God since that time, several years ago, and is still pursuing God in everything she does.

Yes, angels do exist! My friend did not call the angels to her aid, she called on their Master and hers, Jesus Christ, Son of God! God sent them in human form so they would not stand out in the crowd, yet they had the strength needed, the wisdom needed, and the instructions from God Himself to do what was necessary to minister to His children!

Do angels exist today? I think we've proven that they do. And I think we've covered what angels can do: anything God commands and enables them to do. But there are some other things that you need to know about angels:

1. Angels are not children of God. The fallen angels would never want to call God Father, though they may call Lucifer Father, as many Satan worshippers do. Even the holy angels cannot call God their father because they were created, not born.

2. Angels cannot testify of salvation by grace. While the angels rejoice when people are saved and glorify God who saved them, they cannot personally testify to something they have not experienced.

3. Angels have no experiential knowledge of the indwelling of God. Since God seals believers when they accept Christ, such sealing would be unnecessary for the angels who never fell and who therefore don't need salvation.

4. Angels do not marry or procreate. In Matthew 22:30, Jesus points out that in the resurrection they neither married nor are given in marriage but are like the angels of God in heaven.

5. Angels enjoy far greater power than men, but they are not all-powerful. In 2 Thessalonians 1:7,

---

Paul refers to "the mighty angels of God." The word mighty here, we get from the English word dynamite. In material power, angels are God's dynamite. In 2 Peter we read, "Angels who are greater in might and power than men do not bring a revile in judgment against them before the Lord" (2 Peter 2:11, NASB).

6. There is a conjecture about angel choirs. We at least assume that angels do and can sing, even if the Scripture do not pointedly say so. It is likely that John saw a massive heavenly choir (Revelation 5:11–12). What Scripture does this tell us is that angels worship before the throne, and although singing is not the only way of worshipped it is a very important way that we worship and that the angels would worship and have a voice.

The one question we have not answered is "Is there an angel of death?" Nothing in my research of Scripture or the other twelve books I reviewed indicates there is an angel of death. However, I cannot for a moment believe that in our moment of need, God would leave us without comfort. Since the number 2 job of the angels is to minister to God's children (number 1 being worshipping at the throne of God), I'm sure we will have a sufficient number around us, delivering us into Jesus's arms.

And lastly, no, a bell ringing does not indicate an angel has earned His wings.

Chapter 31

You Have an Enemy

Whether or not you believe it, you have an enemy. Whether or not you have accepted the Lord as your Savior, you have an enemy. You may not have thought about it much, but your enemy is there. Your enemy is watching you, just to make sure you don't make the best decision of your life and turn to Jesus. Your enemy, Satan, is smart and he is evil. He is not all-knowing. He cannot read your mind. He knows what's going on in your life, by listening to what comes out of your mouth! He hears what you talk to your friends about; he especially listens when you mumble about your spouse! Satan has used the same tactics for years against believers and not yet believers. He is not omnipresent so he cannot be everywhere at once, like God can, but scripture tells us he travels all over the earth doing whatever he can to destroy us.

"Be sober, be vigilant; because your adversary the devil walks about like a roaring lion, seeking whom he may devour" (1 Pet. 5:8, NKJV).

Your enemy also presents (manifests) himself to you in ways that you may not recognize him. Frequently when we are "under attack" our vision gets blurred. We may see that coworker who was trying to sabotage everything we do as our enemy. Or if that ex-spouse tries to take the kids, we may see him/her as our enemy. Or the drunk driver who kills, or anyone who has done anything to hurt us. They all may appear to be our enemy, but they are not. Those attacks may be the result of bad decisions that we made or that someone else made. The attacks may be our enemy at work through those bad decisions or through the circumstances. So when we are under attack we need to remember this: We need to go into battle against the *true* enemy.

We only have one enemy; he has different names. If you go back to Chapter 24 and read the paragraph on Lucifer, you know his name before he fell from heaven. That's right, our enemy was the most beautiful, talented angel in heaven. He was in charge of the worship, so God anointed him with magnificence beyond compare. But Lucifer wasn't satisfied with that. His pride got the better of him and he began to plot how to take over heaven. That is a simplification for our purposes here, but it is truth. God gave him every chance to turn his plan around, then Lucifer chose to rebel, and in so doing he took approximately one-third of the angels of heaven with him when God cast him out of heaven. The angels that went with him are generally called *fallen angels* or *demons*. Satan created his counterfeit of God's "government." The fallen angels make up Satan's "army."

Satan is the most common name for our enemy. He is also called the great deceiver, father of lies, destroyer, tempter. He is quite frequently called the devil, but he does not wear a red suit, have red horns or a long pointy tail. Remember he was the most beautiful angel at one time. Remember also that he is a counterfeiter, so he can make himself appear as something beautiful and good, but he is not.

"…Satan himself transforms himself into an angel of light" (2 Cor. 11:14, NKJV).

When Lucifer fell from heaven, he began his long-term plan against God. What better way to "get even" with a Father than to attack his children? Satan's plan is to infect, tarnish, and destroy everything that God created. A major part of His plan is focused around destroying the family unit and the very order that God created.

He has already accomplished so much. Look at how many abortions have disrupted God's plan for families. As a Christian counselor, I have been heartbroken by women who have lived with the guilt of their decision for years, before they were able to accept God's forgiveness. The divorce rate is higher than it has ever been and is even higher in Christian marriages than in non-Christian ones. Satan deceives people into believing there is a better spouse out there somewhere. Those marriage statistics have swayed many couples into living together, as opposed to marriage. Many people have turned to alternative lifestyles, in hopes of finding love there.

"If a man lies with a male as he lies with a woman, both of them have committed an abomination. They shall surely be put to death. Their blood shall be upon them" (Lev. 20:13, NKJV).

This doesn't mean that anyone who is in a homosexual lifestyle will be brought up on charges and killed. It means the natural process of "their blood upon them" is death, as in HIV—AIDS. In case you hadn't noticed, it seems that every time man finds a drug that "cures" the effects of this lifestyle, another disease is found!

The good news is that God is bigger, better, and more powerful than our enemy could ever hope to be. God uses His power for good and not for evil. God's plan will eventually put an end to Satan's tactics once and for all, but for now, we have a loving God who gives us everything we need to not only survive the attacks of our enemy but to thrive through them and become stronger. He gave us spiritual armor to protect us from our enemy's attacks (Chapter 22).

The only *offensive* weapon we will ever need is the "sword of the Spirit" or the Bible—the written Word of God. Every possible issue that our enemy throws your way is covered in the Bible. The more we know the Bible, the more we can trust God to "bring it to our minds" when we need it.

"But the Helper, the Holy Spirit, whom the Father will send in My name, He will teach you all things, and bring to your remembrance all things that I said to you" (John 14:26, NKJV).

These are the words of Jesus, Son of God, the Word made flesh!

"In the beginning was the Word, and the Word was with God, and the Word was God" (John 1:1, NKJV).

When you look at these two verses together, we have a promise that anything in Scripture will be brought to our "remembrance" (our memory), but if we haven't read the Bible, it doesn't work. *How can we remember something that we never saw or read or heard?* That's one reason it is so important to read and study God's Word! Here's another reason:

"Therefore submit to God. Resist the devil and he will flee from you" (James 4:7, NKJV).

The word *will* in the original language of the New Testament means *must*. This is the 1-2-3 of getting our enemy out of our hair!

1. Submit to God—No one rejoices over the word *submit*, but it's not as hard as you might think. Obedience is easy to someone you know loves you, is out for your good, and in fact, *created you!* "And we know that all things work together for good to those who love God, to those who are the called according to His purpose" (Rom.

8:28, NKJV). We can submit knowing that God is working behind the scenes on our behalf.

2. Resist the devil—Resist, in the original language, is *anthistēmi* (anth-is'-tay-mee) and it means to stand against, to oppose, withstand. We have to stand our ground! *Then...*

3. He (the devil) will flee from you—The word *will*, in the original language of the New Testament, means *must*. He doesn't have a choice! That word *flee* means *run, as if in fear!* Even Satan has to abide by God's rules!

The most important weapon that God gave us is Jesus Himself. Have you ever thought of Jesus as a weapon? He is not a weapon to be used lightly. He is the Captain of the Host of angels who God has charged with your care!

"For He shall give His angels charge over you, To keep you in all your ways" (Ps. 91:11, NKJV).

Christians today sometimes miss it. We don't realize how much power we have access to, when our enemy's attacks come our way!

> And these signs will follow those who believe: In My name they will cast out demons; they will speak with new tongues; they will take up serpents; and if they drink anything deadly, it will by no means hurt them; they will lay hands on the sick, and they will recover. (Mark 16:17–18, NKJV)

Those are the words of Jesus! They are a promise! We *will* cast out demons, if we believe in Him, and use the authority of the name of Jesus. The power of the name of Jesus is a topic in itself of many books, so I won't go into a lot of detail here. But if you pray in the name of Jesus, in accordance with God's Word, it will not take long for you to see for yourself just how powerful that name is! (Also see Chapter 32.)

> Therefore God also has highly exalted Him and given Him the name which is above every name, that at the name of Jesus every knee should bow, of those in heaven, and of those on earth, and of those under the earth, and that every tongue should confess that Jesus Christ is Lord, to the glory of God the Father. (Phil. 2:9–11, NKJV)

Whenever we are dealing with a powerful enemy, we must use every weapon in our arsenal. In that way, this is one of the most important chapters in this book. Understand that we as children of God and servants of the Lord are under the protection of the absolute ultimate power—God.

> "No weapon formed against you shall prosper, And every tongue which rises against you in judgment You shall condemn. This is the heritage of the servants of the LORD, And their righteousness is from Me," Says the LORD. (Isa 54:17, NKJV)
> He who dwells in the secret place of the Most High Shall abide under the shadow of the Almighty. I will say of the LORD, "He is my refuge and my fortress; My God, in Him I will trust." (Ps. 91:1–2, NKJV)

Chapter 32

Let It Be Known

To set the scene for our story in this chapter, I will remind you of King Ahab. He has the nickname of "The Wicked King" and he truly lived up to that nickname. He and his wife Jezebel were the most cruel tyrants you could imagine. Everything they did was done with the motive of strengthening their alliance with the pagan god Balaam. They disobeyed everything God asked them to do because they couldn't see what was in it for them.

The Israelites are always caught in the middle, aren't they? They have to make a choice between following God or following their king. God set things up that way, so when the king did "what was right in God's eyes" there was really no conflict! It was an easy choice because following the king *was* following God. But in the minds of the Israelites, the most dangerous choice was following God, because this physical king that they could see had a huge army, and this wicked king was really quick about chastising with the sword anyone who disobeyed and didn't follow his orders and his way of life. They had forgotten the power of God and became complacent and followed the human king.

Ahab was king of Israel while Elijah was prophet. Ahab calls Elijah the "troubler of Israel" in 1 Kings 18:17. Elijah responds by saying, "It's you and your father who have troubled Israel and forsaken the commandments of God and followed the Baals." Elijah challenges Ahab to gather all the people of Israel on Mount Carmel and include the 450 prophets of Baal and Jezebel's 400 prophets of Asherah. So King Ahab does that. Elijah addresses the people, confronting them, saying, "How long will you falter between two opinions? If the LORD *is* God, follow Him; but if Baal, follow him." But the people answered him not a word (verse 20).

Can't you picture the tribe of Israel standing in front of this prophet with the king standing right there? What are they gonna say? They have this army of prophets who are loyal to this wicked king. They know the quick temper of this wicked king. But the only thing they see on the opposing side is this prophet. And Elijah understands that and puts into motion an object lesson that God has laid on Elijah's heart.

> Then Elijah said to the people, "I alone am left a prophet of the LORD; but Baal's prophets are four hundred and fifty men. Therefore let them give us two bulls; and let them choose one bull for themselves, cut it in pieces, and lay it on the wood, but put no fire under it; and I will prepare the other bull, and lay it on the wood, but put no fire under it. Then you call on the name of your gods, and I will call on the name of the LORD; and the God who answers by fire, He is God." So all the people answered and said, "It is well spoken." (1 Kings 18:22–24, NKJV)

So that's what they do. Elijah gives the prophets of Baal first choice of bulls, so the people watching understand there is no trickery going on here. King Ahab's side butchers the bull and places the wood and put the pieces of the bull on the wood.

But they don't set fire to it. They call on the name of Baal from morning till noon, asking him to appear to show his power, and he doesn't. So then they start to dance, hoping that will bring his presence and it doesn't.

> And so it was, at noon, that Elijah mocked them and said, "Cry aloud, for he is a god; either he is meditating, or he is busy, or he is on a journey, or perhaps he is sleeping and must be awakened." So they cried aloud, and cut themselves, as was their custom, with knives and lances, until the blood gushed out on them. And when midday was past, they prophesied until the time of the offering of the evening sacrifice. But there was no voice; no one answered, no one paid attention. (1 Kings 18:27–29, NKJV)

The word translated as *prophesied* here means they sang a prediction, desperately calling Balaam to do what he needs to do to prove himself. So they turned it into a song, but it didn't happen. But *there was* no voice; no one answered, no one paid attention. Then it's Elijah's turn to go to work:

"Then Elijah said to all the people, 'Come near to me.' So all the people came near to him. And he repaired the altar of the LORD *that was* broken down" (1 Kings 18:30, NKJV).

This altar had been torn down by King Ahab's men, because it honored Jehovah God and not Balaam.

> And Elijah took twelve stones, according to the number of the tribes of the sons of Jacob, to whom the word of the LORD had come, saying, "Israel shall be your name." Then

> with the stones he built an altar in the name
> of the LORD; and he made a trench around
> the altar large enough to hold two seahs of
> seed. And he put the wood in order, cut the
> bull in pieces, and laid it on the wood, and
> said, "Fill four water pots with water, and
> pour it on the burnt sacrifice and on the
> wood." Then he said, "Do it a second time,"
> and they did it a second time; and he said,
> "Do it a third time," and they did it a third
> time. So the water ran all around the altar;
> and he also filled the trench with water. (1
> Kings 18:31–35, NKJV)

Elijah has them pour water over the bull *and* the wood, saturating it until it fills the trough and overflows, so there is not much chance that this wood will start on fire. If this were a natural fire, there would be no chance at all! But Elijah is confident in the power of his God—the power of *our God* to do what He said He would do. Remember, Elijah is doing what God has told him to do.

> And it came to pass, at the time of the offer-
> ing of the evening sacrifice, that Elijah the
> prophet came near and said, "LORD God of
> Abraham, Isaac, and Israel, **let it be known**
> this day that You are God in Israel and I am
> Your servant, and that I have done all these
> things at Your word. Hear me, O LORD,
> hear me, that this people may know that
> You are the LORD God, and that You have
> turned their hearts back to You again." (1
> Kings 18:36–37, NKJV; emphasis mine)

Elijah calls to God, but he doesn't ask him to light the fire. Instead he simply asks God to *let it be known* that God is God. Show yourself strong. Show these people that you are God and I am your servant and that I did all this at Your word because You asked me to do it. Then he asks the Lord to hear Him that the people may see that God had already turned their hearts back to him. Elijah knew God well enough; God knew Elijah well enough; they had done sacrifices together before so that they knew who was supposed to do what. Elijah was supposed to build the altar and put the sacrificial animal on the altar and God's part was to consume the sacrifice by fire.

"Then the fire of the LORD fell and consumed the burnt sacrifice, and the wood and the stones and the dust, and it licked up the water that was in the trench" (1 Kings 18:38, NKJV).

God knew His part and He did what He was supposed to do. God knows His part in your life. But you have to set the groundwork for Him to be able to do it. You have to lay the wood. You have to find the bull—you have to search your heart, look through your life and find the sin there, and lay it on the wood for God to consume.

If you willingly lay that sin on the fire for sacrifice, he will consume it, remove it completely and entirely from your life. When He does that your work is not complete. You need to do your part, in keeping that sin out of your life, in keeping your life pure. And one of the most important parts of your work is to do what Elijah asked God to do.

Remember Elijah didn't ask God to light the fire. He asked God to "let it be known." That's what *we* need to do. We need to let it be known to all those around us. Let it be known that God is God and we are His servants. And this is how God cares for His servants.

Whenever we let it be known that God has healed us, provided for us, saved us—it is called giving God the glory.

Glorifying God. When I open a service in prayer, I generally invite the Lord to join us and "be glorified." That's what it's all about. Those in attendance are invited to speak up and share praise reports, to glorify Him. Then we sing worship songs, we are glorifying Him. So every day that He gives us breath, with everything He does for us, let's "let it be known!"

Chapter 33

Generational Sin

What is a curse? The *Nelson's Illustrated Bible Dictionary* defines a curse "as a prayer for injury, harm or misfortune to fall on someone." This is a good definition, but it is only partly correct. A curse can also come from a pronouncement against someone, not just a prayer. But even more so, the primary way a curse can come into your lives can be through personal choices that are sinful and law breaking in nature. When we sin, we can and often do open our lives to the effect of curses. So, to be perfectly clear here, a curse is a spiritual reality, existing in someone's life. A curse is real. It is a spiritual reality that is mentioned almost two hundred times in the Bible and it may be the reason you struggle with certain things and cannot find lasting victory.[22]

My father was a brilliant musician. He couldn't read a note of music. He played by ear and learned how to play a banjo when he was three years old. The banjo sat on a chair beside him and he played up on the neck. As he grew up, he learned a lot of other musical instruments, and actually played piano on his TV show called *Keyways to Heaven*, for most of his Christian life.

That talent came from somewhere... I never heard my grandmother sing or play an instrument, so I assume it wasn't from her. But his dad died before any of us kids were born. Now his brothers were all musical as well, so we have decided that it probably came from his dad. But that would only be one generation. Since we can't look into the past with much detail, let's look into the more recent generations. My brother and sister could play piano, but that talent to play an instrument skipped my baby sister and me, although we can both sing. But my son can play anything you put in front of him! That is a legacy that we take part in. It was passed down from generation to generation.

Now if my father had chosen not to play music in our home, it never would have been received or continued. That legacy would have been lost. Or if my son decides not to play anymore, it would be lost. You may have a tremendous heritage in the Lord. Your grandparents and their grandparents brought with them a love and reverence for the Lord God that has flowed from their generation through the second and third and landed in you—the fourth and the fifth. You have made the choice to continue that legacy and carry it forward. Some of us have a godly heritage that has a hiccup in the bloodline, but it still got through. And for some of you, you are the beginning of a godly heritage for the third and fourth generations of your own family. It is *your* choice to maintain that legacy and help it flourish.

> I will open my mouth in a parable; I will utter dark sayings from of old, things that we have heard and known, that our fathers have told us. We will not hide them from their children, but tell to the coming generation the glorious deeds of the LORD, and his might, and the wonders that he has done. He established a testimony in Jacob and appointed a law in Israel, which he commanded our fathers to teach to their children, that the

next generation might know them, the children yet unborn, and arise and tell them to their children, so that they should set their hope in God and not forget the works of God, but keep his commandments; and that they should not be like their fathers, a stubborn and rebellious generation, a generation whose heart was not steadfast, whose spirit was not faithful to God. (Ps. 78:2–8, NKJV)

Exodus 20:5 is probably the most well-known verse regarding curses to future generations: "For I, the LORD your God, am a jealous God, visiting the iniquity of the fathers upon the children to the third and fourth generations of those who hate Me" (NKJV).

This verse is frequently misrepresented because of ignoring the last five words: "of those who hate me." "But showing mercy to thousands, to those who love Me and keep My commandments" (Exod. 20:6).

Curses are real. They are real in the United States. They are real in Bible preaching churches. They are real in church and very possibly they are real in your life. This can sound scary at the onset, but this is just because the parts of the church with the greatest western influences have lost sight of many biblical truths that have some of the greatest impact on our daily lives. One of those impacts is curses.

The Bible deals with curses on an individual and even national level. It also, however, deals with this on an ancestral or generational level and that's why we are studying generational curses. Just as good talents and legacies can be passed on from generation to generation, the negative traits and sins can be as well. Something else my father was good at was being angry. He was never a violent man, but he had a temper that came out of his mouth. He passed that trait on to his kids. My brother fought with it until the day he died. My sisters and I still occasionally struggle with it.

"Know this, my beloved brothers: let every person be quick to hear, slow to speak, slow to anger" (James 1:19, NKJV).

We make choices every day. Sometimes we win and sometimes we don't. But we know that God is on our side. When I get up in the morning, I *must* make the choice to not let anger win today. I know that if I remember to do that, my choice aligns with what God's Word says, then anger will not win... sometimes I forget that. But just as I have a choice to let that negative family trait be passed on to my son and his daughters, I also have the choice to be sure that the godly heritage from my mother's side of the family lives on. And that legacy is strengthened now, with the salvation of my father in his later years.

> Now the works of the flesh are evident: sexual immorality, impurity, sensuality, idolatry, sorcery, enmity, strife, jealousy, fits of anger, rivalries, dissensions, divisions, envy, drunkenness, orgies, and things like these. I warn you, as I warned you before, that those who do such things will not inherit the kingdom of God. (Gal. 5:19–21, NKJV)

This scripture gives us a fairly complete list of sins. These are probably included in those that might have been "visited upon the third and fourth generations." Many religious circles refer to this type of sin as a generational curse. These things are the evils that our enemy would love to use to work his destruction in us and our families for generations to come.

How curses can happen:

1. A curse can come through appointed direct pronouncement made against someone. We see this in the story of Balaam in the book of Numbers. Balak tried to pay Balaam to have him curse the nation of Israel. After God's command, Balaam didn't, but it is a biblical truth that an attempt was made to curse Israel. I believe God placed this story in the Bible so that we would learn to seek the Holy Spirit for how these things work.

2. Disobedience—another passage of scripture demonstrates another way curses can come into our lives: "Behold, I set before you today a blessing and a curse: the blessing, if you obey the commandments of the LORD your God which I command you today; and the curse, if you do not obey the commandments of the LORD your God, but turn aside from the way which I command you today, to go after other gods which you have not known" (Deut. 11:26–28, NKJV).

   This was when Israel is preparing to go into the promised land. Moses gathered them and pronounced to them the voice of the Lord declaring that God pre-established in advance blessings and curses. They exist in the spiritual realm. They are accessed through personal and corporate choices: personal being our own individual choices, corporate being on behalf of our church, our nation, etc. If we follow the commands of God, we are placed in a place of pre-established blessing. The blessings God pre-established on our behalf. Consequently, if we don't listen to the voice of the Lord we place ourselves in a place of pre-established curse. Blessing would bring life, peace, prosperity; curse would bring harm, divine resistance, and even death. God has given us a free will so the choice is always ours.

3.   In a recent study in the book of Proverbs, one particular verse lodged itself in my heart, so I studied a bit, and stumbled onto a third possible cause of curses: "Like a flitting sparrow, like a flying swallow, So a curse without cause shall not alight" (Prov. 26:2, NKJV).

This is a profound verse. Solomon draws a comparison between birds and a curse. He says that like a sparrow or a swallow, a curse without proper cause cannot "get in." A bird simply cannot land where it pleases. There must be an open place and accessibility for a bird to roost. It's the same for a curse. If a curse has been sent against you, it cannot "get in" without an opening. If someone releases a curse against you, it will not gain an effect on you if there's no place in you for it to land. This is why Jesus said to bless those who curse you.

Theologian Albert Barnes translates this verse as "The causeless curse, though it may pass out of our ken (view), like a bird's track in the air, will come on the man who utters it." The bird landing or the curse "getting in" means there is a place in you that is an open door. An open door is a place in your soul that is open for harmful things or curses to move in and out. Those open doors can be caused by unconfessed sin, besetting sin woundedness, unforgiveness, bitterness, and other generational issues. If there is a sin that you are committing on a regular basis and you try again and again to let it go, and it keeps creeping back: that's a besetting sin (Heb. 2:1). This can open a doorway inside your soul for the enemy to get in. If you've been wound up through the loss of a loved one, a painful betrayal, or you harbor hatred toward someone, those too can cause openings in your soul. It is in the place of these open doors that the enemy and evils done against us can find a place of habitation. This is how it can happen with the generational curse or a curse that has been passed down through the ancestry of one's life.

By the same token, we pass on to our children many of our dispositions, both good and evil. That's why God established the law that says,

> And the LORD passed before him and proclaimed, "The LORD, the LORD God, merciful and gracious, longsuffering, and abounding in goodness and truth, keeping mercy for thousands, forgiving iniquity and transgression and sin, by no means clearing the guilty, visiting the iniquity of the fathers upon the children and the children's children to the third and the fourth generation." (NKJV)

It's one thing to accept the fact that I will be punished for the sinful acts or choices of my ancestors, but it's quite a different thing to know that a sin or curse gets into my kids because I have not repented! We have the power within us to stop these things in their tracks. Jesus *in you* makes that true. If you are a child of God, the same power that raised Jesus Christ from the grave is in *you*. You have the greatest power in the universe inside of you. You can break any generational curse because God enables you to. Through Christ Jesus, you can overcome any problem. You have the power to build your faith—you do that every time to choose to go to a Bible study or to Sunday school or to a church service. You have the power to build your faith to the point where you can stare evil in the face and be fearless. You have the *power* of *faith* to *overcome*.

Search your family! Just sit and think a while about your family. Ask God to reveal to you patterns of behavior—good or bad—that may be generational curses. They can be something as obvious as divorce, alcoholism, or something hidden like physical abuse. Whatever you find there, right it down on a piece of paper. Then pray a prayer to renounce it. Something like this:

Father in heaven, I thank you for revealing to me the issues that my ancestors have fallen prey to. In the name of Jesus, I renounce the sin of _____ (alcoholism, divorce, etc.). I repent of my own participation in this sin and I break the spiritual tie it holds between my ancestors and myself. I also break the tie of that sin between myself and my descendants, now existing and those to come. In the name of Jesus, I renounce any claim the sin of _____ and declare myself and my descendants free from it. I thank you for delivering me and my family from all sin. In Jesus's name, Amen.

Do the same for any additional sins God reveals to you in prayer. Any time you feel that the sin is recurring, pray again! Eventually Satan will get the idea! Your part is to continually resist temptation in the areas God leads you to renounce, and here's how:

1. Pray, knowing that God is listening and answers your prayers.

2. Claim the promises in Scripture. "Therefore submit to God. Resist the devil and he will flee from you" (James 4:7). This is one of those conditional promises. If...then...if you submit to

God, then Satan will flee. Submitting to God, simply put, means obedience. Know what God is asking of you—read Scripture, and do it, obey. The wording of the second phrase is actually "Satan shall flee." The word *shall* was used as a legal term; if the word *shall* was used, it was a must—no choice, no alternative. So our promise is if we submit to God, Satan has no choice but to flee…from us because God is in us.

3. Praise—God inhabits the praises of His people. Our enemy can't stand for God to be praised, so again, He leaves so He doesn't have to hear it. So when you feel weak, sing a song of praise!

Breaking generational curses is not an exercise to be taken lightly. Please contact your local Bible-believing church for assistance!

Chapter 34

Accepted in the Beloved

I once visited with a dear friend when we found ourselves talking about a few women that we love dearly, who appear to be suffering from the same affliction. As a counselor, I call it rejection syndrome. Maybe you know someone who has it. Here are some of the symptoms:

- Perfectionism

- Performance oriented
- Workaholic

- Jealous
- Undependable/seemingly irresponsible
- Angry/Hostile
- Judgmental/Bitter
- Depressed/mood swings
- Mischievousness

- Dissatisfied/unsettled

- Dominant/overbearing
- Exaggerates/lies

- Withdrawn

- Unaffectionate/overly affectionate
- Negative/disagreeable
- Unattached/careless
- Excessive talker/very quiet
- Avoids heart issues

- Reads into conversations
- Chameleon-like character
- Harsh character
- Insecure/fear of being rejected
- Needs constant affirmation/reassurance
- Feels unworthy
- Self-rejection/hate/condemnation
- Speaks highly of self/Haughtiness
- Drug/alcohol abuse

These aren't all of the symptoms, but this list is pretty revealing, isn't it? Emotionally, they are all over the page! If I were inclined to betting, I'd guess that everyone reading this has or has had at least a few of these symptoms. When we have symptoms of a health issue, what do we generally do? We go to the doctor for help, right?

> Blessed be the God and Father of our Lord Jesus Christ, who has blessed us with every spiritual blessing in the heavenly places in Christ, just as He chose us in Him before the foundation of the world, that we should be holy and without blame before Him in love, having predestined us to adoption as sons by Jesus Christ to Himself, according to the good pleasure of His will, to the praise of the glory of His grace, by which He made us accepted in the Beloved. (Eph. 1:3–6, NKJV)

Accepted by the Beloved—the Beloved is capitalized, so who is it that we are talking about here? Of course, Jesus or God. The verse says that we are accepted in the Beloved. We are accepted into Christ Jesus. Does that sound like rejection to you? The opposite of rejection is acceptance. In order that we no longer behave, act, or live like we are rejected, we must accept that acceptance into our hearts. We are not rejected, so we need to remove the "rejection syndrome" from our lives!

Freedom from rejection comes from renewing our minds, according to the Word of God. Now, I can tell you that if you are suffering from rejection syndrome, you may have had it for a long time, so that it has become part of the foundation of your life and your belief system. Maybe, it's time to begin building your life on a new foundation. There are only two foundations that your life can be established upon: the World or Christ.

"Therefore, having these promises, beloved, let us cleanse ourselves from all filthiness of the flesh and spirit, perfecting holiness in the fear of God" (2 Cor. 7:1, NKJV).

Paul exhorts us to cleanse ourselves from all defilement, including the spirit of rejection. That cleansing comes by renewing our minds and *choosing* to leave the old life and our old ways behind and step into a new life...a new house. To build your house on a new foundation, you must go through a process. I watch a show called *Flip and Move*. The teams buy houses and move them off the lots, then renovate and resell them. Sometimes as they renovate, they find they have to tear everything down to the foundation, and sometimes they even have to rebuild the foundation. Houses become corrupt with termites, wood rot, any number of things. The damage must be treated or totally rebuilt. The materials used and the workmanship must ensure that the foundation be a strong one that will endure.

Through the process of rebuilding our foundation, only one foundation will prevail—either the World or Christ. We want that foundation to be Christ, right?

Step 1. Revelation: The first step in the process of rebuilding your foundation is called Revelation and has two parts:

A. Counting the Cost—"Now great multitudes went with Him. And He turned and said to them, 'If anyone comes to Me and does not hate his father and mother, wife and children, brothers and sisters, yes, and his own life also, he cannot be My disciple. And whoever does not bear his cross and come after Me cannot be My disciple. For which of you, intending to build a tower, does not sit down first and count the cost, whether he has enough to finish it—

lest, after he has laid the foundation, and is not able to finish, all who see it begin to mock him, saying, "This man began to build and was not able to finish." Or what king, going to make war against another king, does not sit down first and consider whether he is able with ten thousand to meet him who comes against him with twenty thousand? Or else, while the other is still a great way off, he sends a delegation and asks conditions of peace. So likewise, whoever of you does not forsake all that he has cannot be My disciple'" (Luke 14:25–33, NKJV).

When you first gave your life to Jesus, you may have weighed the cost of turning away from your old life, by kicking some old habits or maybe establishing new friends. Maybe it's time to revisit that decision. Have you remained firm? Maybe it's time to re-establish that position.

B. Establish your source. This is similar to going to the store and deciding what your supplies are going to be.

> You are of your father the devil, and the desires of your father you want to do. He was a murderer from the beginning, and does not stand in the truth, because there is no truth in him. When he speaks a lie, he speaks from his own resources, for he is a liar and the father of it. (John 8:44, NKJV)

> The thief does not come except to steal, and to kill, and to destroy. I have come that they may have life, and that they may have it more abundantly. (John 10:10, NKJV)

> But now after you have known God, or rather are known by God, how is it that you turn again to the weak and beggarly elements,

to which you desire again to be in bondage?
(Gal. 4:9, NKJV)

Basing your decision not just on those three verses, but also remembering everything that you have learned about Christ Jesus, what do you want your source to be? Jesus, of course! So your source is Jesus and His Word.

Step 2. Repentance: Generally you don't build a new house on top of the old, so repentance can be viewed as tearing down the old house—getting rid of all that defilement, the old foundation. Sometimes the teams on my show are able to reuse some of the old materials, sometimes it all gets thrown away. *We're not re-using anything!* We are starting fresh.

Repentance defined is "to be sorry, and stop doing the action you regret." Generally, we say to repent means to turn your back on the sin, which means that when you do that, you will be facing God again.

There is no special prayer to pray; you just tell God that you are sorry for your sin, and you live in a way that honors God, instead of returning you to that sin. When you are repenting, remember also to repent of bitterness and unforgiveness toward others.

"Brethren, I do not count myself to have apprehended; but one thing I do, forgetting those things which are behind and reaching forward to those things which are ahead, I press toward the goal for the prize of the upward call of God in Christ Jesus" (Phil. 3:13–14, NKJV).

It is impossible for us to move forward in good health and freedom, if we continually look back, and that's what we do if we are harboring unforgiveness toward someone.

Step 3. Reconciliation: Lay the new foundation. This follows naturally with that repentance and forgiveness that is required in rebuilding our foundation. Re-establish healthy relationships. Leave unhealthy ones behind.

Step 4. Restoration: Begin building the new house. At this point, you have torn down the old foundation, laid a new one, and now you are ready to rebuild. Satan wants nothing more than to keep you in his grip. He will do all he can to snatch God's Word from your heart. He wants it to seem difficult to live for Jesus and follow God.[23]

> Listen! Behold, a sower went out to sow. And it happened, as he sowed, that some seed fell by the wayside; and the birds of the air came and devoured it. Some fell on stony ground, where it did not have much earth; and immediately it sprang up because it had no depth of earth. But when the sun was up it was scorched, and because it had no root it withered away. And some seed fell among thorns; and the thorns grew up and choked it, and it yielded no crop. But other seed fell on good ground and yielded a crop that sprang up, increased and produced: some thirtyfold, some sixty, and some a hundred. ...And He said to them, "Do you not understand this parable? How then will you understand all the parables? The sower sows the word. And these are the ones by the wayside where the word is sown. When they hear, Satan comes immediately and takes away the word that was sown in their hearts. These likewise are the ones sown on stony ground who, when they hear the word, immediately receive it with gladness; and they have no

root in themselves, and so endure only for
a time. Afterward, when tribulation or persecution arises for the word's sake, immediately they stumble. Now these are the ones
sown among thorns; they are the ones who
hear the word, and the cares of this world,
the deceitfulness of riches, and the desires for
other things entering in choke the word, and
it becomes unfruitful. But these are the ones
sown on good ground, those who hear the
word, accept it, and bear fruit: some thirty-
fold, some sixty, and some a hundred." (Mar.
4:3–20, NKJV)

Now is when you must particularly be on guard to protect
the new or renewed seed of hope you have. Your enemy, Satan,
will come and try to immediately steal your hope by bringing
more conflict into those newly mended relationships. When
that happens, you return to your source—God's Word:

So I will restore to you the years that the
swarming locust has eaten, The crawling
locust, The consuming locust, And the chew-
ing locust, My great army which I sent among
you. (Joel 2:25, NKJV)

Trust in the LORD with all your heart,
And lean not on your own understanding.
(Prov. 3:5, NKJV)

And before you know it, you will be shouting "Hallelujah!
Look what God is doing!"

Step 5. Revival: Possess your new home. Move in to it!

"You who laid the foundations of the earth, So that it should not be moved forever" (Ps. 104:5 NKJV).

In Deuteronomy 23, there is a passage that made me very uncomfortable. Paraphrased, it says *that there are some people who may join in covenant relationship—the relationship between you and God is that covenant we talked about earlier—they may join in covenant relationship but they may not join in the fellowship of the saints—as we are right now, as we do on Sunday mornings, if they or their ancestors for ten generations back have done certain things.*

Among that list of "certain things" are pagan rituals that would not apply to our culture today. But among those things that would keep us out of fellowship is forbidden marriages, illegitimate children, and children from prostitution or rape. Now, I realize that his passage has little to do with God's promises for us, but there is a principle here that we need to address, at this point: We, as grafted-in children of Abraham, accept the laws, as well as the promises of the Old Testament. Yet, when a law seems uncomfortable to adhere to, we set that one aside as if it isn't there, and say that it was only meant for Old Testament Israelites. That we would accept *part* of God's Word as truth and set aside other parts breaks the law of adding to or taking away from God's Word. And *that* can result in our being removed from God's book of life, so I went to the source.

I was on my knees and basically wrestled with God as Jacob did, until I got my answer to my question: How can we commit to living by your laws, Lord, when some of them just don't apply to today's culture? How can I, as a divorcee, keep covenant with you and not be allowed to fellowship with my church family? And our great God answered me, "Now, my child, you understand grace."

The reason I felt the need to include that little aside is because we frequently cheat ourselves out of God's great abundance because we think we may be unworthy, because of our past mistakes. God says, "You are forgiven. You are my child. Understand grace."

> Therefore, having been justified by faith, we have peace with God through our Lord Jesus Christ, through whom also we have access by faith into this grace in which we stand, and rejoice in hope of the glory of God. And not only that, but we also glory in tribulations, knowing that tribulation produces perseverance; and perseverance, character; and character, hope. Now hope does not disappoint, because the love of God has been poured out in our hearts by the Holy Spirit who was given to us. (Rom. 5:1–5, NKJV)

Pray, receiving grace, thanking Him for His promises of grace and all the other promises He has made to us. Help us to focus on Him throughout the day and focus on the way He sees His children, as royalty.

You are a solid rock and will not be easily moved. Rejection no longer has the hold on you that it once did, because your foundation—your *new* foundation—your new house is built on the Rock, Jesus Christ. There will be floods and winds come against your house, but your house shall stand. Jesus is your everlasting source. No one can ever take that away from you. You are accepted in the Beloved.

Chapter 35

Wound Recovery

Truth—generally speaking, it does our heart good to hear the truth…scripture even tells us the truth will set us free. You fall and hurt your leg so you go to the doctor. He examines you. Your leg is not broken. Yes, you took quite a tumble and the pain is still there, but your heart feels better, just knowing your leg is not broken. But you've also heard it said that the truth hurts, right? To continue with that scenario, the bone in your leg isn't broken, but the muscles are torn. You might be immobile longer than if it had been broken. Either way, you're dealing with the truth. When it comes to things like our physical health, that first diagnosis can change; initial X-rays didn't show a break. But a second X-ray might show a fracture. The truth itself didn't change. Your knowledge of the truth changed. There was no lie involved when the doctor said "no break," but deeper examination revealed deeper truth.

Sometimes it takes deeper examination to discern the truth from a lie…a second look and sometimes a third and a fourth, to reveal whether or not a truth is absolute truth or not. If that broken leg is what is called a compound fracture, the bone is sticking out of the skin. Doesn't take a second look to know that it is broken. But something can be broken on the inside and never show a sign on the outside of anything at all being out of place. So if there is no sign of anything wrong, we don't always look closer, do we? Until we see or feel the symptoms: fever, pain, inability to function, lack of mobility or energy. When those things occur, then we start taking stock of our physical health to get to the truth of what might be wrong or broken... can we repair it ourselves? Eat better? Drink more water? Get more exercise? Get more rest? Or do we need a doctor? And when we go to the doctor, are we going to do what that doctor recommends? Because if we don't, the wound will only fester and never heal properly.

In emotional or spiritual wounds, the symptoms are frequently the same. Extreme cases cause us to be unable to eat or sleep, sometimes unable to function and move forward. And the remedy isn't so easily visible as with physical wounds. If our leg is hurt, we go to the doctor, get X-rays and do whatever the doctor says.

If our heart is broken or our spirit is wounded, the Doctor (capital D) doesn't have a clinic, He has the Church. Our Great Physician can heal our physical wounds through doctors, hospitals, and medicines, or He can heal us supernaturally. He can heal our emotional and spiritual wounds through His Word and His love and through His Church.

The first thing we must do when we are wounded is admit that we're hurt. Face the truth. Sometimes people hurt people. It may be intentional or it may be accidental, but either way, we can be hurt by other people's actions or words. If we feel the symptoms, we have to admit there is an injury, so we can take that second look to get to the bottom of things and find the truth. Why are we hurt? What happened?

When you realize that there was indeed an injury, it just keeps getting worse and worse because it has been left untreated. And we may never know the real cause of the injury in the first place, because the wound itself can't or won't speak up. The wound is now revealed and it is time to cleanse it and treat it and heal.

Satan is good at his job. That's one of those truths that isn't pleasant to hear, but it is still a truth. He has been God's enemy since the beginning of time, so he has worked at his job forever. When you gave your life to Jesus, Satan became your enemy too. And although you may not have even realized it, he began right then and there, to weaken you, immobilize you, deceive you, and do whatever he can to either stop you from doing anything Jesus wants you to do, or to destroy your Christian witness.

Your Christian witness—Scripture tells us that faith without works is dead (James 2:20). What I say and what I do as a Christian is all anyone else gets to see. They can't look into my heart and see that when I was nine years old, I went forward at an altar call in church camp and asked Jesus to be my Lord and Savior. And if I tell people that they still have the choice whether or not to believe it. But actions speak louder than words, don't they? So if I speak truth and not lies, if I am loving and kind to people even when they might not be so loving and kind to me, if I help to heal hurts instead of causing more wounds or pouring salt in wounds, that is my Christian witness. If I tell lies, gossip, or do things that are cruel or hurtful toward other people, that negatively affects my Christian witness.

Our salvation isn't earned by these works or acts, it is displayed by them. So if Satan can tarnish our Christian witness, he has succeeded at his job. And like I said, Satan is good at his job. But God is better at His! And He is always right there by our side, always, when our peace is threatened by our enemy. He is always there with His healing balm to ease the pain and begin the healing process, even before we know the full truth of the injury revealed by that closer examination.

The Christian witness of every Christian has come under attack at one time or another. Because that's what our enemy does. I want to share with you some of the scriptures revealed to me when my husband and I came under attack. These are just a few that help to prevent further pain and infection.

- (This is when Joseph is reunited with his brothers after they threw him in the pit and changed his entire life) "But as for you, you meant evil against me; *but God* meant it for good, in order to bring it about as it is this day, to save many people alive" (Gen. 50:20, NKJV).

  Whether God had it planned all along or Satan took hold of those brothers is a matter for theologians to determine, but the act was meant for evil. *But God*—those two words can stand alone and above all issues that come against us. Because God is in it with us, just as He was with Joseph. And God's plan will always prevail. It's a huge comfort to know that!

- "And we know that all things work together for good to those who love God, to those who are called according to His purpose" (Rom. 8:28, NKJV).

  God works all things for His glory and my good…His glory and your good, if you love God. Because if you love God, you are called to His purpose. If Satan can get your mind off God and what God wants for you and your life, he is succeeding. *But God*…is more powerful.

- (This is to Jehoshaphat when he was facing three armies.) "You will not need to fight in this battle. Position yourselves, stand still and see the salvation of the LORD, who is with you, O Judah and Jerusalem! Do not fear or be dismayed; tomorrow go out against them, for the LORD is with you" (2 Chron. 20:17, NKJV).

Sometimes, we are told to put on the armor of God and go into battle. When that happens, God is the captain of the host and leads us. Sometimes the battle belongs to the Lord. We are to stand and see...stand and watch God work.

- "For the Lord GOD will help Me; Therefore I will not be disgraced; Therefore I have set My face like a flint, And I know that I will not be ashamed. He is near who justifies Me; Who will contend with Me? Let us stand together. Who is My adversary? Let him come near Me. Surely the Lord GOD will help Me; Who is he who will condemn Me? Indeed they will all grow old like a garment; The moth will eat them up" (Isa. 50:7–9, NKJV).

These verses tell us that when it is our character or our Christian witness that is under attack, we must be faithful. We can stand together in our beliefs and trust that God has the final word. God has led me to some obscure verses during trying times. That was one of them. I knew I'd read them, but I had totally forgotten them. Just proves John 14:26—the Holy Spirit brings to our remembrance the things we have learned in His Word.

- "And who is he who will harm you if you become followers of what is good? But even if you should suffer for righteousness' sake, you are blessed. 'and do not be afraid of their threats, nor be troubled.' But sanctify the Lord God in your hearts, and always be ready to give a defense to everyone who asks you a reason for the hope that is in you, with meekness and fear; having a good conscience, that when they defame you as evildoers, those who revile your good conduct in Christ may be ashamed" (1 Pet. 3:13–16, NKJV).

These scriptures gives us the soothing balm we need, but they also tell us how we are to act and how to conduct ourselves in a manner that honors God and protects our Christian witness (good conduct)—or they tell us to stand firm because He is going to do that, and how we are to maintain a good conscience.

Our recovery from such wounds begins when we examine the wound in truth and love, and pour healing balm into the wound through God's Word. Our healing continues when we begin making the choice to forgive those who have hurt us and we examine ourselves and repent of our part, in how we reacted or responded.

There is no formula to healing, no timetable. No two wounded people are going to heal in quite the same way. There is one thing that every wounded believer has in common: He is not alone. God is still in control and He is right there guiding our healing. And He wants you to be healthy and successful.

It is God's plan that the children of God learn from the incident so that when we see other brothers and sisters who are suffering or who have suffered, and we can come alongside them and bring them through the pain to healing, like He brought us through, and that helps us to continue to heal.

My husband closes every service with the wise admonition to "go and be the church." Helping other wounded folks heal is part of what it means to "go and be the church." That's what we as a body must continue to do to regain health and to grow and to continue to be the strong body God has called us to be. That's what every individual believer must do, to be healthy, to grow and be a strong believer in Christ.

To repeat 2 Chron. 20:17: "Position yourselves, stand still and see the salvation of the LORD, who is with you, O Judah and Jerusalem! Do not fear or be dismayed…for the LORD is with you" (NKJV).

Chapter 36
Give Them What They Deserve?

If you have ever lived through the devastation of someone deeply hurting you, you probably didn't want to hear the words, "Vengeance is mine, saith the Lord." But if you are a Christian, you didn't have to hear them, they came into your heart at the very moment that you toyed with the idea of getting even.

In many of my roles (pastor's wife, pastor's assistant, counselor, church leader), I have been privy to some severe wounds that Christians can inflict on other Christians. Sometimes those wounds appear totally accidental. Remorse, repentance, and reconciliation were immediately sought and received, and God's kingdom suffered a bump and perhaps a bit of a bruise that healed fairly quickly.

In other situations, whether the wounds were inflicted with no ill intent or were intended for serious damage, there was harm done. If there was no attempt at getting to the truth of what happened; if there was no advancement made toward repentance or forgiveness, then indeed, there was no reconciliation made. The damage is done.

God has made it clear to my husband and myself that He specifically called us and trained us (especially my husband) to help hurting churches heal. Sometimes warriors get hurt. Praise God that in our own wounds, God has covered us; He has protected us and made sure that any wounds inflicted on us were covered by His love, mercy, and especially by His healing balm. The more serious any wounds that we have received were the more healing balm He administered to us through His Word, through His Holy Spirit, through His people, and through the wonderful worship songs that are so dear to both of us. I must say that throughout our journey, Hutch has always been ready to go "full steam ahead," without much rest or rehab needed in between. Myself, not so much.

My husband has always recognized my need to recuperate from hurts inflicted upon us. God has always honored our choice to "take a break," when the wounds were more than I felt we could handle. After one particularly difficult healing, I can remember telling my Lord that I wasn't sure I ever wanted to pastor a church again. He spoke to me, comforted me, and put me in a nurturing church for healing, for nearly three years, before he called us to another church. We always worked in secular jobs, in between churches, and that's where we were, making a decent living, when we were approached to pastor another church. The initial excitement in both of us was instantly shadowed, for me, by a sense of foreboding. Was I up for it? The concern only lasted momentarily though, because deep down both of us always knew we were waiting on God. Whenever He wanted us, we would go. We started praying to be sure it was where God wanted us to go.

It was, and we did. We were instantly welcomed into this little church family. These were solid Christian folks, well-versed in Scripture and hungry for whatever adventure God would lead them into through this new pastor and his wife. In Genesis 24, Abraham sends his trusted servant to find his son, Isaac, a wife. When the servant realizes he has come directly to the woman who is part of Abraham's family, who is to be Isaac's wife, he rejoices: "And he said, 'Blessed be the LORD God of my master Abraham, who has not forsaken His mercy and His truth toward my master. As for me, being on the way, the LORD led me to the house of my master's brethren'" (Gen. 24:27, NKJV).

It fits our situation so beautifully! God led us to the house of "our Master's" family! We were loved as if we were family, the moment we arrived.

We had tremendous support from the beginning, and we had a few who weren't too sure either of us knew what we were doing! Less than two years into our service, Satan stepped in and started wreaking havoc. I won't go into details, but Satan can use anyone and he certainly had a field day. Our little church was endangered and God's warriors stepped into battle. Throughout the turmoil, Hutch and I repeatedly heard the Lord's instruction through Scripture, that this battle was not ours. As the song goes, "The Battle Belongs to the Lord."

"You will not need to fight in this battle. Position yourselves, stand still and see the salvation of the LORD, who is with you, O Judah and Jerusalem!" (2 Chron. 20:17, NKJV).

People in our congregation contacted us with encouragement, when we felt our hands were tied. The trauma built up for several months but came to a head, with the church council calling for our resignation! Men of God stepped in and went into battle for my husband and counseled him. Women of God that I knew—even women who did not go to my church—were by my side nearly any time of the night or day that I needed a friend. My dear girlfriends took the time to take pictures on their phones of a particularly applicable daily devotional and sent them to me, which were so encouraging!

"But as for you, you meant evil against me; but God meant it for good, in order to bring it about as it is this day, to save many people alive" (Gen. 50:20, NKJV).

God Himself continually surrounded us with His comforting angels, as well as His huge warring ones! I am pleased to say that the church body rallied and refused our resignation. Through their hard work and the guidance of our regional executive minister, God's will was carried out and we were vindicated. The council was found to be in error and was removed, and a new council put in place.

This was a different scenario that I was used to. The hurting churches God had led us to in the past were not ones that we were called to as permanent pastors. We were interim. We knew it going in. But this was not an interim position. We had fallen in love with the people in this church and the community, and we weren't planning on leaving any time soon. So once the immediate threat to this church was over, we were still here and still hurting, as was our church family. We were healing together from this nearly mortal wound that our enemy, Satan had inflicted on us.

"But if you do not forgive, neither will your Father in heaven forgive your trespasses" (Mark 11:26, NKJV).

Scripture tells us that we must forgive those who hurt us. So much of what Hutch preached from the pulpit for nearly the next year was covering forgiveness. It's not easy to forgive, and believe me, we knew that, because at times, neither of *us* felt much like forgiving either. Most of the congregation didn't know the entirety of what went on behind the scenes. Hutch and I and the new leadership agreed that it would serve no purpose to share details, and could very well further injure this tender and still hurting church that we love.

There were times when I cried into the night, wondering why we didn't see any justice. It wasn't long, however, that God led me to pray for those who were involved. My decision to be obedient did more to help me heal than I could ever have imagined. Over a year later, I don't think much about it anymore. "But God" brings it to mind how blessed I am to have the family of God that I have.

With every heartache I have ever survived, God has used my pain. When He healed me of it, He *always* led me to write it down so I could remember it. Why would I want to remember my pain? So God can use me to help someone else. My healing has *always* come by helping someone else heal. I fully expect God will be consistent and use this, the most devastating hurt I have ever been dealt, to help someone else heal. What lessons in the learning throughout this process!

In a recent devotional, God sparked my heart, first by reminding me of several verses that were so encouraging to me during that time:

> O my God, I trust in You; Let me not be ashamed; Let not my enemies triumph over me. Indeed, let no one who waits on You be ashamed; Let those be ashamed who deal treacherously without cause. (Ps. 25:2–3, NKJV)
>
> Do not gather my soul with sinners, Nor my life with bloodthirsty men, in whose hands is a sinister scheme, And whose right hand is full of bribes. But as for me, I will walk in my integrity; Redeem me and be merciful to me. (Ps. 26:9–11, NKJV)
>
> When the wicked came against me To eat up my flesh, My enemies and foes, They stumbled and fell. (Ps. 27:2, NKJV)

Then the next day, a friend of mine had loaned me her copy of *23 Minutes in Hell,*[24] so I started reading it. I highly recommend the book, but it is not an easy read! After reading just one chapter, I had a very vivid picture of the pit of hell, and my heart was broken for all lost souls. Needing to feel encouraged (as God's Word always does for me), I picked up the devotional for the next day: "A Psalm of David. To You I will cry, O LORD my Rock: Do not be silent to me, Lest, if You are silent to me, I become like those who go down to the pit" (Ps. 28:1, NKJV).

Again "the pit!" The fiery picture leapt back into my mind, so I quickly continued reading:

> Do not take me away with the wicked And with the workers of iniquity, Who speak peace to their neighbors, But evil is in their hearts. Give them according to their deeds, And according to the wickedness of their endeavors; Give them according to the work of their hands; Render to them what they deserve. Because they do not regard the works of the LORD, Nor the *operation of His hands*, He shall destroy them And not build them up. (Ps. 28:3–5, NKJV; emphasis mine)

God's Words throughout the Psalms, Chapters 25–28 kept reminding me of the evil turmoil He delivered us through during that time. I remembered vividly the wickedness spearheaded by one person. I remembered how that person totally manipulated those on the council and a few who attended our church.

David's descriptions in this prayer struck home in my memory. How loving and generous that person was when we first moved here, and yet how evil the plan of the heart became when it was discovered that Hutch would not be manipulated. How clearly God's words were disregarded unless they were twisted into something suitable for the intended evil purposes. That person totally tried to destroy us because we are God's servants and are 100 percent on board with "the operation of His hands."

This passage cries out for God to give them their just desserts, to give them what they deserve, to punish them, to bring justice. A part of me understands David's cry for justice. There is also a part of me that cries out for something else. I flashback to that intense picture of the pit! I wouldn't want anyone to be condemned to that! The biggest part of me (what I hope is the best part of me) begs for God to heal all of those who took part in the evil attempt at ungodly leadership of His church. Yet there is another part of me still that is a little bit afraid that my human nature may step in. I do not want to be like Jonah and not want God to extend his love and forgiveness toward them. *"Oh, Lord God, I am so very grateful and happy that you are in charge and I am not."*

It wasn't but a day or two after I wrote that journal entry based on that devotional, that an acquaintance called and was horribly upset by a situation in her life. She was in a position where she couldn't remove herself from someone who was inflicting serious mental anguish into her life. I was able to share this only because God had brought it all to my remembrance, as He promises to do, when I needed it.

God is truly faithful. He only allows us to go through pain, so that we can learn and turn it around for our good, and His glory! Next time you are hurt, trust God to (1) see you through it, (2) heal you, (3) and to protect you and let Him use you to heal someone else. It is *so* much better than "giving them what they deserve."

Have you been hurt? Whether by a person inside or outside of the church, God wants us to heal. The old saying goes, "Hurt people hurt people." As a counselor, that line has gone through my mind hundreds of times. As I am listening to someone's story, knowing they are begging for help, I realize and understand that line is so true. In teaching lay counselors for God's service, the line is completed: "Hurt people hurt people, but healed people heal people." Of course it is God who ultimately heals us, but our jobs as counselor is to lead those broken hearts to God's plan for their healing.

When we use our past hurts to help others heal, our own healing becomes complete. Our healing can be stifled when we choose to "suffer in silence." That doesn't mean we're supposed to bad-mouth the person who has wounded us. While we are wounded, we tend to strike out. That does nothing toward our healing, and more often than not, makes matters worse, and quite often it leads to actions on our part, that *we* need to ask God to forgive *us* for. Our healing begins by taking the wound to our Lord and Savior Jesus Christ.

Spend some time doing that. He is our Comforter. He is the One most qualified to heal your hurt, because He was witness to it. He already knows the hurt, the intent, and your pain. If you are still suffering, call your pastor, or his wife, a godly friend, or someone you feel comfortable with. Set up an appointment and be honest with them to begin your healing. Your healing will progress at whatever pace God sees necessary and you continue to be open and pliable. (Remember God can work so much better with soft clay than hardened.) It may be complete after that first meeting. You may have to return for more help. Trust that God wants you healed. Remember also that your goal is to be healed. It is not to see the other person punished. (Remember the opening thought: "Vengeance is mine saith the Lord.")

Chapter 37

Holiness—the Lord's Supper

In this book, I've written quite a lot about being totally devoted to God, about destroying sacred pillars in our lives, about putting God first, about influencing other people to do the same thing, about being obedient to God, about giving our tithes in our offerings so that God's kingdom can be advanced. All those things are a part of being totally devoted to God. Another facet to cultivate in our journey to become totally devoted to God: holiness. It is defined as a sacred place or thing, a consecrated, dedicated, or hallowed place or thing.

In all of Genesis the word *holy* or *holiness* does not even exist. Nor do the words pure, sanctified, sacred, dedicated, or hallowed. None of those words which we use to define the word holy or holiness is even in scripture until the first mention of it, when the Lord God himself says it. It's when Moses is approaching the burning bush. God is presenting himself to a mere mortal man.

"Then He said, 'Do not draw near this place. Take your sandals off your feet, for the place where you stand is holy ground'" (Exod. 3:5, NKJV).

God is holy. The very ground He walks on, if He were walking on the ground, is holy. Moses cannot approach too closely because God is holy and man is not. Moses was not holy.

He was guilty of sin. Is that a definition of holiness? Can you be holy if you have sin in your life?

Moses's life was not an easy one, but throughout his life he grew to know what holiness was. He became consecrated, dedicated, set apart to God because of God's holiness. Moses walked in close proximity to God. God placed him in the cleft of the rock to protect him with His own hand as God's glory passed by him. That's as close as anyone ever got to God, until Jacob wrestled with Him in Genesis 32:22–32. So I'm willing to go out on a limb and say that Moses knew God and understood holiness. But does that mean Moses was holy? In fact the definition itself says a sacred place or thing, so can a person even be holy?

Leviticus 19:2 tells us that God says, "You shall be holy, for I the Lord your God am holy" (NKJV).

If it were not possible to live a holy life, God would not have commanded it. To be holy means to be separated to God—for *His* purpose. God's nature itself defines holiness. That's what Moses grew to know personally. Being set apart to God makes us holy. We're not made holy by doing good things. We are made holy by faith in Christ Jesus, just as we are saved by faith.

Little by little, as we grow and live with the Lord we will become more like Him. As we think about Jesus, learn about Him and pray to Him, as we spend more time with Him, and seek to follow His example we become more like Him. We begin to think like Him and act like Him and to *love* like Him. We become like Him because we are set apart to him and that is true holiness.

If you are a Christian, your life ten years from now should be considerably different from what it is now. Your motives and desires as you draw closer to God should be continuously more holy. We can only achieve a certain degree of holiness in this life. It comes from God, as we grow closer to Him and we become more like Him. Although perfection is not totally attainable in this life, it is something we should continually strive toward and aim for, for Christian maturity and holy living are the substance of our being a responsible son or daughter of God.

Mature holiness is seen in people who have stopped being concerned about their own needs and have entered into God's big vision, so that a hurting world can be transformed. Having said that, I want you to keep in mind none of us are holy. We are a work in progress. We will be until we see Jesus face-to-face.

> But let a man examine himself and then let him eat of the bread and drink of the cup for whoever eats and drinks in an unworthy manner eats and drinks judgment to himself not discerning the Lord's body. For this reason, many are weak and sick among you and many sleep. For if we would judge ourselves, we would not be judged, but when we are judged, we are chastened by the Lord that we may not be condemned with the world. (1 Cor. 11:28–32, NKJV)

If we allow ourselves to go through life living however we want to, and never stop to look at our hearts and see how our actions and our motives please or displease God, we risk being chastised by the Lord and condemned with the world.

We need to keep ourselves holy, and Scripture here is telling us how to do that. We take a good look at ourselves and judge ourselves as if God is judging us to see what is in our hearts that we need to clean up, repent of, and turn away from before we come to the Communion table.

Repent—to turn back (hence, away) as if in change (not necessarily with the idea of returning to the starting point), to bring home again, to cease, to convert, deliver again, draw back, to get oneself back, pull in again, recompense, recover, refresh. We do it an injustice when we say it means to turn away from sin; it does, but it's so much more than that.

Just as the act of water baptism outwardly declares the inward expression of salvation through the blood of Jesus, each time we approach the communion table, we declare that we have examined our hearts and repented and thereby renewed our communion with God. Each observance of the Lord's Supper is a powerful occasion for the confession of our renewed faith. Each time we partake in the bread and the cup, we confess not only that we believe but also that we have not forgotten.

Verses 24 and 25 say "in remembrance of Me." It involves more than just a memory. The word *remembrance* suggests an active "calling to mind" of what Jesus did on our behalf. The Lord's Supper is not a ritual but an active renewed confession of Jesus's death, our acknowledgment of the horrible pain and suffering He bore on our behalf and a true appreciation of the full redemption power that Jesus availed to us on that cross.

> For I received from the Lord that which I also delivered to you: that the Lord Jesus on the same night in which He was betrayed took bread; and when He had given thanks, He broke it and said, "Take, eat; this is My body which is broken for you; do this in remembrance of Me." In the same manner He also took the cup after supper, saying, "This cup is the new covenant in My blood. This do, as often as you drink it, in remembrance of Me." (1 Cor. 11:23–26, NKJV)

Scripture doesn't dictate when we take communion, only that when we do, we remember what Jesus did for us. Most evangelical churches celebrate this holy sacrament once a month. If you don't know when your church serves communion, call and ask. Then prepare for it. Don't take the elements lightly. Examine your heart. In prayer, ask the Lord God to show you if there is anything that he wants you to take care of before you partake of the elements.

If you don't have a relationship with the Lord, this precious bread and cup means nothing. It will not save you. But if you want to have that relationship right now you can do that between you and God. Just invite Him into your heart and tell Him that you believe in all that He did for you, all that you've been reading talking about, that He gave his life for you that you would not spend eternity separated from God.

Chapter 38

The Names of God

According to best-selling author Ann Spangler,[25] there are twenty-six names of God in Scripture, and that doesn't count the ones for Jesus Himself. I believe there are more than that, but I've pick out several that I have known firsthand.

In the Jewish culture, people named their children carefully. Their names always meant something. In Scripture, Sarah laughed when she was told at age ninety that she would have a baby. When that prophecy came true, she named her son Isaac, which means "laughter." Names matter. You have many names. I know a woman named Arlene. My friend Sue calls her Mom. Another friend, Betty, calls Arlene, Sis. Gaye calls her Aunt Arlene. Emily calls her Grandma. If you look up the definition of Arlene, it means pledge or promise. So no matter what someone calls us, our name means something. Out of curiosity, I looked up what my name means in Hebrew. It means innovative, dynamic, supportive, and understanding. Often they think about others and not about themselves. They are kind, sympathetic, generous, support and help, direct, with confidence. They may be prone to stubbornness and dominance. The names of God are like that. They depict who He is or what He does. And like my definition, sometimes it takes more than a word or two to explain them. The Hebrew language is like that.

The names of God reveal His character to His people. No matter what concern you have, there is a name of God—a characteristic of God that covers it, and frequently more than one. It isn't vital that you remember all of the names He has. But it can be reassuring to you, to know that if you are praying for a healing, He has a specific name for that—but let's start at the beginning.

"In the beginning God created the heavens and the earth…" (Gen. 1:1, NKJV).

God the creator. Elohim—the word contains the idea of God's creative power. It is used in Scripture more than 2,500 times, 32 times in Genesis alone, not only depicting God's creative power, but also His sovereignty and authority over everything He has created. You get the idea? More than a word or two was needed to give you the full idea of who Elohim is.

In Genesis 17:1–2 God revealed Himself to Abraham as God Almighty—El Shaddai—"And when Abram was ninety-nine years old, Jehovah appeared to Abram and said to him, I am the Almighty God! Walk before Me and be perfect. And I will make My covenant between Me and you, and will multiply you exceedingly." Mighty—all powerful—literally, the name means "God, the Mountain One." The One for whom nothing is impossible. The longer description prompts your heart to grasp the fullness of the name.

Yahweh—the name Yahweh, if written in English, is YHWH. If your Bible shows the word LORD in all caps, in most instances, that was translated from the word Yahweh. It's in the Old Testament 6,800 times and it was forbidden to even speak the Name. When it was finally spoken (originally only by the priests) it was pronounced Jehovah: "And God said to Moses again, You shall say this to the sons of Israel, Jehovah the God of your fathers, the God of Abraham, the God of Isaac, and the God of Jacob, has sent me to you. This is My name forever, and this is My title from generation to generation" (Exod. 3:15, NKJV).

Jehovah Jireh—Jehovah (the Lord) Will Provide. The root word of Jireh means "to see beforehand." So this name literally means Jehovah sees the need and provides. It's the name Abraham used when he took Isaac up to the mountain to be sacrificed (Gen. 22). He prayed this name so Jehovah Jireh would provide the lamb for sacrifice and spare his son, and that is exactly what God did.

The name "Adonai" means Master. "Oh my soul, you have said to Jehovah, You are my Lord;—you are Adonai—I have no goodness apart from You" (Ps. 16:2).

Remember, the names of God depict His character to us. In this case, this name depicts what He wants our relationship to be. A characteristic He wants in us. He is our Lord and Master. This Hebrew word depicts the word *lord* as owner, superior, to be revered and respected.

Jehovah Shalom—you've heard the word *shalom* before—peace. This name means God our peace. But "peace" usually refers to our inner peace, the calm we feel inside. The word *shalom* goes deeper. Yes, it means our inner peace but also absence from outer conflict; it means safety, completeness, wholeness, wellness. So if you go to Israel and someone greets you with "Shalom," they are extending so much more to you than calmness!

Shalom comes from living in harmony with God. When Gideon was called to serve the Lord as the Mighty Man of Valor we have come to know him as, he was in fact sweeping the floor. When God told Him what He wanted him to do, Gideon was a bit timid about it.

"And Jehovah said to him, Peace to you. Do not fear. You shall not die. Then Gideon built an altar there to Jehovah, and called it Jehovah-shalom" (Judg. 6:23–24, NKJV).

Jehovah Rophe—the Lord Who Heals. Rophe means heal, cure, restore, or make whole. We've called Him the Great Physician. But Jehovah Rophe heals body soul and spirit—physical, mental, and spiritual.

> And he said, If you will carefully listen to the voice of Jehovah your God, and will do that which is right in His sight, and will give ear to His commandments, and keep all His Laws, I will put none of these diseases upon you, which I have brought upon the Egyptians; for I am Jehovah who heals you. (Exod. 15:26, NKJV)

God revealed Himself to the Israelites as the Lord that Heals when they were complaining about having nothing to eat and the waters were bitter. This name doesn't just apply to the person, it also applies to healing the waters (turning the bitter water sweet), healing a nation. It can mean deliverance from death, sin, and demons, as well as sickness in a person.

Jehovah Machseh—God our Refuge, I think of calling 911 when we turn to Psalm 91:1–2: "He who dwells in the secret place of the Most High shall rest under the shadow of the Almighty. I will say of Jehovah, my refuge and my fortress; my God; in Him I will trust" (NKJV).

This name is actually a conglomeration of names, because for each word—refuge, high-tower, fortress, shelter, dwelling place—there is a different Hebrew word. But they all come down to the same thing—a safe place we can run when we are in trouble. But that word "dwelling place"—that means we live there; we with Him, He with us. That's our home, not just a place we run to, but a place where we live, day in and day out.

Jehovah Roi—the Lord My Shepherd. The Bible Study in Forman that I just finished leading was a Shepherd's Look at the Shepherd's Psalm—the 23rd Psalm. So much of our acceptance of the Lord as our Shepherd is dependent on our view of a shepherd (small *s*).

If we know certain things about our "sheep manager," we can accept Him truly as the Lord My Shepherd. For example, if we know that we know that we know that

    a)   He loves us unconditionally;

    b)   He knows where to find the good food and clean cool water;

    c)   He knows the best paths to lead us through; and

    d)   He is strong enough and wise enough to protect us from our enemies, even when that is ourselves.

Then, we are more likely to understand and accept this relationship and know that we can rely on Him.

Abba—the first time I ever heard someone pray to Daddy God, my shackles went up. I felt she was being flippant and disrespectful. She wasn't. She was praying to a Father to whom she was very close, with whom she had a special relationship. Whom she loved and she knew that He loved her.

It's only used in the New Testament—one time you are very familiar with: "And He said, Abba, Father [Daddy God], all things are possible to You. Take away this cup from Me. Yet not what I will, but what You will" (Mark 14:36, NKJV).

I have to admit that I was devastated when my former husband left me. The only way I got through it was to spend time every morning with the Lord and cry on His shoulder. I climbed up on Daddy God's lap every morning and poured out my heart and gained strength for every day. That's the relationship that we can have with our Father in heaven—our Daddy God. That's the relationship He wants us to have with Him. Yes, He wants us to revere him and respect Him. And we need to acknowledge Him as Master of our lives. He wants to be to us, everything that the names of God depict Him as! Our Almighty God, Master, our Peace, our Provider, our Healer, our Strong Tower, our Dwelling Place, our Shepherd, and our Daddy God. And not just these names! God wants to be everything to us and He wants to be Jehovah Shammah very present in our lives. He wants to be our everything!

Chapter 39

Giving and Tithing

The Old Testament priests were not allowed to raise their own sheep or plant their own grain, so their livelihood depended upon the people of Israel being obedient. A portion of the Israelites' offerings was always given to the priests. It was called the first-fruits and was their sole support. Tithe is defined as "tenth." The first mention of it in Scripture is in Genesis 14:20 and was a tithe (tenth) of all the goods plundered from a recent battle:

> Then Melchizedek king of Salem brought out bread and wine; he was the priest of God Most High. And he blessed him and said: "Blessed be Abram of God Most High, Possessor of heaven and earth; And blessed be God Most High, Who has delivered your enemies into your hand." And he gave him a tithe of all. (Gen. 14:18–20, NKJV)

It wasn't until Abraham's grandson Jacob (aka Israel) addressed the tenth later, that it became a covenant/promise to God:

> Then Jacob made a vow, saying, "If God will be with me, and keep me in this way that I am going, and give me bread to eat and clothing to put on, so that I come back to my father's house in peace, then the LORD shall be my God. And this stone which I have set as a pillar shall be God's house, and of all that You give me I will surely give a tenth to You." (Gen. 28:20–22, NKJV)

The building of altars acts as a reminder to the Israelites. Every time Jacob came to this altar, he would be reminded of the promise he made that he would give to God one-tenth of everything God gave to him. It wasn't a command for the Israelites to do likewise. Until God spoke through the prophet Malachi:

> "Bring all the tithes into the storehouse, That there may be food in My house, And try Me now in this," Says the LORD of hosts, "If I will not open for you the windows of heaven And pour out for you such blessing That there will not be room enough to receive it. And I will rebuke the devourer for your sakes, So that he will not destroy the fruit of your ground, Nor shall the vine fail to bear fruit for you in the field," Says the LORD of hosts; "And all nations will call you blessed, For you will be a delightful land," Says the LORD of hosts. (Mal. 3:10–13, NKJV)

The phrase "try me in this" means God is giving His "permission" to test Him, in this promise. This is the only time God invites His people to do this! And He will always pass the test! Shortly after I returned to fellowship with God, I was in a Sunday evening service in my new little church, listening to a teaching on tithes and offerings. The pastor shared some New Testament teachings on giving as well.

"Give, and it will be given to you: good measure, pressed down, shaken together, and running over will be put into your bosom. For with the same measure that you use, it will be measured back to you" (Luke 6:38, NKJV).

I had never been a tither because I was a single mom at the time, and money was tight. My six-hundred-dollar-house payment took half of my net income every month. The rest had to cover a car payment, insurance, gas and groceries, utilities, and the cost of raising a teenage son. Like I said, money was tight. I usually slipped a ten dollar bill in the offering plate, when I could spare it. (That would be an "offering: but not a tithe.) But the pastor had just urged us to trust in God's promise to give back to us, "running over."

The pastor stated that he had purchased the sound system to start this church with his personal credit card, and wanted to take a special offering to pay it off. I knew I had eighty dollars in cash left in my wallet, and my checkbook was bare. One-tenth of my check would have been sixty dollars. I didn't need much in groceries, but I did need to fill my tank before I could make too many trips in to work. I reached in and nervously took three twenties out and slipped them into the envelope. I prayed (silently I hope!), "Lord, you know how badly I need this back," as I dropped the envelope into the offering plate.

That very same week, when I opened my mortgage statement, I was surprised that it wasn't a statement; it was a letter stating that my escrow account had been overpaid and that the mortgage payment for the next month would be transferred from escrow. I would not have to make a house payment! I gave my tenth of sixty dollars, and God blessed me with six hundred dollars! That's definitely "running over!" I have not stopped tithing since then and God has not stopped blessing me! When I make my budget, I take a tenth "off the top." Sometimes, I give a little extra, if I can, but I consider that my offering. I may give my offering to the missionary I saw on TV last week, or to the building fund, but my tithe always goes to the general fund at my church. It is my belief that the tithe should go to where you are fed, spiritually. Then I pray that God will guide the church leaders and give them the wisdom they need to spend His money wisely. Then I trust Him to do that, because it's no longer my money, it's His! I urge you to "test" him, as I did. He will always pass the test!

Chapter 40

Dealing with Loss of a Loved One

If you have lost a loved one, your grief is uppermost in your mind. Your healing should be also. It is important to God. This may be a time when you feel totally alone and unloved. Nothing could be further from the truth. Your time of grieving will reveal to you that more people love you than you even realized. Being alone does not have to be a new normal for you. The goal of your healing is to bring you to a place where you are okay being alone, when you want to be.

"Be strong and of good courage, do not fear nor be afraid of them; for the LORD your God, He is the One who goes with you. He will not leave you nor forsake you" (Deut. 31:6, NKJV).

You were not alone when you got the news, you are not alone now. God promises to be by your side through every tear you shed through the heartbreak. The Holy Spirit is your Great Comforter. He is there with you. God has sent His ministering angels to surround you.

No two people grieve loss in the same way. As a survivor, it is important that you remember you are not alone. Most survivors seek some type of help in dealing with the immediate crisis. Even if you are an independent person and feel you can handle any situation, there may be a time when you can still draw help from others. That help and comfort, even months/years after your loss, could come from clergy, friends, neighbors, professional, relatives, and support groups. Please do not think you are weak when you reach out for help.

Loss of a spouse, whether by death or divorce, changes everything about your life. Your acceptance of those changes determines how you heal. You had no control over *those* changes, so make some positive changes that you do control. They don't have to be major changes. Rearrange your furniture! Don't be afraid to move that old recliner that you never liked in the first place. You can take it in stages and move it into a different room for the time being, but there is no room for guilt here! You need to focus on *your* healing and going where God is leading you. But don't let anyone convince you it's time to "get rid" of anything, until *you* are ready to do that. That, in itself is a step in your healing, and cannot be rushed. When you feel ready, don't let anyone tell you it's too soon either!

Although friends may give great, loving, caring hugs and offer help, you may not think there is a lot they can actually do. However, there *are* some things they *can* do. They can go out to dinner occasionally with you, so that you don't get into the habit of sitting at home and skipping a meal because you are now eating alone. When they invite you out for coffee, take them up on it! You don't have to talk about your feelings unless you want to. They can take you to a movie—a comedy! They can help you keep your focus on God and your future and not your past. (If someone you meet on the street asks, "How you are doing?" be honest and tell them as much as you want to tell them. If you aren't ready to go into any detail, just say something like, "Thanks for asking, but let's talk about something else," or, "Another time, maybe." If they push, just let them know you aren't ready to talk about it right now. A friend who is any decent friend at all will honor your wishes and let it drop.

There are stages to grief, and counselors generally agree on these two things: Everyone must go through each stage of grief, and everyone must go through each stage of grief *at their own pace.* My counselor also stated that there is nothing in "the textbooks" that say you have to go through each stage in order, nor that you won't "re-visit" a stage somewhere in the process.

The Grief Cycle:

1. Shock
2. Denial
3. Anger
4. Emptiness
5. Depression
6. Acceptance
7. Rebuilding
8. Rebuilding
9. Rebuilding
10. New Wholeness

This is not a ten-step process. There may be more rebuilding stages. The point is this: don't give up on yourself. Enlist the help of your friends—plural. Find a support group or create your own. For me, there were several women (many single, widow, or divorced, but a few were also married) from my church that became my Thursday night group. We had pizza, watched a sappy movie, and just encouraged each other. Be honest with them. Then they can better come alongside you and help lead you to new peace in your life.

When you get to the *anger* stage, remember that it is understandable that your anger may be aimed at your spouse. Don't let Satan beat you up because you feel angry! Your anger may be directed at God. God has already sent His Holy Spirit and His angels to comfort you and to minister to you. He knows your anger and is "big enough" to let you be angry. Might I suggest, instead of anger, you consider crawling up in Daddy God's lap and just letting Him comfort you through your tears. Pour out your heart to Him and open your ears to His loving kindness. Trust that He *will* give you a new reason to live and He *will* fill your life again with joy, if you let Him. Anger is one of the stages that I returned to several times over those first few years, but it does get better, I promise.

You had no control over what happened to change your life. During this time of change, there are some positive changes you can make that you *do* have control over, that really do help you heal. Starting a journal is one thing that helped me. Although I had written since I was a child, during this period I was writing *every day!* But this time, I was writing to God, daily, about my hurt, my anger, my guilt, everything I felt throughout my marriage—things I never got to say and do with my husband. Once I wrote them, I felt I had "given" all those emotions to God, for His safekeeping. They were there, any time I wanted to retrieve them, but little by little, I stopped picking them back up and I was able to leave them with God once and for all.

New activities helped also. I went back to college and got my degrees. I was blessed to be working for my church at the time, so my pastors were a tremendous support, and being in the same building most of the time made it a convenient shoulder! But again, little by little, I didn't do so much crying on their shoulders. I was able to lean more and more on God and His Word, and I could actually heal myself becoming me again. A new me, one that could share memories now and again without crying. One who could look back at a few things he didn't get done before he left, and I could forgive him, do them or hire them done, and smile, and go forward, one step at a time.

"And let us consider one another in order to stir up love and good works, not forsaking the assembling of ourselves together, as is the manner of some, but exhorting one another..." (Heb. 10:24–25, NKJV).

Rely on your church family. More than likely, they would love to help you, but *you* are the one who holds the reins. Tell them how they can help. I poured a lot of my time into church activities—taught at Vacation Bible School, sang a lot of specials at church, wrote articles for our local newspaper. Those were things that I hadn't done with my husband. Those were *my* interests. Pursue the interests that you, perhaps, left behind.

There was a time in my mourning when I was angry at myself for loving him too much. In truth, a marriage can only work when we *do* love each other "too much." God created us to love our spouses; to forgive them when they messed up, even if they never apologized. I became angry because of all the plans we had made that were now never going to happen. I had to forgive him for leaving before we had completed our life together. Then, I had to forgive myself for being angry about it! And I had to forgive God, even though I knew, deep in my heart, that God had not taken my husband from me.

Mourning is unique to everyone. Support by family is invaluable. But we also can be overwhelmed by family who are also mourning. Understand that family members have to mourn in their own way, in their own time, also. You may have to lovingly separate yourself occasionally from them in order to facilitate your own healing. Don't feel guilty! If you are advancing in your healing, when one of them calls you, be wise. Do you feel strong enough to keep them from pulling you back into a stage of grief that you have already accomplished?

Give yourself some grace when you feel like you aren't doing this "grief thing" correctly. There is no wrong way. The only right way is to keep your eyes on God, step-by-step, one day at a time, continually trusting Him that there are better days ahead! There is hope!

"This I recall to my mind, Therefore I have hope. Through the LORD's mercies we are not consumed, Because His compassions fail not. They are new every morning; Great is Your faithfulness" (Lam. 3:21–23, NKJV).

Suffering the loss of a spouse will bring loneliness. How you handle it can mean healing or stifling. My advice as a counselor is to let people know they are entitled to a "pity party." I put two conditions on it: It can't last more than fifteen minutes, and Jesus must be invited. Remember to take time for yourself and not just "keep busy." Taking time to take a refreshing walk by yourself, relax in a hot tub, participating in an activity alone are good ways to cope with the loneliness, rather than hiding or running from it. When you are comfortable being alone, consider yourself healed, even though you may not want to *always* be alone! We all need to be alone occasionally, without feeling lonely.

God has a plan for you that is not determined by whether you are single, married, widowed, or divorced. Spending time with God will help you understand that you were created specifically for that plan. Time with your Creator is just what the "doctor ordered" for you to become whole again, and ready, able and willing to go forward into that plan.

"For I know the thoughts that I think toward you, says the LORD, thoughts of peace and not of evil, to give you a future and a hope" (Jer. 29:11, NKJV).

Chapter 41
Daily Thoughts to Ponder

1. Newness—Genesis 19

I look out my dining room window at a magnificent thirty-foot Colorado Blue Spruce tree. Although it has been standing for about twenty years, I have admired it for only the past few years, since we moved to this wonderful small town in Southeast North Dakota. To me, it is still new, still fresh. Although the tree and I will (hopefully) both continue to get older, I pray that my perspective doesn't, that I continue to see that tree as new.

As we begin each new chapter of our lives, it is important that we see this era as a new one. Going into a new year with our old attitudes and mind-sets can only hinder our progress. Our walk with God is an adventure that changes and evolves every day—every moment. If our eyes are looking at unfinished issues from our past, we can't see clearly what God is calling us to see today. And if we can't see what He wants us to see, how can we do what He wants us to do?

When God brought Lot and his wife out of Sodom, into their adventure, they were told to look forward. Lot's wife could not go forward without looking back just one more time (Gen. 19:24) and God stopped her in her tracks. She was turned to a statue of salt, and Lot continued the adventure without her.

No matter what the last year was like for you, go forward. If it was good, don't look back. If it was bad, don't look back. If it was a combination, as most of us experienced, don't look back.

Look forward with new hope, leaving the past behind! Take a moment to—once and for all—write down those things that you're having trouble leaving behind. Write them briefly and pray the prayer at the end of the page.

_____

_____

_____

_____

_____

_____

_____

_____

_____

_____

_____

_____

_____

_____

_____

Father in heaven, I thank you for guiding me and strengthening me through the issues I have listed here. I give them to You now, knowing that You are faithful and willing to heal, fix, or deal with them. I trust that You alone are able to keep me from taking them back. In Jesus's name, Amen.

2.   Roots—Matthew 13

This morning, that beautiful Blue Spruce in my backyard is laden with several inches of pure wet snow, each long elegant branch bending under the weight, some bending so far as to rest on the ground. Just as it was in the first season I saw it as such, it is breathtaking. The weight of the winter weighs heavy, but the underlying strength enables bending, giving, never breaking.

The roots to that tree extend deep into the ground establishing solid ground, solid footing. Those roots didn't grow that deep by chance. When that tree was planted, it was cared for, nurtured. The tree was watered, received plenty of sunshine, fertilized, and it endured a lot of hardship in the way of harsh North Dakota winds!

In the parable of the sower (Matt. 13) Jesus teaches the disciples the importance of deep roots. But they don't grow deep on their own. We must nurture our spiritual roots to grow deep. Studying God's Holy Bible, attending a Bible-believing church, and meeting regularly with like-minded believers are the three top methods to learn how to live God's Word, and that is the key to nurturing our roots. Studying God's Word is crucial but truly studying it, not just reading the words. Both reading and studying will prove invaluable to those roots!

Daily studies like this one help us to make studying God's Word become a daily habit. God's Word is living and breathing and applies to absolutely everything you might go through in your life. I have discovered that during those brief interruptions in my life when my daily studies lapsed, problems went unanswered. When, in reality, the answer lay in the daily study that I had omitted! What a lesson I learned, when I forced myself to get back into my daily study, only to find the answer there, waiting for me.

"Bible in a Year" reading schedules are also a valuable tool, but don't let them replace your daily study, as they are surface reading only. Scripture tells us that God will bring us the remembrance (of His Word) when we need it (John 14:26). But you have to read it before you can remember it!

Write your thoughts to God here:

_____

_____

_____

_____

_____

_____

_____

_____

_____

_____

_____

_____

_____

_____

_____

_____

_____

_____

_____

_____

Father God, I ask you to lead me in my Bible studies. Help me to understand what I read and give me a hunger for more! Show me where you want me to read today and where you want me to study today. Thank you. In Jesus's name, Amen.

3.   Deeper Roots—2 Timothy 3

Attending a church that believes in the entire Word of God is essential to keeping those roots healthy and strong. It is important that you choose a church that teaches the truth and teaches the wiles of evil so that you will not be caught off guard by the enemy. And believe me you do have an enemy! But that's another study for another day. (See Chapter 25)

One of the dangers Scripture warns us of is not to follow leaders who preach and teach what man wants to hear, as opposed to what God says. There are preachers, teachers, and evangelists who are quite popular who teach the truth in its entirety. But there are also those who teach just enough biblical truth to make it sound like the full gospel story, when in reality, it teaches a false, incomplete gospel, which can lead us away from Christ and the life He wants us to live.

These teachers generally focus on one principle of the Bible—i.e., healing, prosperity, etc.—and distorts it to the point where that principle is taken out of proportion or out of context. Sadly, many of them were right on target scripturally, in the early stages of their ministries, and have become tainted by our enemy's influence. It might be any number of human nature factors that caused such a slide: greed, pride, desire for fame, etc.

The only way to guard against such false teachers is to know Scripture! The more you know the Bible, the more those false teachings will "not sit right" in your spirit, when you hear them.

"All scripture is given by inspiration of God, and is profitable for doctrine, for reproof, for correction, for instruction in righteousness" (2 Tim. 3:16).

We, as Christians, must believe and live by all of God's Word, not just those parts that appeal to us or those that are popular or deemed important by special interest groups.

_____
_____
_____
_____
_____
_____
_____
_____
_____
_____
_____
_____
_____
_____
_____
_____
_____

Dear Lord God, Please help me to commit myself to reading Your Word. Help me to understand what I read there so that I can truly live by all of it, not just the parts that I like! Thank you, Lord. Amen.

4.   Stronger Roots—1 John 1

After choosing a church that believes in and adheres to the entire Bible, regular attendance and membership in that church serves to guide you through your Bible knowledge and to help grow those deep roots you're after.

In addition to Bible study, teachings and messages from the pastor, those roots are strengthened by being with "like-minded believers." My parents used to tell us, "Be careful of the company you keep." It means that you pick up habits from those you spend time with. Those habits may be good ones or terrible ones, but we take on manners and behaviors of those people we associate with. Social behaviors are learned.

To learn to live the Christian life called for in Scripture, you'll want to (1) read the Manual (Bible) and (2) see the example of those who attend church with you.

"But if we walk in the light, as he is in the light, we have fellowship with one another, and the blood of Jesus his Son cleanses us from all sin" (1 John 1:7).

Association with other Christians is a way to see, in action, how other Christians live. Because Christians are still human, some of the actions you observe may not be what Christ would prefer. After all, we are all still a work in progress, and perfection doesn't come until Jesus returns! More often, you will see human examples of God's love, mercy, grace, compassion—all those traits God instills in your heart, that show through your life, when those roots are in good shape.

Serving in your church helps those roots to grow stronger. Don't wait to be asked to serve. In your prayers (tomorrow's study) ask God to reveal to you what it is He wants you to do in your church. The list below is not an exhaustive list. It includes

just some of the ministries your church may need your help
with:

- Greeter
- Servant Leader
- Sound
- Children's Dept.
- Youth
- Music
- Hospitality

- Décor
- Bulletin
- Facility/Grounds
- Communion setup
- "Son-shine"
- Cleaning

Don't be surprised if you feel God is leading you into serving in a way that you don't see above or in your church. Talk to your pastor or an elder/deacon! And if you don't feel qualified or equipped to serve, remember that God enables you to do what He calls you to do! Step up!

_____
_____
_____
_____
_____
_____
_____
_____
_____
_____

Dear Lord, Please help me to understand when You lay something on my heart. Please guide me to how I can be of service to You by serving in your church. Thank you, Lord. I am getting excited about this! Amen.

5. Healthier Roots—Matthew 6

There are so many books on prayer, and every one of them will tell you a different method of praying. They are all wrong and they are all right. If you adhere to each one of the methods prescribed, you will be praying prayer after prayer after prayer. And while there is certainly nothing wrong with spending all day in prayer, most of us have other demands on our time each day. Besides, Scripture tells us not to be repetitive in our prayers ("And when you pray, do not heap up empty phrases as the Gentiles do, for they think that they will be heard for their many words" [Matt. 6:7].) If I were to pray all day, I have no doubt I would repeat myself and just re-word things I had already prayed about. How about you?

For today, let's keep it simple. Prayer is conversation with God. God hears your heart anyway, so you don't have to be too concerned with the wording of your prayers. The child's prayer, "God is great, God is good, and we thank Him for this food," is simple enough for a child to understand. It teaches a child that God understands whatever we say in our prayers. As a more mature Christian, our simple prayers of grace over a meal can be a bit more in line with our adult status, but they don't have to be more complicated. Prayers you hear at group functions may be something like this: "Father in heaven, we give thanks for all that You provide for us. We ask that you bless it to our bodies. Amen." At groups of service you might here a phrase added: "Bless it to the nourishment of our bodies, for your continued service," or something similar to that. Around the family table, prayer may be, "Dear Lord, thank you for this food and the hands that prepared it. Amen" The point is, it doesn't much matter! God hears all the prayers mentioned above and hears the hearts of those who prayed them.

I've taken table grace as my examples so far. But let's look at an easy format to prayer, to help *you* remember what you want your ACTS of prayer to be:

A—Adoration: Acknowledge that you know who God is, that you respect His authority, power. Voice your adoration and love for Him! He is worthy of it!

C—Confession: God knows what you may need to confess, but you need to confess it to Him.

T—Thanksgiving: Thank Him for what He has done, is doing; and promises to do in your life. Thank Him for the very opportunity to approach Him in prayer!

S—Supplication: The last thing in your prayer is the request that is burdening your heart. Although He already knows it (because He sees your heart), the Lord tells us in Scripture that we have not because we ask not (James 4:2b).

_____
_____
_____
_____
_____
_____
_____
_____
_____
_____
_____

Dear Lord, Teach me to pray. Help me to understand that prayer is just communication with You. Help me to learn how to speak to You and also to learn how to hear from You. Thank You. Amen.

6.　　Vine and Branches

"I am the vine, you are the branches. He who abides in Me, and I in him, bears much fruit; for without Me you can do nothing" (John 15:5).

These are the words of Jesus. Quite often in Scripture Jesus taught in parables so that the disciples had to think and ask Him questions, in order to understand. This analogy explained to the disciples that He was their lifeline. They, as "branches," needed to be connected to Jesus, the "Vine." Today, Jesus is still the Vine, and we are the branches. Although Jesus no longer walks the earth as a man, we still must be connected to Him, through His Holy Spirit, in order to accomplish God's plan for our lives. We do that through spending time in God's Word, the Bible. The lessons we can learn throughout every verse of Scripture help us to live as Jesus wants us to—to be an example to others, of what the Christian life should be like.

Any time a branch is broken from the vine, it withers and dies. Christ Jesus is truly our lifeline. He will never cut us off, but we can do that ourselves, by our own choice.

_____

_____

_____

_____

_____

_____

_____

_____

_____

_____

_____

Dear Lord, Please be my vine and help me learn how to be a branch, forever and always attached to you! Amen.

7.   The Perfect Prayer—Matthew 6

Don't feel embarrassed if you don't know how to pray. Even Jesus's disciples asked Him to teach them to pray (Luke 11:1). And who better to teach us. These are Jesus's words:

> And when you pray, you shall not be like the hypocrites. For they love to pray standing in the synagogues and on the corners of the streets, that they may be seen by men. Assuredly, I say to you, they have their reward. But you, when you pray, go into your room, and when you have shut your door, pray to your Father who is in the secret place; and your Father who sees in secret will reward you openly. And when you pray, do not use vain repetitions as the heathen do. For they think that they will be heard for their many words. Therefore do not be like them. For your Father knows the things you have need of before you ask Him. (Matt. 6:5–8)

Then, Jesus gave us this prayer. Sometimes it is called the Lord's Prayer, sometimes the Model Prayer:

> In this manner, therefore, pray: Our Father in heaven, Hallowed be Your name. Your kingdom come. Your will be done On earth as it is in heaven. Give us this day our daily bread. And forgive us our debts, As we forgive our debtors. And do not lead us into temptation, But deliver us from the evil one. For Yours

is the kingdom and the power and the glory
forever. Amen. (Matt. 6:9–13)

When we pattern our prayers after this one, we acknowledge who God is, verbalize that we know God is our Father, and
worthy of praise (the word *hallowed* does this!). "Thy Kingdom
come, Thy will be done" tells God that we agree with His plan.
"Our daily bread" is our petition. It means physical food, but
also spiritual food. It means what we need to live every day. And
it tells God we trust Him for tomorrow's bread without praying
for it today! It asks for God to forgive us, but also to help us
to forgive those who sin against us. And this model prayer asks
God to protect us from the temptations we meet in life and
from our enemy. Then, lastly, it declares that we accept by faith
that God's kingdom and power and glory will last forever!

Now, take a moment, and with that in mind, say that
prayer from your heart. Write your thoughts here:

_____

_____

_____

_____

_____

_____

_____

_____

_____

_____

_____

Lord God, please teach me to pray.

8.   Worship

Webster's Dictionary of American English (1828) gives a detailed definition of the act of worship. I've condensed it here:

Worship: Chiefly and eminently, the act of paying divine honors to the Supreme Being; or the reverence and homage paid to him in religious exercises, consisting in adoration, confession, prayer, thanksgiving, and the like. The worship of God is an eminent part of religion. To adore; to pay divine honors to; to reverence with supreme respect and veneration. To respect; to honor; to treat with civil reverence. To honor with extravagant love and extreme submission; as a lover.

Yes, I promise you I did condense it. But when you talk about worship, there are many aspects to consider. One of the most important aspects to consider is the object of our worship—the one True Living God, Jehovah, our Father, Jesus Christ, His Son.

"But you shall destroy their altars [to pagan gods], break their sacred pillars, and cut down their wooden images (for you shall worship no other god...)" (Exod. 34:13–14a, NKJV).

If you read the chapter in this book entitled "Sacred Pillars," you have a good picture of what the beginning of this passage means. The Israelites were told and reminded repeatedly of the greatness of God, and He and He alone was to be praised (another word for worship). But many of the kings in charge of those Israelites were greedy and turned to the pagan gods they thought could give them more. They frequently learned (too late) that those pagan gods demanded a price way too high. Jehovah God, even today, commands love, to Him and to each other, but to no other "god."

The definition continues with three important parts of worship:

Prayer—Acts of adoration—Service.

Our common perception of worship is the music, and indeed that is a part of it. Our singing to the Lord, whether through traditional hymns or contemporary ones, as long as the object of our praise is God/Jesus, those acts of adoration are a part of our worship.

_____

_____

_____

_____

_____

_____

_____

_____

_____

_____

_____

_____

_____

_____

_____

_____

_____

Lord God, teach me the way to worship You. Show me what is acceptable praise. Help me please to restrict my worship to You and You alone. There is none like You, Lord. Lead me to heartfelt, sincere and acceptable worship. Amen.

9.   Salt and Light

"You are the salt of the earth; but if the salt loses its flavor, how shall it be seasoned? It is then good for nothing but to be thrown out and trampled underfoot by men. You are the light of the world. A city that is set on a hill cannot be hidden" (Matt. 5:13–14).

Salt: we wouldn't consider setting a table for guests without it. We are very much aware of flavoring our foods with salt. Imagine your favorite baked potato without salt. Or those wonderful scrambled eggs, but no salt. Bland, almost tasteless? Verse 13 is not telling us to grab our salt shakers and throw salt on people. These scriptures are telling us, as Christians, to flavor the world. We were not all created alike. We're not to try to be alike. We are to embrace how differently God created us, because it is in those very differences that we can reach others who feel they are "different," even to the point that they feel they don't fit in anywhere. Who better to reach that person that a Christian who might be a bit "different."

The disciples were occasionally compared to "salt" because of the savory doctrines they preached. Those doctrines were in agreement with Scripture, but very new to the culture of that time. This is why Christ used this example when addressing His disciples: "You are the salt of the earth." Salt is not only a flavoring, it is also used as a preservative. This is another reason Christ addressed them as such. Everything Christ charged His disciples to do can be viewed as a "preservative" for our eternal souls!

But if the salt loses its flavor, we today would throw it out. You can't re-flavor salt. It's useless. In Bible days, the salt wouldn't go to waste. Once it lost its flavor, it was used to crudely "pave" the streets of Israel.

"Then Jesus spoke to them again, saying, 'I am the light of the world. He who follows Me shall not walk in darkness, but have the light of life'" (John 8:12, NKJV).

As followers of Christ, this applies to us. We have the light of life. He didn't give it to us to "hide it under a bushel," but to shine our light to everyone we meet, so that they "want what we have," that being the love of Jesus Christ.

_____

_____

_____

_____

_____

_____

_____

_____

_____

_____

_____

_____

_____

_____

_____

_____

_____

_____

_____

Lord, help me to be the salt and light to the world that You have called me to be. Help me to always represent You well, so that the lost want what I have—You in my heart. Amen.

10.   Jew and Gentile

To simplify these terms, the descendants of Abraham were Jewish, born into the Israelite "tribe." The Old Testament covenants were made between the Jews and Jehovah God. God made a covenant with Abraham that he would have so many children that his descendants would number more than the sands of the earth. Abraham's grandson, Jacob was renamed Israel. He had twelve sons who became the leaders of the twelve tribes of Israel. Of course, that made them all Jews. When Jesus walked on the earth, He preached the truth of salvation to the Jews, many of whom rejected Him. Scripture tells us that when that happened, He began to share His "Good News" teaching first His disciples, then to Gentiles across the land.

The Jews are considered God's "chosen" people, but only "Messianic" Jews—Jews who have accepted Jesus as the Messiah are, in fact, chosen. When Jesus died on the cross, He died for all people, not just the Jews. That means, if you have accepted Jesus as your Savior, you are a child of God and are an heir with those *Messianic* Jews and are also "chosen!"

_____

_____

_____

_____

_____

_____

_____

_____

Lord, help me to learn more about You and Our Father in heaven, about the Jews and the Gentiles. Help me to live as a child of God. Amen.

11.   Fruit of the Spirit

In Galatians 5:19–20 we are given a list of sins. This is not necessarily an exhaustive list, but Paul calls them the "works of the flesh," which means these sins are committed when we allow our flesh to rule us instead of living according to the Holy Spirit leading us. "Now the works of the flesh are evident, which are: adultery, fornication, uncleanness, lewdness, idolatry, sorcery, hatred, contentions, jealousies, outbursts of wrath, selfish ambitions, dissensions, heresies, envy, murders, drunkenness, revelries, and the like." Verse 21 tells us how seriously God takes these actions: "of which I tell you beforehand, just as I also told you in time past, that those who practice such things will not inherit the kingdom of God" (NKJV).

Then, in God's mercy and love, the next two verses tell us how to "walk in the Spirit." "But the fruit of the Spirit is love, joy, peace, longsuffering, kindness, goodness, faithfulness, gentleness, self-control" (Gal. 5:22–23, NKJV). If we strive to live in the fruit of the Spirit, we will better equip ourselves to live the Christian life that pleases Christ Jesus.

Lord God, please show me how to live according to the fruit of the Spirit. Please guide me as I strive to walk in the Spirit. In Jesus's name, I pray, Amen.

12.   Forgiveness

When you gave your life to Jesus, every sin you had ever committed, whether telling a little white lie or a big bold one, stealing a postage stamp or an automobile, whether you disrespected God's servant or murdered someone, those sins were covered by the blood of Jesus. No matter how long ago that was, you have sinned since then. Even we Christians sin. We are human too.

The difference between Christians who sin and "not-yet Christians" who sin is one thing—one *major* thing: "If we confess our sins, He is faithful and just to forgive us our sins and to cleanse us from all unrighteousness" (1 John 1:9).

Many Christians live in defeat, because they feel they can't live up to the example Jesus set for us. Newsflash: None of us can! That's why God gave us a way out of that stigma! This doesn't give us a license to go through life sinning, because we know we can confess and be forgiven.

The verses just before the one above gives us the bigger picture:

> If we say that we have fellowship with Him, and walk in darkness, we lie and do not practice the truth. But if we walk in the light as He is in the light, we have fellowship with one another, and the blood of Jesus Christ His Son cleanses us from all sin. If we say that we have no sin, we deceive ourselves, and the truth is not in us. If we confess our sins, He is faithful and just to forgive us our sins and to cleanse us from all unrighteousness. (1 John 1:6–9)

When we "confess" our sins, we don't need to tell the preacher or the priest or the deacon—we need to tell God. The definition from *Webster's 1828 Dictionary*: "To own, acknowledge or avow, as a crime, a fault, a charge, a debt, or something that is against one's interest, To declare a belief in and adherence to, to admit or assent to in words; to disclose faults, or the state of the conscience."

Confession and repentance often go hand-in-hand. When we confess we admit our sin. When we repent, we confess and turn away from our sin back to God. Sometimes, when our sin has hurt someone, it may be necessary for us to go to that person and apologize. Remember that our apology doesn't change the results of our sin, so it might be necessary to make amends, i.e., pay for any physical damage done to that person's property or medical bills that our sin has caused. Remember also, that the person we sinned against is not required to accept our apology; you are required to make it.

Dear Lord. I have sinned, by

_____

_____

_____

_____

_____

_____

_____

_____

_____

_____

Please forgive me, and show me how to make amends for my sin, if that is what you require of me. I ask that you help me to turn from this action and keep my eyes on You. In Jesus's name, amen.

13.   Unforgiveness

When we sin against someone and go to them in repentance, acceptance of our apology is not a given. On the flipside, when someone sins against us, we are wise, and in fact, we are commanded to forgive. In other words, whether or not the person who sins against us apologizes, we are required to forgive them.

"For if you forgive men their trespasses, your heavenly Father will also forgive you. But if you do not forgive men their trespasses, neither will your Father forgive your trespasses" (Matt. 6:14–15, NKJV).

This is the command. If we forgive, we are forgiven. The wisdom in forgiving comes also from what our body physically does to itself if we do *not* forgive. The phrase has been used frequently, that unforgiveness eats us up inside. Trust me, it's true. It takes a lot of energy to harbor unforgiveness, and that energy is wasted! It prevents us from using that energy to do things that are constructive rather than destructive! It is a choice, sometimes made more than once, to forgive. Not forgiving someone for something keeps you in bondage to that person.

In his pamphlets, Neal Anderson, Freedom in Christ Ministries,[26] offers a worksheet that walks the reader through an intense process of healing for those who have harbored unforgiveness. In it, he advises the reader to forgive God. Obviously, God has never done anything against anyone that requires forgiveness. But if your perception of something that happened has made you angry with God, maybe you should. (For example, if you are angry with God over your divorce, now might be a good time to ask God to forgive you (1) for blaming Him, (2) for your part in the divorce.) Take a moment to list anyone you can think of, even if you think you have already forgiven them.

Then "tell God" you forgive them in the statement below your list.

_____

_____

_____

_____

_____

_____

_____

_____

_____

_____

_____

_____

_____

_____

_____

_____

_____

_____

_____

_____

_____

Lord, I choose to forgive _____ for _____
_____. I thank You for enabling me to forgive that person, and I ask You to help me go forward in freedom, without the chains of unforgiveness. And I thank You for forgiving me. Amen.

14.   The Eyes of the Lord

People in the Church today quite often can get into a "rut." We go through the motions of a "good little Christian" by going to church every Sunday and sometimes to Bible Study or midweek service. We even go so far as to serve as usher when our turn comes around. We really enjoy the potlucks that are lined up now and then and we never forget to give our offering.

After all, that's about all there is to being a Christian, right? Wrong! If your neighbor looks at your life and this is what he sees, he probably agrees, you are living the Christian life. If God looks at your life, would He agree? Trust me, He *is* looking at your life.

"I will instruct you and teach you in the way you should go; I will guide you with My eye" (Ps. 32:8).

Notice the last phrase in that verse. God guides you with His eye. That doesn't mean it is a judgmental eye; it means He sees. God sees everything. If what you know He sees disturbs you, you might want to examine your own life. We all should! When we go forward monthly (or however often your church serves Communion) to accept the elements of the Lord's Supper, we should have already examined our lives, made any apologies necessary, and taken care of the heart issues that God leads us to address…*before* we take Communion.

God sees all. He sees the good in you as well. He sees the good works you do, and His Word tells us to not "brag" about the times that we help someone. After all, our motive for helping someone should be to please God, not man, so God is the only one that matters! God sees the wounds you suffer and stay silent about, and He sends His ministering angels to ease your pain and comfort you.

"For the eyes of the LORD run to and fro throughout the whole earth, to show Himself strong on behalf of those whose heart is loyal to Him" (2 Chron. 16:9a).

This verse tells us that God looks throughout the earth to show favor to those who are loyal to Him—to His children! To you! He is there to defend you, provided for you and to bless you! That's our God!

_____

_____

_____

_____

_____

_____

_____

_____

_____

_____

_____

_____

_____

_____

Thank you, Lord, for reminding me that You see me in my troubles and You help me. Thank you for showing me that I need to keep my thoughts pure and examine my heart before I approach the Communion table, and for guiding me into the life You want me to live. Help me to keep my eyes on You and not get in a rut where You are concerned! Amen.

15.   Priorities

Early on in Scripture, as we learn about God, we learn that He insists on being number 1 in our lives. That is an admirable goal to strive for, but it isn't an easy one to accomplish! You may be thinking, "If I don't put my job first, I won't have it very long." Or "If my wife isn't #1 in my life, I'll be in big trouble!" I understand those thoughts, but let me explain to you why they represent misplaced loyalties.

If my work comes first, that means I put God and my family after my job. So if I skip church to take on a second shift at work, to make more money, I am breaking several of God's "commandments." By putting my job ahead of God, I am making my job more important than God, which is making my job a god in my life. When I do that a few Sundays in a row, I may decide that church isn't that important anyway, which means I have put God ever further down in my list of priorities. The enemy of our soul will be delighted! But if we give Satan a little room, he wedges himself in and stretches that room wider and bigger, and before you know it, you are further from God that you thought you could ever be. Those few dollars earned are not worth it! God promises to provide for you. Let Him! Trust Him!

Scripture sets up marriage in a very simple pattern: "For the husband is head of the wife, as also Christ is head of the church; and He is the Savior of the body. Therefore, just as the church is subject to Christ, so let the wives be to their own husbands in everything" (Eph. 5:23–24).

When our families are set up scripturally, there is no doubt about the priorities! Christ is the head of the family; husband, the head of the wife; wife, the head of the children. That's a simplification, because the wife and children are still under the authority of Christ. But it works! God is #1. Spouse is #2. Kids are #3. Job is #4. Trust me—better yet, trust God! His plan works!

_____

_____

_____

_____

_____

_____

_____

_____

_____

_____

_____

_____

_____

_____

_____

_____

_____

_____

_____

_____

Lord, I ask You to help me align my family to Your Word. Help me to live in a way that makes it obvious to my family that I love You and I put You first. In Jesus's name, Amen.

16.   Discouragement and Depression

"Oh, Lord, I don't know where to begin!" If your prayers have ever started something like that, welcome to the club! Living the Christian life doesn't mean we will never encounter bumps in the road. Life on this earth is quite different from life in the Garden of Eden. When Adam and Eve shared that apple, everything changed.

God created this beautiful garden for them (and us) to live in. It was a garden of peace and contentment, joy with every breath of sweet clean air. Every step they took was accompanied by sights, sounds, and smells we can only imagine. God loved them so much that He created this paradise for them to live in. They didn't even have to work for food! It was already there. All they had to do was pick it off the tree and eat...but not *that* tree.

> And out of the ground the LORD God made every tree grow that is pleasant to the sight and good for food. The tree of life was also in the midst of the garden, and the tree of the knowledge of good and evil... but of the tree of the knowledge of good and evil you shall not eat, for in the day that you eat of it you shall surely die. (Gen. 2:9, 17; NKJV)

It would be easy to believe that when God said those words to them, they didn't understand what death was. They hadn't encountered anything like that yet. But they knew God, and up to that point, they had never disobeyed, never questioned. We aren't told in Scripture how big their beautiful home was. We don't know how long it might have taken Eve to get around to that tree during her exploring. It might have been weeks. It might have been years. She may have gone directly to that tree, as soon as God said not to. As soon as they ate that forbidden fruit, everything changed—forever.

Before	After
Food on every tree wherever they went	Work the (sometimes rocky) ground for food
Animals were friendly, content	Animals were dangerous, sometimes vicious
Adam and Eve walked freely with God	Adam and Eve broke fellowship with God
The perfect marriage, contentment	Discouragement, depression, envy, irritation
No sickness, pain-free childbirth expected	Germs arrived, pain during childbirth a promise
No death	Death—not immediate, but definite: physical and spiritual

The changes above aren't the only ones that occurred, but they are some major ones. Life was no longer easy. The pain, sickness, death, discouragement, depression—all the negative issues that we deal with today came into the world with one act of disobedience. The good news is we can have it back! When we gave our lives to Jesus, that beautiful life once again became our inheritance.

Discouragement is just as much a part of the Christian's life, as it is a not-yet-believer's, so you are not alone. The difference is, we have a loving Father to turn to. When we pray, we are communicating with Daddy God. Remember He loves you and does not want you to dwell in the negative emotions that you are feeling right now. Tell Him how you feel and spend some time with Him!

_____
_____
_____
_____
_____
_____
_____
_____
_____
_____
_____
_____
_____
_____
_____
_____
_____
_____
_____
_____
_____
_____
_____

Dear Lord, please take away my (discouragement, depression, anger) and restore my joy. Help me to keep my eyes on You and not what I see that discourages me, I want to remember that this earth is not my home, that I will spend eternity with You in paradise. I know that this pity party is over! Thank You! Amen.

17.   Where Are You Looking?

I lived in Texas for over twenty years. I loved it there. I got accustomed to the fact of life that I rarely even had to wear a jacket. I did not even own a heavy winter coat and I liked that! In truth, I didn't even own a raincoat! For approximately 360 days out of a year, I didn't need one! Then, I married my husband and moved to Washington State. Beautiful plush green everywhere you look. But I definitely needed a raincoat. In fact I needed one approximately 360 days out of the year!

Life has sunshine and rain. That's true no matter who you are or where you live.

Jesus tells us in Matthew 5:45b "…that our Father makes His sun rise on the evil and on the good, and sends rain on the just and on the unjust" (NKJV).

When life seems to "get us down," one of the best ways we can overcome it is to look *out* instead of *in*. As children growing up, my sisters and brother and I were taught that there was always someone whose pain or sorrow was worse than our own. It may seem like a simple thought, but it is so true. If we focus on our own problems, they become bigger than life.

As an adult, I have learned to take that a step further. When I see someone who *is* in a plight worse than my own, I can focus on them, helping if I can, but at least encouraging them through it. My healing has come from helping others, repeatedly during my lifetime! Sometimes that offer of assistance has developed into a delightful friendship and we have been able to encourage each other along the way!

Again, let God know how you feel and ask Him to open your eyes to someone else you might reach out to.

_____

_____

_____

_____

_____

_____

_____

_____

_____

_____

_____

_____

_____

_____

_____

_____

_____

_____

_____

_____

_____

_____

Lord God. Please help me to look out and not in. Lead me to someone that I can encourage today. I ask that You help me to stop feeling sorry for myself and trust that You have a plan for me, today and always. Thank you. Amen.

18.   The Trinity

If you do a search in your Bible, you will not find the word *trinity* anywhere. It refers to the triune (3) Godhead of Father God, Jesus, and the Holy Spirit. Even for Christians, this is a hard word to explain, although we generally understand it in our hearts and we accept it by faith.

"In the beginning God created the heavens and the earth" (Gen. 1:1, NKJV).

The word for *God* used here is Elohim. It is used in the plural sense, meaning the godhead, the trinity—all three were present at creation. In the same sense, it was also used in verse 25, "let us make man in our image."

"You shall have no other gods before Me" (Exod. 20:3, NKJV).

Jesus is God. He is part of the Trinity. When we worship Jesus, we are not going against this first commandment.

It's a little confusing, but it started "in the beginning" and continues to be. Understanding it completely isn't a must. Accepting it is. You can accept it by faith now, trusting that God will help you to understand it.

God the Father sent Jesus the Son in a physical body, to earth, to die on the cross for our sins. When that was accomplished, Jesus told the disciples He would send a Comforter (the Holy Spirit). Obviously there are ions between those events, but that is, in a nutshell, the connection. They are all God (singular) in different capacities. You cannot accept One without the other Two, nor would you want to. If you were to do that, you would be eliminating two-thirds of everything that was created for and in us!

_____
_____
_____
_____
_____
_____
_____
_____
_____
_____
_____
_____
_____
_____
_____
_____
_____
_____
_____
_____
_____
_____

Father God, thank you for sending your Son, Jesus, to die on the cross for me. Dear Lord Jesus, thank You for choosing to die for my sin. Holy Spirit, please come and help me to understand all I need to know now, and help me to trust that I will learn more as You enable me. Amen.

19.   Your Testimony

Your testimony is your story of what God has done and is doing in your life. It is what you yearn for other people to know, so that they might be encouraged to live for Jesus, as you do. I would suggest that you write out every detail of your story, and then shorten it to a quick five-minute "speech" to share with others. As you get to know people, there will be other opportunities to share the long version. Look for them. But also look for those quick God moments or "divine appointments" along the way! Telling your testimony to someone is a part of "witnessing" to them. When you witness to someone, you want to tell them the part of *your* testimony that might connect with what they are going through, to encourage them that there is hope in Christ Jesus. For example, as someone who has gone through divorce, I can witness to someone that God not only helped and comforted me through it, but He also forgave me of my part in it *and* He gives me the boldness to help others.

Before I found Jesus:

_____
_____
_____
_____
_____

How and when I found Jesus:

_____
_____
_____
_____
_____

After I found Jesus:

_____

_____

_____

_____

_____

What part of my testimony does God want me to use and who does He want me to witness to right away?

_____

_____

_____

_____

_____

_____

_____

_____

_____

_____

_____

Lord, I thank You for coming into my life. Thank You for plucking me out of my sin and healing me from that life. Show me how to share Your love with others. Show me how to have Your mercy and grace toward those who have not yet come to You. Lead me Lord, today, to those You want me to touch with Your love.

20.   Failure

The word *failure* does not appear anywhere in scripture in reference to God. My take on that is that it is impossible for God to fail! *Webster's 1828 Dictionary* defines failure this way:

> 1. A failing; deficiency; cessation of supply, as the failure of crops. 2. Omission; non-performance; as the failure of a promise. 3. Decay, or defect from decay; as the failure of memory or of sight. 4. A breaking, or becoming insolvent; as in the failure of a bank. 5. A failing; a slight fault, as in a fault in the foundation.

Nowhere in that definition is the word used to describe a *person's* lack of ability to do something. But that word has evolved since then, to mean a lot more: A student fails, a marriage fails, a person's heath fails. Nothing positive. Unless an evil plan fails!

It is Satan's evil plan to destroy you. But when we belong to Jesus, Satan's plan fails.

"He who trusts in his riches will fall, But the righteous will flourish like foliage" (Prov. 11:28, NKJV).

When we trust in God, the word *failure* doesn't need to be in our vocabulary! In the CEV this verse says "the man who trusts in his own wealth will fail..."

"The thief does not come except to steal, and to kill, and to destroy. I have come that they may have life, and that they may have it more abundantly" (John 10:10, NKJV).

What is it that you may have failed at? I failed at marriage. (See Chapter 1.) Looking back, I can see that part of that failure was because of my own decisions to be selfish and do things my way. I had to repent of those sins and God forgave me. Repentance doesn't undo the damage. I had to live with the consequences of my sin.

If you failed at something, consider these thoughts:

- Did you fail at something God had sanctioned?
- If you consider something a failure, is it possible that it was never intended to happen?
- Did you fail or did you give up?

If you failed, it is possible that whatever it was you failed at wasn't what God wanted. It wasn't in His will. It is not possible for God to fail. If He assigned something to you, He enabled you to do it. Take another look. The outcome may not have been what *you* thought it should be, but if God sanctioned it, it was accomplished, as *He* had planned. Thank Him for using you to accomplish His will. Ask God about it! Your enemy, Satan, condemns you so you don't feel worthy of God's love or you think (as I did) that God can't use you. Please don't believe Satan's lies.

_____

_____

_____

_____

_____

_____

_____

Father God, I feel like a failure, because _____
_____ My enemy is condemning me because of it. I repent of my part in it and ask You to help me get past it and go forward, victorious in You. In Jesus's name, Amen.

21.   Pride, Rebellion, and Other Sins

I have caught myself in the sin of rebellion (see Chapter 2).
I hope I learned my lesson. I repented and asked my husband's
forgiveness, and moved forward. But there are so many more
sins! Our enemy lays traps for us to fall into, let alone the fact
that I am, after all, human!

Only one man who walked the face of the earth was perfect: Jesus. When anyone believes they are perfect, they sin—
the sin of pride and deceit. No one lives without sin. No one
can go through life without sinning. There are lists in Scripture
to help guide us. From Exodus, in the Old Testament, the Ten
Commandments given to Moses by God (paraphrased).

1.   You shall have no other gods before Me.
2.   You shall not make for yourself a carved image.
3.   You shall not take the name of the LORD your God in vain.
4.   Remember the Sabbath day, to keep it holy.
5.   Honor your father and your mother, that your days may be long upon the land which the LORD your God is giving you.
6.   You shall not murder.
7.   You shall not commit adultery.
8.   You shall not steal.
9.   You shall not bear false witness against your neighbor.
10. You shall not covet your neighbor's house; you shall not covet your neighbor's wife, nor his male servant, nor his female servant, nor his ox, nor his donkey, nor anything that is your neighbor's.

Then in the New Testament, Jesus gave two commandments, which encompass all of those ten.

> "Teacher, which is the great commandment in the law?" Jesus said to him, "You shall love the Lord your god with all your heart, with all your soul, and with all your mind." This is the first and great commandment. And the second is like it: "You shall love your neighbor as yourself." (Matt. 22:36–39)

Sins can be generally covered by this list:

> Now the works of the flesh are evident, which are: adultery, fornication, uncleanness, lewdness, idolatry, sorcery, hatred, contentions, jealousies, outbursts of wrath, selfish ambitions, dissensions, heresies, envy, murders, drunkenness, revelries, and the like; of which I tell you beforehand, just as I also told you in time past, that those who practice such things will not inherit the kingdom of God. (Gal. 5:19–21, NKJV)

A list of all the individual sins could take pages and hours for me to write and you to read. Scripture keeps it simple: "Your Word I have hidden in my heart, That I might not sin against You" (Ps. 119:11, NKJV).

The fellowship we share with Father God develops a relationship with Him that moves our hearts to *want* to be pure, to never sin again. Knowing that we are human, God made a way, through Jesus Christ, for our sin to be forgiven. When we give our lives to Jesus, our sin, all of our sin, is forgiven. When we do sin, we have instructions: "If we say that we have no sin, we deceive ourselves, and the truth is not in us. If we confess our sins, He is faithful and just to forgive us our sins and to cleanse us from all unrighteousness" (1 John 1:8–9).

_____
_____
_____
_____
_____
_____
_____
_____
_____
_____
_____
_____
_____
_____
_____
_____

Dear Lord, I ask Your forgiveness for my sin of _____. I ask You to help me remain close to You, so I see the sin before I go forward. Give me the wisdom and boldness to say "No" when I need to and when to walk away, when I should. Thank you. In Jesus's name. Amen.

22.   Grace, Mercy, and Blessing

> Grace is when God gives us good things that we don't
> deserve.
> Mercy is when He spares us from bad things that we
> do deserve.
> Blessings are when He is generous with both.
> "My grace is sufficient for thee" (2 Cor. 12:9, NKJV).

Grace: 1. Favor; good will; kindness; disposition to oblige another. 2. The free unmerited love and favor of God, the spring and source of all the benefits men receive from him. 3. Favorable influence of God; divine influence or the influence of the spirit, in renewing the heart and restraining from sin. 4. The application of Christ's righteousness to the sinner. 5. A state of reconciliation to God. 6. Virtuous or religious affection or disposition, as a liberal disposition, faith, meekness, humility, patience, proceeding from divine influence.

"Mercy and truth preserve the king; and his throne is upheld by mercy" (Prov. 20:28, NKJV).

Mercy: 1. That benevolence, mildness or tenderness of heart which disposes a person to overlook injuries, or to treat an offender better than he deserves; the disposition that tempers justice, and induces an injured person to forgive trespasses and injuries, and to forbear punishment, or inflict less than law or justice will warrant. In this sense, there is perhaps no word in our language precisely synonymous with mercy. That which comes nearest to it is grace. It implies benevolence, tenderness, mildness, pity or compassion, and clemency, but exercised only towards offenders. Mercy is a distinguishing attribute of the Supreme Being. 2. An act or exercise of mercy or favor. 3. Pity; compassion manifested towards a person in distress.4. Clemency and bounty. 5. Charity, or the duties of charity and benevolence.6. Grace; favor. 7. Eternal life, the fruit of mercy.

8. Pardon. 9. The act of sparing, or the forbearance of a violent act expected. The prisoner cried for mercy. To be or to lie at the mercy of, to have no means of self-defense, but to be dependent for safety on the mercy or compassion of another, or in the power of that which is irresistible; as, to be at the mercy of a foe, or of the waves.

"This is the blessing wherewith Moses—blessed the children of Israel" (Deut. 33:1, NKJV).

Blessing: 1. A solemn prophetic benediction, in which happiness is desired, invoked or foretold. Any means of happiness; a gift, benefit or advantage; that which promotes temporal prosperity and welfare, or secures immortal felicity. A just and pious magistrate is a public blessing. The divine favor is the greatest blessing. 2. Among the Jews, a present; a gift; either because it was attended with kind wishes for the welfare of the giver, or because it was the means of increasing happiness.

Dear Heavenly Father, I thank You for these gifts. I thank You that I don't have to choose one, but that they are each a part of Your gift to me. Help me to appreciate them always and to never forget to treat other people with grace and mercy and bless them every chance I get. In Jesus's name, Amen.

23.   Healing

"Is anyone among you sick? Let him call for the elders of the church, and let them pray over him, anointing him with oil in the name of the Lord" (James 5:14, NKJV).

My husband and I arrived at our present church two and a half years ago. The majority of our church family are what I call my "elderlies." Many are folks who have been raised in the church. They are faithful in reading the Word, and they believe by faith, everything they read there. Several months after we "landed," the daughter of one of those dear elderlies came up to Pastor at the end of service and asked him to pray for "Mom's shoulder," as she was in horrible pain. "Mom" was ninety-two years old at the time, and she looked pale and fragile as she answered his call to come forward for prayer. He anointed her with oil and the whole congregation prayed for her pain to cease. The next Sunday, as is his norm, Pastor Hutch asked if anyone cared to share a praise report. "Mom" was the first to stand, fragile but focused, and announced loudly and clearly that God healed her shoulder last week!

Scripture is true. Scripture works. Why some people receive their healing and others don't, only God knows. He is sovereign. Sickness is not a sign of sin and not a punishment for sin, although sin may have been the cause of the sickness (e.g. HIV, AIDS). If you or someone you love is looking to God for a healing, trust God's leading. Contact a church that believes in the Bible—*all* of the Bible—and let God be God!

_____
_____
_____
_____
_____
_____
_____
_____
_____
_____
_____
_____
_____
_____
_____
_____
_____
_____
_____
_____
_____
_____
_____

Lord God, I know You can heal me. You can heal anyone in any way You choose. I ask that You show me how to receive my healing, and I will give You the glory for it! Thank You. In Jesus's name, Amen.

24.   Handling Conflict

Whether or not you can see a wound, doesn't mean it isn't there. Any wound must be treated. If a conflict is left unattended, it can cause wounds, sometimes severe ones. God knew there would be conflict among His children, so He gave us a perfect plan to attend to any conflicts that might arise in the body of Christ—in your church. (They work in your families too.)

> If your brother sins against you, go and tell him his fault, between you and him alone. If he listens to you, you have gained your brother. But if he does not listen, take one or two others along with you, that every charge may be established by the evidence of two or three witnesses. If he refuses to listen to them, tell it to the church. And if he refuses to listen even to the church, let him be to you as a Gentile and a tax collector. (Matt. 18:15–17, NKJV)

Some of the articles you have read in these daily devotionals are critical to allowing God's plan to work. The attributes of mercy and grace are imperative to forgiving and healing from conflicts within the church, and in other relationships as well.

Sometimes it isn't easy to even want to resolve conflicts, but remember God will never ask you to do something that He won't enable you to do.

"Jesus looked at them and said, 'With man it is impossible, but not with God. For all things are possible with God'" (Mark 10:27, NKJV).

Forgiving someone who has hurt you is impossible, in the flesh. But not when you trust God. When you make the choice to be obedient to His Word and choose to forgive, it is possible.

But you have to make the choice—to forgive, to let it go—and to let God be the one to handle the situation.

_____

_____

_____

_____

_____

_____

_____

_____

_____

_____

_____

_____

_____

_____

_____

_____

_____

_____

_____

_____

Dear Lord God. It is my humble prayer that You heal my wounded and broken heart. Heal those wounds that have been inflicted and help me to forgive those who inflicted them. Show me the treatment plan, Lord, and nudge me to pursue health. Pour Your healing balm into my heart. I ask Your forgiveness for allowing any offense to fester. In Jesus's name, Amen.

25.   Setting Boundaries

> Then Laban said to Jacob, "Here is this heap
> and here is this pillar, which I have placed
> between you and me. This heap is a witness,
> and this pillar is a witness, that I will not pass
> beyond this heap to you, and you will not
> pass beyond this heap and this pillar to me,
> for harm" (Gen. 31:51–52, NKJV)

Jacob and Laban had major disagreements (see Chapter 8) and they both agreed to set this boundary that was marked with the heap of stones and a pillar. Neither would cross the boundary without the permission of the other. Jacob was married to both of Laban's daughters and he and his father-in-law both knew that there was never going to be peace without boundaries.

Boundaries are important. Physical boundaries protect your property from outsiders. Spiritual boundaries are crucial to your walk with the Lord. If you associate with anyone whose religious beliefs are different from yours, your spiritual boundaries must be solid and firmly in place.

Emotional boundaries are necessary too to protect your heart. The conflicts that you may endure, whether you were right or wrong, can leave scars. Even after each party in the conflict has forgiven and been forgiven, it is sometimes necessary to maintain boundaries to prevent further injury. Sometimes we call it "putting up walls."

The walls should not be permanent ones, because they can indicate a lack of total healing and can actually deter your healing. If you are in a position, in a relationship, in which you feel you are vulnerable to further injury, approach your pastor or trusted church leader. They can help you heal through tearing down the walls, as you heal.

_____

_____

_____

_____

_____

_____

_____

_____

_____

_____

_____

_____

_____

_____

_____

_____

_____

_____

_____

_____

_____

_____

_____

Lord God, I trust You to help me keep my boundaries in place until I heal from the hurt I have endured. I ask You to help extend mercy and grace to those outside my boundaries. Please help me to heal and forgive and I believe You will tear the wall down as I heal. In Jesus's name. Amen.

26.   Leadership

Jesus recruited twelve disciples. The very word *disciple* explains their positions. Strong's Concordance defines the word as a learner, that is, pupil. We consider them as *followers*. Except for Judas, they walked with Jesus the entire time He walked the earth, learning by His by teachings and from His examples. Most of them became *leaders*.

After Jesus ascended to heaven, the continuing of ministry and beginning the new church was entrusted to the disciples. But unlike Jesus, they weren't able to keep up with everything Jesus had been doing. The healings and the everyday ministry to the people was overwhelming, and not to mention, the following was growing. They enlisted help, which became the first "elder team."

> Then the twelve summoned the multitude of the disciples and said, "It is not desirable that we should leave the word of God and serve tables. Therefore, brethren, seek out from among you seven men of good reputation, full of the Holy Spirit and wisdom, whom we may appoint over this business; but we will give ourselves continually to prayer and to the ministry of the word." And the saying pleased the whole multitude. And they chose Stephen, a man full of faith and the Holy Spirit, and Philip, Prochorus, Nicanor, Timon, Parmenas, and Nicolas, a proselyte from Antioch, whom they set before the apostles; and when they had prayed, they laid hands on them. Then the word of God spread, and the number of the disciples multiplied greatly in Jerusalem, and a

great many of the priests were obedient to the
faith. (Acts 6:2–7)

This is God's model of the church. A leadership team—all
of whom are believers in the Word of God. It is a good format
for our churches today. Even today, there are churches structured
after this example. Depending on the size of the church, there is a
leadership team, generally led by the lead pastor and several other
leaders. For example Christian education director would be in
charge of children and adults Sunday schools, Bible studies, etc.
Church government changes within denominations. But it was
all set up so that the pastor was not charged with doing all the
work. If done correctly, and in God's will, the church leadership
consists of godly men and women who are intent on serving God
and God's children. Ideally, they are generally chosen by God
(anointed) and "confirmed" the church body.

The leadership is accountable to the members of the congregation and the pastor, but even more importantly, they are
responsible to God, for both the physical and financial steward-
ship of the church, *and* the spiritual health of the church body.
They have a lot on their plates, because quite often, these are
volunteer positions (except for possibly the pastor and church
secretary) and have other jobs. Their time is frequently juggled
between home, family, and church responsibilities. And they are
human and fallible, and the entire church membership should
be praying for them!

If you would like to be considered for a leadership role in your
church, go to the (probably monthly) meeting and let them know.
If you think there is a concern in the church that needs attention,
same advice.

If you or someone you know has been wounded by a leader
in your church, the article called "Dealing with Conflict" is a
good guideline to follow. You should know that if you are pre-

sented with a problem, and you tell a friend, and another friend and another, that is gossip. You become a part of the problem. Remember you are all children of God. Pour on the mercy and grace and step in, *in love,* and be a part of the solution, whatever God may determine that to be.

_____
_____
_____
_____
_____
_____
_____
_____
_____
_____
_____
_____
_____
_____
_____

Lord God, if You are calling me to be a part of leadership in my church, I accept. Please guide me into the next step. I ask that You help me to know what to do about the situation I am concerned or hurt about. I lift my church leadership up to You. I ask You to guide them and protect them and their families from our enemy's attacks, whether those attacks come from within or without. Thank You, Lord, for helping me to be a part of the solution and not the problem. In Jesus's name, Amen.

27.   Follow the Leader

In our lives, we are all followers and we are all leaders. As followers, we often have little say so in who our leaders are. A student rarely gets a chance to choose his professor. When we do have choices we need to pray about the decision before we make one. When we choose a church, for example, quite often the biggest influence in our decision is the pastor—the leader. When we are followers, if we follow blindly, we can follow our leader into deep trouble.

My father used to tell a story of a time when he and a friend of his were driving semis through Colorado during the winter. His friend was in front because he knew the roads better than Daddy did. During the trip, a snowstorm hit and the wind made visibility close to zero. They were close to their destination, so they didn't stop. The way Daddy told the story, "He drove off into a ditch, and I drove off right behind him."

That's what can happen when we don't pay attention to where our leaders are leading us. We need to be wise, but we also need to rely on God to choose our leaders for us. We also need to pray for wisdom for our leaders and protection for the path they are leading us on.

We are also leaders. If we are parents, our children follow us. If we are the teachers that the students follow, we have a huge responsibility to lead them in wisdom, to places of safety. It is our responsibility to seek God's face continually, so that no matter who it is that is following us, they need to be able to trust that we have their best interest at heart, always. As leaders, we need to remember that those who follow us aren't just watching us during the workday or while we are at church. Frequently they are watching us 24-7 and they learn more by watching our example than by anything we verbally try to teach them.

I was told one time that I was an amazing woman of God, based on someone who was watching me when I didn't realize they were. Thank God I handled that situation well, even with my wounded heart! I pray God "covers" me when I am not quite "on my game!" I'm not saying "put on a show" when you know you're being watched. I'm saying *be the best role model you can be at all times.* If you mess up, admit it to your followers at the moment. They will learn even more when you show them how to apologize and own up to your mistakes.

Dear Lord, help me to choose my leaders wisely. Help me to pray for them daily. I ask, Lord, that You help me to give them grace and mercy when they make mistakes. I ask too, Lord, that You make me a good example for those who are following me. Help me to be true to who You are calling me to be, so I can represent You well, and those who follow me will want that same relationship with You. In Jesus's name I pray. And I thank You, Lord. Amen.

28.   Servanthood

Christ gave us the perfect example of a servant.

"If I then, your Lord and Teacher, have washed your feet, you also ought to wash one another's feet. For I have given you an example, that you should do as I have done to you" (John 13:14-15, NKJV).

In these verses He gave His disciples the demonstration by washing their feet and then He told them to do it. He also told them that He had come to earth to serve: "...just as the Son of Man did not come to be served, but to serve, and to give His life a ransom for many" (Matt. 20:28, NKJV).

We don't go around shoving people's feet into a basin to wash them. But we *can* find ways to serve. My first "choice" would be to have you serve in your church, and in all honesty, God chose it before I did: "I beseech you therefore, brethren, by the mercies of God, that you present your bodies a living sacrifice, holy, acceptable to God, which is your reasonable service" (Rom. 2:1, NKJV).

Generally speaking, churches today are always looking for someone to serve, whether it be someone who loves kids stepping in to the Sunday school teacher position, or someone with a gift for computers to volunteer to print the bulletins, or a lover of music stepping up to lead worship or sing in the choir, or even someone to clean the building! Often these are paid positions, but in smaller churches, that's not always the case.

Ask God what you might be gifted to do and where He wants you to serve! After all, Jesus didn't say, "Well done, my good and faithful; pastor, Sunday school teacher, worship leader, or singer. He said, "His lord said to him, 'Well done, good and faithful servant; you have been faithful over a few things, I will make you ruler over many things. Enter into the joy of your Lord'" (Matt. 25:23, NKJV).

_____

_____

_____

_____

_____

_____

_____

_____

_____

_____

_____

_____

_____

_____

_____

_____

_____

_____

_____

_____

_____

_____

_____

_____

Dear Lord, I want to serve You. Give me a servant's heart, I pray. Lead me to the church You want me to go to and show me where You want me to serve You. Thank You! In Jesus's name, Amen.

29.   Peace

"But the fruit of the Spirit is love, joy, peace…" (Gal. 5:22, NKJV).

Peace is defined as prosperity, quietness, rest. When our spirits are agitated, we say we've lost our peace. According to Scripture, God *is* our peace. When we are content with God, we are at peace. But living in what we call a "fallen" world means we, and therefore our peace, are subject to innumerable attacks! So how do we protect and maintain our peace? Read on.

"Then He arose and rebuked the wind, and said to the sea, 'Peace, be still!' And the wind ceased and there was a great calm" (Mark 4:39).

There was a terrible storm raging. All Jesus had to do was to speak to it. "Peace! Be still!" The world may have changed, but Jesus hasn't! If Jesus has the power to speak peace into existence in this horrible storm, don't you think He can bring *and keep* peace in your life?

"Jesus Christ is the same yesterday, today, and forever" (Heb. 13:8, NKJV).

The storm Jesus spoke to wasn't a concern to Jesus, but it was to the disciples. They were fishermen, they knew the seas, but this storm scared them! It wasn't until the disciples voiced their fears that He addressed the issue.

"But He was in the stern, asleep on a pillow. And they awoke Him and said to Him, 'Teacher, do You not care that we are perishing?'" (Mark 4:38).

Of course, He cared. He still cares. All we have to do is talk to Him, even now, and He will answer it. While you are waiting for His answer, ponder on these verses:

> Be anxious for nothing, but in everything by
> prayer and supplication, with thanksgiving, let

your requests be made known to God; and the peace of God, which surpasses all understanding, will guard your hearts and minds through Christ Jesus. Finally, brethren, whatever things are true, whatever things are noble, whatever things are just, whatever things are pure, whatever things are lovely, whatever things are of good report, if there is any virtue and if there is anything praiseworthy—meditate on these things. The things which you learned and received and heard and saw in me, these do, and the God of peace will be with you. (Phil. 4:6–9)

_____
_____
_____
_____
_____
_____
_____
_____
_____
_____
_____
_____

Father in heaven, thank You for this word to my heart. Help me to get it down into my spirit, that I don't have to tolerate the storms in my life. Dear Lord Jesus, I ask You to calm the storm and keep my focus on You so I can live in the peace of God. Thank You. In Jesus's name, Amen.

30. Community

What do you consider your community? Your subdivision? Your kids' coach and team? How about your church? Your neighbors?

> And you shall love the Lord your God with all your soul, with all your mind, and with all your strength. This is the first commandment. And the second, like it, is this: "you shall love your neighbor as yourself." There is no other commandment greater than these. (Mark 12:30–31, NKJV)

Your community can be whoever you *allow* it to be. God created woman so man wouldn't be alone. We weren't created to be "an island." God has gifted you with gifts and talents that He wants you to use to help people and to advance His kingdom. You can't do that if you live a life of solitude.

Open yourself up to friendships, whether individual friendships or groups, to stay social! Book clubs, painting classes, cooking or baking classes, community theater, pinochle or bridge clubs, Bible studies. Volunteer at local schools, nursing homes, and hospitals. Put yourself out there in whatever areas you are interested in. Be the person God has created you to be and enjoy life. If your goal is to "just" make new friends or keep from getting bored, go for it! God can move in whatever circle you join!

_____

_____

_____

_____

_____
_____
_____
_____
_____
_____
_____
_____
_____
_____
_____
_____
_____
_____
_____
_____
_____
_____
_____
_____
_____
_____

Lord, I want to be a contributing part of my community. Lead me to where You want me to go. Open and close the doors as You see fit! Help me to glorify You wherever I go. Show me where I can go to feel like I am contributing something of value to my community. Help me to use the talents and gifts You have given me. Thank You. In Jesus's name, Amen.

31.   The Bible

I was given my first Bible just before I went to church camp, at age nine, where I gave my life to Jesus. That was a "few" years ago, but I still remember the first verse I memorized. It was probably the first for many of you: "For God so loved the world, He gave His only begotten Son, that whosoever believeth in Him shall not perish, but have everlasting life" (John 3:16). (The way I learned it.)

I believed it then and I believed it now. There have been at least ten to fifteen "versions" that have been published since then, some of which are "transliterations" and make it easier for a new believer to understand God's Word (The Message, the New Living Translation). They are great "primers," but should be used as such, recognizing that they reveal a vast amount of surface Scripture. Once you've been studying those, in church and in a Bible study, with a wise and anointed teacher, I strongly advise you to "graduate" into a true *version* of the Bible. I prefer the New King James Version (NKJV), but truth be known, I also love the New American Standard Bible (NASB). I often defer to the Scofield Bible.

As I study to teach, I generally have several versions available, either on e-sword (free computer Bible) or scattered across my desk. Suffice it to say, *I love the Word of God!* It is my firm belief that once you get to know Scripture, you will come to feel you are spending time with a trusted friend! Enjoy!

_____

_____

_____

_____

_____

_____
_____
_____
_____
_____
_____
_____
_____
_____
_____
_____
_____
_____
_____
_____
_____
_____
_____
_____
_____
_____
_____

Dear Lord, please guide me into Your Word. I want to know You, and I believe that I can do that best by studying the Bible. Show me where to start. Give me a burning desire to spend time there every morning or every night *or both!* I love You, Lord Jesus. Thank You for loving me. In Jesus's name, Amen.

Notes

1   Sheila Cragg, *Woman's Walk with God.*
2   Phillip Keller, *A Shepherd Looks at Psalm 23.*
3   Phillip Keller, *A Shepherd Looks at the Good Shepherd and His Sheep.*
4   Henry and Richard Blackaby, *Hearing God's Voice.*
5   Joanna Weaver, *Having a Mary Heart in a Martha World.*
6   Dr. Mark Virkler, *Communion with God.*
7   Robert Munger, *My Heart—Christ's Home.*
8   Mark Buchanan, *The Rest of God.*
9   Dr. David Jeremiah, *Escape the Coming Night.*
10 Martha Peace, *Becoming a Titus Two Woman.*
11 Martha Peace, *The Excellent Wife.*
12 Webster's Dictionary 1828
13 Judson Press—Bible Journeys—(Spring 2017)
14 Mel Gibson's movie: *The Passion of the Christ*
15 Sandra L. Dixon, *I Am L-O-V-E-D (I Am Living and Overcoming Victoriously Even Divorced).*
16 Charles Spurgeon
17 Horacio G. Spafford and Phillip P. Bliss, "It Is Well with My Soul."
18 Kevin J. Conner, *The Foundations of Christian Doctrine: A Practical Guide to Christian Belief.*
19 Ptolemy Tomkins and Tyler Beddoes, *Proof of Angels.*
20 E. Lonnie Melashenko with Brian Jones, *Angels Among Us.*
21 Billy Graham, *Angels.*
22 Joe Brock, *An Introduction to Generational Sins and Curses.*
23 Lisa Morgan, *Accepted in the Beloved.*
24 Bill Weise, *23 Minutes in Hell.*
25 Ann Spangler, *Praying the Names of God.*
26 Neal Anderson, Freedom in Christ Ministries.
27 Graham Cooke, Morning Star Ministries.
28 Brian Hardesty, Valley Community Church, Burlington, WA.

Bible Reading Schedule

01-Jan	Gen 1-2	Psalm 1	Jer 1-2	08-Feb	Ex 27-28	Psalm 39	Neh 7
02-Jan	Gen 3-4	Psalm 2	Jer 3-4	09-Feb	Ex 29-30	Psalm 40	Neh 8
03-Jan	Gen 5-6	Psalm 3	Jer 5-6	10-Feb	Ex 31-32	Psalm 41	Neh 9
04-Jan	Gen 7-8	Psalm 4	Jer 7-8	11-Feb	Ex 33-34	Psalm 42	Neh 10
05-Jan	Gen 9-10	Psalm 5	Jer 9-10	12-Feb	Ex 35-36	Psalm 43	Neh 11
06-Jan	Gen 11-12	Psalm 6	Jer 11-12	13-Feb	Ex 37	Psalm 44	Neh 12
07-Jan	Gen 13-14	Psalm 7	Jer 13-14	14-Feb	Ex 38	Psalm 45	Neh 13
08-Jan	Gen 15-16	Psalm 8	Jer 15-16	15-Feb	Ex 39	Psalm 46	1 Chron 1
09-Jan	Gen 17-18	Psalm 9	Jer 17-18	16-Feb	Ex 40	Psalm 47	1 Chron 2
10-Jan	Gen 19-20	Psalm 10	Jer 19-20	17-Feb	1 Kings 1	Psalm 48	1 Chron 3
11-Jan	Gen 21-22	Psalm 11	Jer 21-22	18-Feb	1 Kings 2	Psalm 49	1 Chron 4
12-Jan	Gen 23-24	Psalm 12	Jer 23-24	19-Feb	1 Kings 3	Psalm 50	1 Chron 5
13-Jan	Gen 25-26	Psalm 13	Jer 25-26	20-Feb	1 Kings 4	Psalm 51	1 Chron 6
14-Jan	Gen 27-28	Psalm 14	Jer 27-28	21-Feb	1 Kings 5	Psalm 52	1 Chron 7
15-Jan	Gen 29-30	Psalm 15	Jer 29-30	22-Feb	1 Kings 6	Psalm 53	1 Chron 8
16-Jan	Gen 31-32	Psalm 16	Jer 31-32	23-Feb	1 Kings 7	Psalm 54	1 Chron 9
17-Jan	Gen 33-34	Psalm 17	Jer 33-34	24-Feb	1 Kings 8	Psalm 55	1 Chron 10
18-Jan	Gen 35-36	Psalm 18	Jer 35-36	25-Feb	1 Kings 9	Psalm 56	1 Chron 11
19-Jan	Gen 37-38	Psalm 19	Jer 37-38	26-Feb	1 Kings 10	Psalm 57	1 Chron 12
20-Jan	Gen 39-40	Psalm 20	Jer 39-40	27-Feb	1 Kings 11	Psalm 58	1 Chron 13
21-Jan	Gen 41-42	Psalm 21	Jer 41-42	28-Feb	1 Kings 12	Psalm 59	1 Chron 14
22-Jan	Gen 43-44	Psalm 22	Jer 43-44	29 Feb	1 Kings 13	Psalm 60	1 Chron 15
23-Jan	Gen 45-46	Psalm 23	Jer 45-46	01-Mar	1 Kings 14	Psalm 61	1 Chron 16
24-Jan	Gen 47-48	Psalm 24	Jer 47-48	02-Mar	1 Kings 15	Psalm 62	1 Chron 17
25-Jan	Gen 49-50	Psalm 25	Jer 49-50	03-Mar	1 Kings 16	Psalm 63	1 Chron 18
26-Jan	Ex 1-2	Psalm 26	Jer 51	04-Mar	1 Kings 17	Psalm 64	1 Chron 19
27-Jan	Ex 3-4	Psalm 27	Jer 52	05-Mar	1 Kings 18	Psalm 65	1 Chron 20
28-Jan	Ex 5-6	Psalm 28	Lam 1	06-Mar	1 Kings 19	Psalm 66	1 Chron 21
29-Jan	Ex 7-8	Psalm 29	Lam 2	07-Mar	1 Kings 20	Psalm 67	1 Chron 22
30-Jan	Ex 9-10	Psalm 30	Lam 3	08-Mar	1 Kings 21	Psalm 68	1 Chron 23
31-Jan	Ex 11-12	Psalm 31	Lam 4	09-Mar	1 Kings 22	Psalm 69	1 Chron 24
01-Feb	Ex 13-14	Psalm 32	Lam 5	10-Mar	2 Kings 1	Psalm 70	1 Chron 25
02-Feb	Ex 15-16	Psalm 33	Neh 1	11-Mar	2 Kings 2	Psalm 71	2 Chron 1
03-Feb	Ex 17-18	Psalm 34	Neh 2	12-Mar	2 Kings 3	Psalm 72	2 Chron 2
04-Feb	Ex 19-20	Psalm 35	Neh 3	13-Mar	2 Kings 4	Psalm 73	2 Chron 3
05-Feb	Ex 21-22	Psalm 36	Neh 4	14-Mar	2 Kings 5	Psalm 74	2 Chron 4
06-Feb	Ex 23-24	Psalm 37	Neh 5	15-Mar	2 Kings 6	Psalm 75	2 Chron 5
07-Feb	Ex 25-26	Psalm 38	Neh 6	16-Mar	2 Kings 7	Psalm 76	2 Chron 6

17-Mar	2 Kings 8	Psalm 77	2 Chron 7	04-May	Num 6	Psalm 124	Obad 11-12
18-Mar	2 Kings 9	Psalm 78	2 Chron 8	05-May	Num 7	Psalm 125	Obad 13-14
19-Mar	2 Kings 10	Psalm 79	2 Chron 9	06-May	Num 8	Psalm 126	Obad 15-16
20-Mar	2 Kings 11	Psalm 80	2 Chron 10	07-May	Num 9	Psalm 127	Obad 17-18
21-Mar	2 Kings 12	Psalm 81	2 Chron 11	08-May	Num 10	Psalm 128	Matt 1-2
22-Mar	2 Kings 13	Psalm 82	2 Chron 12	09-May	Num 11	Psalm 129	Matt 3-4
23-Mar	2 Kings 14	Psalm 83	2 Chron 13	10-May	Num 12	Psalm 130	Matt 5-6
24-Mar	2 Kings 15	Psalm 84	2 Chron 14	11-May	Num 13	Psalm 131	Matt 7-8
25-Mar	2 Kings 16	Psalm 85	2 Chron 15	12-May	Num 14	Psalm 132	Matt 9-10
26-Mar	2 Kings 17	Psalm 86	2 Chron 16	13-May	Num 15	Psalm 133	Matt 11-12
27-Mar	2 Kings 18	Psalm 87	2 Chron 17	14-May	Num 16	Psalm 134	Matt 13-14
28-Mar	2 Kings 19	Psalm 88	2 Chron 18	15-May	Num 17	Psalm 135	Matt 15-16
29-Mar	2 Kings 20	Psalm 89	2 Chron 19	16-May	Num 18	Psalm 136	Matt 17-18
30-Mar	Joel 1	Psalm 90	2 Chron 20	17-May	Num 19	Psalm 137	Matt 19-20
31-Mar	Joel 2	Psalm 91	2 Chron 21	18-May	Num 20	Psalm 138	Matt 20-21
01-Apr	Joel 3	Psalm 92	2 Chron 22	19-May	Num 21	Psalm 139	Matt 22-23
02-Apr	Lev 1	Psalm 93	2 Chron 23	20-May	Num 22	Psalm 140	Matt 24-25
03-Apr	Lev 2	Psalm 94	2 Chron 24	21-May	Num 23	Psalm 141	Matt 26
04-Apr	Lev 3	Psalm 95	2 Chron 25	22-May	Num 24	Psalm 142	Matt 27
05-Apr	Lev 4	Psalm 96	2 Chron 26	23-May	Num 25	Psalm 143	Matt 28
06-Apr	Lev 5	Psalm 97	2 Chron 27	24-May	Num 26	Psalm 144	Mark 1
07-Apr	Lev 6	Psalm 98	2 Chron 28	25-May	Num 27	Psalm 145	Mark 2
08-Apr	Lev 7	Psalm 99	2 Chron 29	26-May	Num 28	Psalm 146	Mark 3
09-Apr	Lev 8	Psalm 100	2 Chron 30	27-May	Num 29	Psalm 147	Mark 4
10-Apr	Lev 9	Psalm 101	2 Chron 31	28-May	Num 30	Psalm 148	Mark 5
11-Apr	Lev 10	Psalm 102	2 Chron 32	29-May	Num 31	Psalm 149	Mark 6
12-Apr	Lev 11	Psalm 103	2 Chron 33	30-May	Num 32	Psalm 150	Mark 7
13-Apr	Lev 12	Psalm 104	2 Chron 34	31-May	Num 33	Prov 1	Mark 8
14-Apr	Lev 13	Psalm 105	2 Chron 35	01-Jun	Num 34	Prov 2	Mark 9
15-Apr	Lev 14	Psalm 106	2 Chron 36	02-Jun	Num 35	Prov 3	Mark 10
16-Apr	Lev 15	Psalm 107	Hosea 1-2	03-Jun	Num 36	Prov 4	Mark 11
17-Apr	Lev 16	Psalm 108	Hosea 3-4	04-Jun	Deut 1	Prov 5	Matt 12
18-Apr	Lev 17	Psalm 109	Hosea 5-6	05-Jun	Deut 2	Prov 6	Matt 13
19-Apr	Lev 18	Psalm 110	Hosea 7-8	06-Jun	Deut 3	Prov 7	Mark 14
20-Apr	Lev 19	Psalm 111	Hosea 9-10	07-Jun	Deut 4	Prov 8	Mark 15
21-Apr	Lev 20	Psalm 112	Hosea 11	08-Jun	Deut 5	Prov 9	Mark 16
22-Apr	Lev 21	Psalm 113	Hosea 12	09-Jun	Deut 6	Prov 10	Luke 1
23-Apr	Lev 22	Psalm 114	Hosea 13	10-Jun	Deut 7	Prov 11	Luke 2
24-Apr	Lev 23	Psalm 115	Hosea 14	11-Jun	Deut 8	Prov 12	Luke 3
25-Apr	Lev 24	Psalm 116	Amos 1-2	12-Jun	Deut 9	Prov 13	Luke 4
26-Apr	Lev 25	Psalm 117	Amos 3-4	13-Jun	Deut 9	Prov 14	Luke 5
27-Apr	Lev 26	Psalm 118	Amos 5-6	14-Jun	Deut 10	Prov 15	Luke 6
28-Apr	Lev 27	Psalm 119	Amos 7-9	15-Jun	Deut 11	Prov 16	Luke 7
29-Apr	Num 1	Psalm 119:89	Obas 1-2	16-Jun	Deut 12	Prov 17	Luke 8
30-Apr	Num 2	Psalm 120	Obad 3-4	17-Jun	Deut 13	Prov 18	Luke 9
01-May	Num 3	Psalm 121	Obad 5-6	18-Jun	Deut 14	Prov 19	Luke 10
02-May	Num 4	Psalm 122	Obad 7-8	19-Jun	Deut 15	Prov 20	Luke 11
03-May	Num 5	Psalm 123	Obad 9-10	20-Jun	Deut 16	Prov 21	Luke 12

Date				Date				
21-Jun	Deut 17	Prov 22	Luke 13	08-Aug	Judges 7	Ezekiel 11	Acts 17	
22-Jun	Deut 18	Prov 23	Luke 14	09-Aug	Judges 8	Ezekiel 12	Acts 18	
23-Jun	Deut 19	Prov 24	Luke 15	10-Aug	Judges 9	Ezekiel 13	Acts 19	
24-Jun	Deut 20	Prov 25	Luke 16	11-Aug	Judges 10	Ezekiel 14	Acts 20	
25-Jun	Deut 21	Prov 26	Luke 17	12-Aug	Judges 11	Ezekiel 15	Acts 21	
26-Jun	Deut 22	Prov 27	Luke 18	13-Aug	Judges 12	Ezekiel 16	Acts 22	
27-Jun	Deut 23	Prov 28	Luk 19	14-Aug	Judges 13	Ezekiel 17	Acts 23	
28-Jun	Deut 24	Prov 29	Luk 20	15-Aug	Judges 14	Ezekiel 18	Acts 24	
29-Jun	Deut 25	Prov 30	Luk 21	16-Aug	Judges 15	Ezekiel 19	Acts 25	
30-Jun	Deut 26	Prov 31	Luke 22	17-Aug	Judges 16	Ezekiel 20	Acts 26	
01-Jul	Deut 27	Esth 1	Luke 23	18-Aug	Judges 17	Ezekiel 21	Acts 27	
02-Jul	Deut 28	Esth 2	Luke 24	19-Aug	Judges 18	Ezekiel 22	Acts 28	
03-Jul	Deut 29	Esth 3	John 1	20-Aug	Judges 19	Ezekiel 23	Rom 1	
04-Jul	Deut 30	Esth 4	John 2	21-Aug	Judges 20	Ezekiel 24	Rom 2	
05-Jul	Deut 31	Esth 5	John 3	22-Aug	Judges 21	Ezekiel 25	Rom 3	
06-Jul	Deut 32	Esth 6	John 4	23-Aug	Ruth 1	Ezekiel 26	Rom 4	
07-Jul	Deut 33	Esth 7	John 5	24-Aug	Ruth 2	Ezekiel 27	Rom 5	
08-Jul	Deut 34	Esth 8	John 7	25-Aug	Ruth 3	Ezekiel 28	Rom 6	
09-Jul	Josh 1	Esth 9	John 8	26-Aug	Ruth 4	Ezekiel 29	Rom 7	
10-Jul	Josh 2	Esth 10	John 9	27-Aug	Mal 1	Ezekiel 30	Rom 8	
11-Jul	Josh 3	Zeph 1	John 10	28-Aug	Mal 2	Ezekiel 31	Rom 9	
12-Jul	Josh 4	Zeph 2	John 11	29-Aug	Mal 3	Ezekiel 32	Rom 10	
13-Jul	Josh 5	Zeph 3	John 12	30-Aug	Mal 4	Ezekiel 33	1 Cor 1	
14-Jul	Josh 6	Hagg 1-2	John 13	31-Aug	Job 1	Ezekiel 34	1 Cor 2	
15-Jul	Josh 7	Zech 1	John 14	01-Sep	Job 2	Ezekiel 35	1 Cor 3	
16-Jul	Josh 8	Zech 2	John 15	02-Sep	Job 3	Ezekiel 36	1 Cor 4	
17-Jul	Josh 9	Zech 3	John 16	03-Sep	Job 4	Ezekiel 37	1 Cor 5	
18-Jul	Josh 10	Zech 4	John 17	04-Sep	Job 5	Ezekiel 38	1 Cor 6	
19-Jul	Josh 11	Zech 5	John 18	05-Sep	Job 6	Ezekiel 39	1 Cor 7	
20-Jul	Josh 12	Zech 6	John 19	06-Sep	Job 7	Ezekiel 40	1 Cor 8	
21-Jul	Josh 13	Zech 7	John 20	07-Sep	Job 8	Ezekiel 41	1 Cor 9	
22-Jul	Josh 14	Zech 8	John 21	08-Sep	Job 9	Ezekiel 42	1 Cor 10	
23-Jul	Josh 15	Zech 9	Acts 1	09-Sep	Job 10	Ezekiel 43	1 Cor 11	
24-Jul	Josh 16	Zech 10	Acts 2	10-Sep	Job 11	Ezekiel 44	1 Cor 12	
25-Jul	Josh 17	Zech 11	Acts 3	11-Sep	Job 12	Ezekiel 45	1 Cor 13	
26-Jul	Josh 18	Zech 12	Acts 4	12-Sep	Job 13	Ezekiel 46	1 Cor 14	
27-Jul	Josh 19	Zech 13	Acts 5	13-Sep	Job 14	Ezekiel 47	1 Cor 15	
28-Jul	Josh 20	Zech 14	Acts 6	14-Sep	Job 15	Jonah 1	1 Cor 16	
29-Jul	Josh 21	Ezekiel 1	Acts 7	15-Sep	Job 16	Jonah 2	2 Cor 1	
30-Jul	Josh 22	Ezekiel 2	Acts 8	16-Sep	Job 17	Jonah 3	2 Cor 2	
31-Jul	Josh 23	Ezekiel 3	Acts 9	17-Sep	Job 18	Jonah 4	2 Cor 3	
01-Aug	Josh 24	Ezekiel 4	Acts 10	18-Sep	Job 19	Micah 1	2 Cor 4	
02-Aug	Judges 1	Ezekiel 5	Acts 11	19-Sep	Job 20	Micah 2	2 Cor 5	
03-Aug	Judges 2	Ezekiel 6	Acts 12	20-Sep	Job 21	Micah 3	2 Cor 6	
04-Aug	Judges 3	Ezekiel 7	Acts 13	21-Sep	Job 22	Micah 4	2 Cor 7	
05-Aug	Judges 4	Ezekiel 8	Acts 14	22-Sep	Job 23	Micah 5	2 Cor 8	
06-Aug	Judges 5	Ezekiel 9	Acts 15	23-Sep	Job 24	Micah 6	2 Cor 9	
07-Aug	Judges 6	Ezekiel 10	Acts 16	24-Sep	Job 25	Micah 7	2 Cor 10	

25-Sep	Job 26	Nahum 1	2 Cor 11	13-Nov	1 Sam 16	Isaiah 30	Heb 5
26-Sep	Job 27	Nahum 2	2 Cor 12	14-Nov	1 Sam 17	Isaiah 31	Heb 6
27-Sep	Job 28	Nahum 3	2 Cor 13	15-Nov	1 Sam 18	Isaiah 32	Heb 7
28-Sep	Job 29	Habakkuk 1	Gal 1	16-Nov	1 Sam 19	Isaiah 33	Heb 8
29-Sep	Job 30	Habakkuk 2	Gal 2	17-Nov	1 Sam 20	Isaiah 34	Heb 9
30-Sep	Job 31	Habakkuk 3	Gal 3	18-Nov	1 Sam 21	Isaiah 35	Heb 10
01-Oct	Job 32	Zech 1	Gal 4	19-Nov	1 Sam 22	Isaiah 36	Heb 11
02-Oct	Job 33	Zech 2	Gal 5	20-Nov	1 Sam 23	Isaiah 37	Heb 12
03-Oct	Job 34	Zech 3	Gal 6	21-Nov	1 Sam 24	Isaiah 38	Heb 13
04-Oct	Job 35	Zech 4	Eph 1	22-Nov	1 Sam 25	Isaiah 39	James 1
05-Oct	Job 36	Zech 5	Eph 2	23-Nov	1 Sam 26	Isaiah 40	James 2
06-Oct	Eccl 1	Zech 6	Eph 3	24-Nov	1 Sam 27	Isaiah 41	James 3
07-Oct	Eccl 2	Zech 7	Eph 4	25-Nov	1 Sam 18	Isaiah 42	James 4
08-Oct	Eccl 3	Zech 8	Eph 5	26-Nov	1 Sam 29	Isaiah 43	James 5
09-Oct	Eccl 4	Zech 9	Eph 6	27-Nov	1 Sam 30	Isaiah 44	1 Peter 1
10-Oct	Eccl 5	Zech 10	Phil 1	28-Nov	1 Sam 31	Isaiah 45	1 Peter 2
11-Oct	Eccl 6	Zech 11	Phil 2	29-Nov	2 Sam 1	Isaiah 46	1 Peter 3
12-Oct	Eccl 7	Zech 12	Phil 3	30-Nov	2 Sam 2	Isaiah 47	1 Peter 4
13-Oct	Eccl 8	Zech 13	Phil 4	01-Dec	2 Sam 3	Isaiah 48	1 Peter 5
14-Oct	Eccl 9	Zech 14	Col 1	02-Dec	2 Sam 4	Isaiah 49	2 Peter
15-Oct	Eccl 10	Isaiah 1	Col 2	03-Dec	2 Sam 5	Isaiah 50	1 John 1
16-Oct	Eccl 11	Isaiah 2	Col 3	04-Dec	2 Sam 6	Isaiah 51	1 John 2
17-Oct	Eccl 12	Isaiah 3	Col 4	05-Dec	2 Sam 7	Isaiah 52	1 John 3
18-Oct	Eccl 13	Isaiah 4	1 Thess 1	06-Dec	2 Sam 8	Isaiah 53	1 John 4
19-Oct	Ezra 1	Isaiah 5	1 Thess 2	07-Dec	2 Sam 9	Isaiah 54	1 John 5
20-Oct	Ezra 2	Isaiah 6	1 Thess 3	08-Dec	2 Sam 10	Isaiah 55	2 John
21-Oct	Ezra 3	Isaiah 7	1 Thess 4	09-Dec	2 Sam 11	Isaiah 56	3 John
22-Oct	Ezra 4	Isaiah 8	1 Thess 5	10-Dec	2 Sam 12	Isaiah 57	Jude
23-Oct	Ezra 5	Isaiah 9	2 Thess 1	11-Dec	2 Sam 13	Isaiah 58	Rev 1
24-Oct	Ezra 6	Isaiah 10	2 Thess 2	12-Dec	2 Sam 14	Isaiah 59	Rev 2
25-Oct	Ezra 7	Isaiah 11	2 Thess 3	13-Dec	2 Sam 15	Isaiah 60	Rev 3
26-Oct	Ezra 8	Isaiah 12	1 Tim 1	14-Dec	2 Sam 16	Isaiah 61	Rev 4
27-Oct	Ezra 9	Isaiah 13	1 Tim 2	15-Dec	2 Sam 17	Isaiah 62	Rev 5
28-Oct	Ezra 10	Isaiah 14	1 Tim 3	16-Dec	2 Sam 18	Isaiah 63	Rev 6
29-Oct	1 Sam 1	Isaiah 15	1 Tim 4	17-Dec	2 Sam 19	Isaiah 64	Rev 7
30-Oct	1 Sam 2	Isaiah 16	1 Tim 5	18-Dec	2 Sam 20	Isaiah 65	Rev 8
31-Oct	1 Sam 3	Isaiah 17	1 Tim 6	19-Dec	2 Sam 21	Isaiah 66	Rev 9
01-Nov	1 Sam 4	Isaiah 18	2 Tim 1	20-Dec	2 Sam 22	Daniel 1	Rev 10
02-Nov	1 Sam 5	Isaiah 19	2 Tim 2	21-Dec	2 Sam 23	Daniel 2	Rev 11
03-Nov	1 Sam 6	Isaiah 20	2 Tim 3	22-Dec	2 Sam 24	Daniel 3	Rev 12
04-Nov	1 Sam 7	Isaiah 21	2 Tim 4	23-Dec	Song 1	Daniel 4	Rev 13
05-Nov	1 Sam 8	Isaiah 22	Titus 1	24-Dec	Song 2	Daniel 5	Rev 14
06-Nov	1 Sam 9	Isaiah 23	Titus 2	25-Dec	Song 3	Daniel 6	Rev 15
07-Nov	1 Sam 10	Isaiah 24	Titus 3	26-Dec	Song 4	Daniel 7	Rev 16
08-Nov	1 Sam 11	Isaiah 25	Philemon 1	27-Dec	Song 5	Daniel 8	Rev 17
09-Nov	1 Sam 12	Isaiah 26	Heb 1	28-Dec	Song 6	Daniel 9	Rev 18
10-Nov	1 Sam 13	Isaiah 27	Heb 2	29-Dec	Song 7	Daniel 10	Rev 19
11-Nov	1 Sam 14	Isaiah 28	Heb 3	30-Dec	Song 8	Daniel 11	Rev 20
12-Nov	1 Sam 15	Isaiah 29	Heb 4	31-Dec	Song 9	Daniel 12	Rev 21

About the Author

As a child, Karen Hutchins was frequently found curled up in a chair in a quiet corner with her journal. Her writing was the perfect outlet for this shy child's dreams and thoughts. After giving her life to Jesus at age nine, in church camp in Troy, Missouri, her writings became more like letters to her new love— Jesus. Although Karen was born and raised in Illinois, she considers herself a transplanted Texan, having lived there for over twenty-one years, after serving her country in the United States Marine Corps during the Vietnam War. Her son, Jason Breshears, and his wife Jen live outside Houston, with their two daughters, Hayley and Hannah.

Throughout the years, life's changes and location moves have affected her writing only minimally. As an adult, Karen "drifted" from her relationship with Jesus. Her daily journaling, which she fondly refers to as "Breakfast with the King" has been instrumental in bringing her back to her core religious beliefs after her divorce. Karen is a tender spirit who has endured tremendous wounds in her life. Her first book, Protective Custody: Miracles Can Happen When God Has You Right Where He Wants You, was inspired by the journal entries she wrote during an extremely difficult five-year period. Karen and Wayne (Hutch) Hutchins married on Valentine's Day 2003 and moved to Washington State. Karen retired in 2016 from the professional world after holding a variety of office positions: bookkeeper, assistant manager of high-rise office buildings, pastor's assistant, Christian counselor, accounts payable manager, and human resources manager. She and Hutch moved to Lisbon, North Dakota, in 2016, where he pastors First Baptist Church of Lisbon and Forman Community Church in Forman, ND. Her cur- rent role with First Baptist Church in Lisbon is a diverse one. She leads worship, teaches Bible studies, and assists her husband with administrative duties. She also leads the Forman Community Church in their weekly Bible study. They are both members of Christian Motorcyclists Association, where they led music as the "Worship Warriors" for several years in the Pacific Northwest. Karen serves as chaplain and adjutant in the local American Legion Post #7 and serves as Department Chaplain for the state of North Dakota. She takes great joy in carrying the United States flag in local parades and in honors ceremonies for fallen veterans.

She is an animal lover, having claimed animals from A to Z (her palomino, Amigo and her large dog, Zeke.) It has been said that Karen knows how to turn lemons into lemonade and tests into testimonies. Her heart's desire is to help God's children to heal. These days, her perfect day starts with "Breakfast with the King" soaking up like a sponge all she can from God's Word, still writing her love letters to God, but on her laptop, listening for God's responses to turn those letters into more encouraging lessons to share!

Join Karen On her Facebook page Monday nights at 7:00 PM CST for the most current lessons that she is sharing today.

CPSIA information can be obtained
at www.ICGtesting.com
Printed in the USA
FSHW011942091120
75561FS